Navigating Environmental Attitudes

Navigating Environmental Attitudes

THOMAS A. HEBERLEIN

OXFORD
UNIVERSITY PRESS

OXFORD
UNIVERSITY PRESS

Oxford University Press is a department of the University of Oxford.
It furthers the University's objective of excellence in research,
scholarship, and education by publishing worldwide.

Oxford   New York
Auckland   Cape Town   Dar es Salaam   Hong Kong   Karachi
Kuala Lumpur   Madrid   Melbourne   Mexico City   Nairobi
New Delhi   Shanghai   Taipei   Toronto

With offices in
Argentina   Austria   Brazil   Chile   Czech Republic   France   Greece
Guatemala   Hungary   Italy   Japan   Poland   Portugal   Singapore
South Korea   Switzerland   Thailand   Turkey   Ukraine   Vietnam

Oxford is a registered trade mark of Oxford University Press in the UK and certain other countries.

Published in the United States of America by Oxford University Press
198 Madison Avenue, New York, NY 10016

© Oxford University Press 2012

Library of Congress Cataloging-in-Publication Data
Heberlein, Thomas A., 1945–
Navigating environmental attitudes / Thomas A. Heberlein.
    p.   cm.
Includes bibliographical references and index.
ISBN 978-0-19-977332-9 (hbk. : alk. paper)—ISBN 978-0-19-977333-6 (pbk. : alk. paper)
1. Environmental management—Psychological aspects.
2. Environmental sciences—Psychological aspects.
3. Environmental sociology. 4. Environmental psychology. I. Title.
GE300.H43   2012
304.2—dc23   2012003300

9 8 7 6 5 4 3 2

Printed in the United States of America
on acid-free paper

In memory of William R. Freudenburg
colleague and friend

One of the anomalies of modern ecology is that it is the creation of two groups each of which seems barely aware of the existence of the other. The one studies the human community almost as if it were a separate entity, and calls its findings sociology, economics, and history. The other studies the plant and animal community, [and] comfortably relegates the hodge-podge of politics to "the liberal arts." The inevitable fusion of these two lines of thought will, perhaps, constitute the outstanding advance of the present century.

—ALDO LEOPOLD, BERLIN (1935)
As quoted in Meine (1988)

Contents

Navigating Environmental Attitudes

1

Attitudes, Rivers, and Environmental Fixes

SOLUTIONS TO GLOBAL warming are not hard. All we have to do is shoot 800,000 Frisbee-sized ceramic disks into space from 20 electromagnetic guns every 5 minutes for 10 years to create a giant sunshade. Or we could have 1,500 ships spray sea water to create white clouds to reflect the sun. Or we could pump tons of sulfur dioxide into the upper atmosphere to imitate the cooling effect of volcanic eruptions. Don't laugh. These geo-engineering projects were actual proposals—some by Nobel Laureates, no less.[1]

Why do scientists and engineers propose such fanciful strategies? Technological fixes are attractive because they bypass human behavior. They require that people do basically nothing. We simply change the environment and go on living much as we have in the past. Problem solved.

Bypassing human behavior to solve environmental problems is nothing new. The United States went to war against the environment in the 1920s and 1930s. The problems then were floods and droughts. Whether caused by nature (rainfall) or humans (changes in land use), rivers flooded and wrought unprecedented damage, or they dried up so much that the city of Tacoma, Washington, had to call on the U.S. Navy for emergency electricity.[2] The technical solution in those days—simpler than shooting billions of Frisbees into space—was building dams across rivers to control their flow, prevent floods, and generate cheap electricity.

The United States spent billions to build thousands of dams, which did what they were supposed to do.[3] That is, downstream areas usually saw more water in the summer, and less water in the spring and fall. However, when geographers evaluated the New Deal dams, they found that flood losses— what we were really trying to control—went *up*, not down.[4] Why? No one who proposed the technological fix anticipated the dams would change human behavior as well as river flows. When rivers didn't flood every year, people figured they, not the rivers, owned the flood plain. This land looked dry to them, so they built houses and moved in. The next time the river claimed the flood plain, it caused more damage than before.[5] The attitudes of the public, believing dams truly controlled rivers, made them more vulnerable than ever to floods.

Attitudes Are Everything

When changing the environment fails, as it so often does, human behavior must change. So we turn to information in hopes people will change their attitudes and behaviors through what I call the "cognitive fix," in contrast to building dams, an example of a technological fix.[6] The cognitive fix for reducing flood losses was to give people flood-plain maps. After all, who would want to live in a flood plain, where houses wash away? However, changing behavior with information is not as simple as it seems.

Designing an effective cognitive fix requires scientific knowledge; not of rivers and dams, but of something less tangible: public attitudes. I have spent most of my career as a social psychologist trying to figure out how attitudes work, how they can be changed, and what they have to do with behavior as we struggle to deal with nature. Finally, I think I have some answers. That's the stuff of this book.

The problem with implementing environmental fixes is not that those proposing such fixes know too little about attitudes. The problem is they know *too much*. As the saying goes: "It ain't what you don't know that gets you into trouble. It's what you know for sure that just ain't so."

Open any newspaper and you will see the word "attitude" in nearly every edition. We want football teams with *winning attitudes*, students with *positive attitudes*, and leaders with *visionary attitudes*. A pitch to climb Mount Everest says, "It's not the altitude, it's the attitude." A hunting magazine asserts, "The difference between a good retrieving dog and a bad one . . . finally comes down to a matter of attitude." Attitude and behavior seem to be about the same thing. A good attitude propels you to the mountaintop. A good attitude launches your retriever from the duck blind at the sound of the shot. These are observable behaviors. We infer they represent an underlying attitude, but that is where we hit thin ice.

As if it were not enough that attitudes are everywhere, everyone proposes changing them. This is particularly true with the environment. Scarcely a day passes without an environmental or scientific group advocating reversals in public attitudes: If people would only change their attitudes, they would carpool to work. We supposedly squander energy because we lack conservation attitudes. We must make people believe in global warming. Attitudes seem to be changing all the time in newspapers. We continually read about attitude adjustments, especially on the sports page. "Attitude Adjustment Reason Packers Are Super Again." Do championships have anything to do with passing, blocking, and running? Apparently not. Attitudes are the key.

In contrast to the popular view of attitudes, the term *attitude* has had another life as the queen concept in social psychology for more than a hundred years. Social scientists who study attitudes view them as stable, rather than changeable. Stability makes them important. What if everyone awoke with new attitudes each morning? Social scientists also think attitudes differ from behavior. Sometimes the two are closely related, but more often they are not. That is a problem.

Although my discipline has learned much about attitudes, this information has not been easily available to those trying to change the environment. Most of these people are trained in engineering, natural sciences, or resource management. Without specialized training in social sciences, they are forced to rely on common views of attitudes, which usually "just ain't so." I have worked on environmental issues with limnologists, environmentalists, park managers, utility executives, wildlife biologists, and conservation biologists, and have found that "attitude" as a scientific concept is not easily understood. In contrast, biologists explain reproduction, wolf behavior, and population change in ways I understand. Even economists make clear why they can use travel costs to free recreation sites as a substitute for price. I also had no trouble following how coarse woody debris affects fish populations, and how phosphorus in the water column increases algae growth.

However, when I had to explain attitudes, I felt like I was trying to describe a ghost. Where were they born? How much do they weigh? How fast do they grow? What is their position? All simple questions—but all difficult to answer. When I once used the ghost metaphor to describe attitudes, one of my cynical and savvy environmental colleagues replied, "Well, I don't believe in ghosts either . . . but I am afraid of them." He was right. If you are trying to solve environmental problems, you better be afraid of attitudes. Even though they are difficult to pin down and perhaps even harder to change, attitudes are fundamental to environmental solutions.

So let's go back and look at how the cognitive fix (trying to change people's behavior by giving them information) worked to reduce flood losses. When river water covers the ground, people see a flood plain's exact location. When dams reduce flood frequency, the flood plain is less visible. In Topeka, Kansas, the U.S. Geological Survey issued maps showing the flood plain. The maps were supposed to replace information once provided by rivers that often flooded.

The Chicago geographers evaluated these new maps as part of their research.[7] The flood-plain maps didn't work. For starters, bankers, real-estate developers with property in the flood plain, and others interviewed by the geographers knew nothing of the maps, although they had been distributed for free and described in newspaper articles. When people were shown maps as part of the research project, few had the skills to read them. Even worse, they discounted the maps' validity. Only one person interviewed even requested a copy. People didn't use the maps and kept building in the flood plain.

As this story illustrates, when solving environmental problems, even simple assumptions about human behavior must be considered and tested.

The Structural Fix

The Kansas case study provided another important lesson: Although techno-logical and cognitive fixes failed, researchers found some promise in a third fix that changes the context of the human behavior. I call this the "structural fix," and it changes the social environment that influences what people do. This fix does not bypass attitudes, but it does not focus on attitude change as the driver of behavioral change. After a large flood, the Federal Housing Administration (FHA) quit guaranteeing mortgages in parts of Topeka, the same community that ignored the flood-plain maps.[8] The FHA *was* required by Congress to take flood risks into account, no matter what the locals thought about flooding. Appraisers completing FHA applications were instructed to include flood in-formation. If a house was destroyed or damaged by floodwaters, banks could not collect on the mortgage insurance. That got the bankers' attention.

Most banks would not take on the flood risk themselves. Without insur-ance, they would be stuck with losses if owners failed to pay their mortgages after their houses washed away. This changed the bankers' behavior without changing their individual attitudes about Topeka's flood risks. As my Univer-sity of Chicago professor, Gilbert White, concluded:

> While the flood hazard map alone may have little influence upon the decision of the property owner to build in a flood plain, it becomes powerful when placed in the hands of a professional appraiser who has been instructed in its use, and even more powerful when the mortgage insurance officers in the Federal Housing Administration and the Vet-erans Administration are instructed to use it.[9]

The agencies and maps together were a positive force in promoting zoning that kept development out of the flood plains. Maps worked when they reached people in a position to attend to the information and the motivation to act on it. The advance in thinking was to move beyond individual home buyers and their personal attitudes toward floods and to consider how "outside" actors with new information could influence housing choices of individuals and families.

The Three Fixes in the Departmental Coffee Room

Flood-plain managers aren't the only ones wanting to educate the public. "Education" is the most common solution for all sorts of environmental problems, even in my department's coffee room. One day a graduate student burst into my office, all in a dither. Acting locally and thinking globally, he was upset about wasted resources right down the hall. He thought the rampant use of plastic-foam cups depleted the world's supply of nonrenewable hydrocarbons. He wanted to "educate the public"—in this case staff, other students, and perhaps the toughest group, faculty members—to use paper cups or china mugs instead. He asked if a sign or perhaps an e-mail about the ravages of plastic foam would solve the problem. He assumed that, if you gave people information, you could change their attitudes and they would behave appropriately (the cognitive fix). The student assumed that people used plastic-foam cups simply because they did not know or care about the environmental damages that resulted from their use. Therefore, it was necessary to change their attitude, or at least provide new information.

I suggested he study the situation more closely and think about alternatives. The next day he came back a bit sheepishly. He had talked to a few people and discovered they didn't care what kind of cup they had as long as they had a cup. He found several reasons his sign might be ignored or have little effect on behavior. What were the environmental impacts of the behavior he advocated? Some "educated" folks in the department might believe paper cups and paper mills create more pollution than plastic-foam cups. Others might believe paper cups create jobs in northern Wisconsin. And what about the water and soap needed for washing mugs? What seemed like a simple environmental problem had become complicated.

The simpler solution was to get rid of the plastic-foam cups, provide only paper cups, and put up a board where people could hang personal coffee mugs and take pride in them, thus changing the situation's context. Plus, the student had only to persuade the department administrator to make the change. By dealing with one person instead of many, he would have a better chance of getting his message across. Better yet would be to volunteer to buy the cups and reserve the right to provide only paper cups, even if they were a bit more expensive. This would make the administrator's job easier. So, the student bought the cups and we drank out of paper cups and china mugs until he graduated. Then the plastic-foam cups reappeared. He had not changed anyone's attitude, only their behavior. That sometimes is enough for a permanent change, but often it is not. Behavior can revert when social influence is removed, which it did in this case.

The Three Fixes for Environmental Problems

The examples of flood control and plastic-foam cups illustrate the three fixes for environmental problems. The first response is often to try changing the environment, by damming rivers and putting a sunshade over the Earth. The two other fixes require changing human behavior. Of course, in many cases, technology—like seat belts in cars—is involved, but the primary targets are humans who should buckle up. The most popular solution is the cognitive fix, the one first proposed in Kansas and by my student. The central idea is to try changing human behavior by providing information, that is, educating the public. The third fix is to change the structure of the situation that influences human behavior, such as with zoning laws, bank regulations, and even physical structures (like providing paper cups)–hence the name, "structural fix." The structural fix worked for rivers and the coffee room.

No matter which fix we use—and this is the important point—attitudes matter. So we need a scientific understanding of how attitudes work, and this knowledge of attitudes must be part of the design of any environmental program. Even technological fixes that try to change the environment directly must be designed to be consistent with public attitudes so the public will bear the cost, risks, and inconveniences of the fix.

I asked my student to come up with a technological fix for the cup problem by changing the coffee, not the people. He drew a blank. He couldn't imagine we could eliminate cups by piping coffee to every desk, that is, producing a network of coffee fountains. Our existing attitudes limit our ability to even think about some fixes—another reason that attitudes are important for all fixes, not just the cognitive fix.

Structural fixes to reduce flood losses required gaining the support and changing the behaviors of gatekeepers; in this case, the gatekeepers were bankers and administrators who had to change the context that affected housing choices. It was not necessary to change the attitudes of every potential homeowner or builder. Identifying actors who can change the situation's structure to influence individual behavior gives them more leverage to change human response.

Table 1.1 compares how each fix works and, more importantly, the role of attitudes and environmental change in each fix. This book focuses on key assumptions of the cognitive fix: how attitudes change, when they do and don't influence behavior, and how we can change them to change behavior. In that process, we will also discover how scientific knowledge of attitudes is vital for any environmental solution—even shooting Frisbees halfway to the moon.

Table 1.1   **Attitudes and the Three Fixes for Environmental Problems**

	Technological	Cognitive	Structural
What Changes	Environment	Human Behavior	Human Behavior
How Change Is Achieved	Technology influences the environment	Information influences human behavior	Structure of the situation influences human behavior
Examples	Dams; Coffee fountains	Flood-plain maps; Signs and information about cups	Flood-plain zoning; Providing only paper cups
Role of Attitudes	Technology must be consistent with dominant public attitudes and values	Attitudes must be changed and attitudes must influence behavior	Structural changes must be consistent with dominant public attitudes and values

Learning from Leopold

To move ahead with our understanding of attitudes, I find it helpful to think of real people and concrete examples. For part of our journey, I enlist Aldo Leopold. If you are a North American forester, wildlife biologist, or one of the many students in environmental classes who has read his classic book, *A Sand County Almanac,* Leopold needs no introduction.[10]

He was born in 1883, studied at Yale, and became one of the first professionals in the U.S. Forest Service. Leopold learned from nature as a young forester and turned to the study of wildlife and ecosystems. His book *Game Management* literally defined the field of wildlife ecology in 1933, and soon after, Leopold became the first professor of game management in the world. Leopold was a founder of the Wilderness Society, president of the Wildlife

Society and the Ecological Society of America, as well as an adviser to President Roosevelt and the New Deal administration on wildlife policy.

But he was more than that. His vision of nature and broadening the human community to include nature united conservationists of the early twentieth century with environmentalists of today. He gave us the idea of a land ethic as a solution for environmental problems. Although many have analyzed his writings and others have documented his life,[11] I use Leopold himself as a case study to understand what environmental attitudes are, how they change, and what they have to do with behavior.

Running the River

Solving environmental problems is like journeying down a river. When you launch your raft or canoe, the river looks clear and easy. However, a couple of bends downriver, you hear the distant roar of rapids. What had seemed an easy trip is now threatened. Attitudes are like rocks in a rapids. Trying to solve environmental problems by changing attitudes is a little like packing dynamite on a canoe trip and trying to blow up every rock in your way. It's better to learn how to read water and avoid collisions with rocks.

Many rocks—indeed the most dangerous ones—are, like attitudes, under water. You cannot see them but must infer them from what you see on the water's surface. How the water slides over some rocks tells you they lie just below the surface and you must adjust your path. Sometimes, when the water curls up and froths, you are fooled into thinking there is danger when it is really the best course. It takes training and experience to read water correctly. We social scientists read the river with surveys and experiments. We can't spot every rock, but we can get you through some rapids you thought were impossible. We can also warn you of disaster ahead on stretches you thought were smooth and sure.

In navigating the river of social change, we must remember that rivers go downstream. If you try to go against the flow, you move with great difficulty. Some attitude-change proposals we examine early in this book try to avoid the rapids by making the river stop and run upstream. Such attempts don't work. Like a real river, water levels on the river of social change rise and fall. At low water, attitude rocks appear, and navigating your raft or canoe through the maze is almost impossible. At high water, rocks disappear into the depths and let you navigate with ease. Dealing successfully with attitudes may not mean avoiding rocks but figuring out how to increase river flow. Furthermore, rapids that look impassable are not always so. Scouting them reveals eddies where the water's force sends the current upstream, not downstream. Sections of quiet water rest behind the boulders. A clever river runner uses these opportunities to work through what once looked like impossible barriers.

Before beginning a river trip, it's wise to sit down with a map and get a feel for the entire journey. In this book, we will first learn how to scout rapids and read water. We will determine what attitudes are, how they change, and what they have to do with one's behavior. With these basics understood, we will look at the key assumption of the cognitive fix: We can change how people act toward the environment simply by giving them information.

In chapter 2, "Reading Water and Minds," I let Leopold describe his attitude toward pine trees, and then we dissect it much as we might a lab specimen. This reveals all parts of the attitude and how the pieces fit together. Leopold illustrates how attitudes are tied to values and explains their horizontal and vertical structures. From Leopold, we turn to attitudes of students in my Environmental Sociology seminar to illustrate the diversity of attitude organization and the key role of emotion. These stories lead to three basic principles—consistency, direct experience, and identity—that I use to help understand attitudes toward these three environmental problems: wolf restoration, ozone holes, and climate change.

In chapter 3, "Attitude Change: Aldo Leopold Meets the Bennington Women," I examine how attitudes change. This is the first assumption of the cognitive fix—attitudes must change in order to change behavior. Leopold's attitude changed from wolf-hater to wolf-lover. College students' attitudes change and persist. New generations have more favorable attitudes toward wolves and the environment. These changes took time. Less well developed attitudes can sometimes change quickly when linked to stronger, more central attitudes. This is where the media can play a role though framing. That attitudes can and do change does not necessarily mean we can change them whenever we choose.

In chapter 4, "Attitudes Are *Not* Everything," we deal with the second assumption of the cognitive fix: Attitudes have a direct influence on what people actually do, not what they say they might do or would like to do. After Leopold changed his attitude toward wolves, he voted to restore bounties on them. Circumstance, like powerful currents, can keep us from going in the direction we choose. Positive attitudes are a necessary, but not a sufficient, condition for pro-environmental behaviors. More specific attitudes exert greater influence than general pro-environmental attitudes, and attitudes based on direct experience heavily influence our behavior.

In chapter 5, "Educating the Public . . . and Other Disasters," I report on a series of field experiments my students and I conducted over a dozen years to test the key assumption of the cognitive fix: that information can change attitudes, and the resulting attitude change leads to an increase in pro-environmental behavior. The cognitive and the structural fixes go toe-to-toe here, and the prize goes to the latter. The good news of this chapter is that our environmental attitudes are often resilient, and big corporations armed with millions of dollars have little success trying to change them.

The next two chapters focus not so much on rocks but on the hydraulics of the river. This is the current that guides our behavior. Understanding how water works is just as important as figuring out where the rocks, or attitudes, lie.

Chapter 6, "NORMS," advances the attitude concept by moving to something that has much more to do with behavior: norms. Internal and external sanctions, beliefs about negative consequences, and feelings of personal responsibility are forces that push our behavior, much as currents push our boats. The failure of people to act consistently with their pro-environmental attitudes often comes when situations or other attitudes deactivate pro-environmental norms. Norms are one kind of structural fix that helps guide pro-environmental behavior. In our investigation of norms, we again turn to Leopold. In his time, he smoked cigarettes and killed and ate wild trout. If he were to continue these behaviors today, he would be paddling upstream against strong currents. Norms change, but not often and seldom quickly. The chapter concludes by exploring how new norms and currents emerge and strengthen over time.

In chapter 7, "Aldo Leopold and the Flying Horse," I carefully look at the land ethic, Leopold's visionary solution to environmental problems. Although the land ethic has been analyzed from ethical, historical, and philosophical perspectives, I think the concepts of social psychology provide fresh insight into its utility and potential. Leopold is, I am afraid, looking for a flood to save us, and starting a flood is not so simple.

Armed with our knowledge of rapids (attitudes) and hydraulics (norms), it is time to get on the river and make the journey to change environmental behaviors.

Chapter 8 is called "Avoiding the Cognitive Fix Keeper Hole." Keeper holes are places where the water swirls, turns on itself, and traps your craft. You go around and around, sometimes upside down, and, occasionally, even drown. The cognitive fix is a big keeper hole. We get caught in it and can't think beyond it. You can avoid keeper holes by designing technical and structural fixes "with attitudes" rather than trying to change attitudes. These case studies show how people quit driving in central Stockholm, conserved vast amounts of energy on a university campus, and stopped power-plant construction in the Pacific Northwest. Another case shows how millions of hotel guests came to turn off their room lights every time they left their rooms.

Chapter 9, "Going with the Flow," shows how to take advantage of existing attitudes. Rather than fighting the river or, worse, trying to make it go upstream, we can go with the flow and work eddies where water is already headed upstream. A clever river runner can catch these eddies and navigate a boulder field.

Chapter 10, "Increasing the Flow: Activating and Creating Norms," shows how we can use structural fixes to create new norms and avoid the rocks by sending more water over the rapids. These strategies hold much more promise for promoting pro-environmental behavior than cognitive fixes alone.

Chapter 11, "Thinking Beyond the Rim," completes our journey. As the sun goes off the river and big rapids are behind us, we catch our breath, relax, and reflect. Which river-running principles did we learn? Can we read the water better next time? How do we design structural fixes that work? How can social and natural sciences partner to better solve environmental problems? Perhaps we can make progress toward realizing what Leopold called "the inevitable fusion" of knowledge about the human, plant, and animal communities.

You might want to think of this book as a practical river guide to environmental attitudes. It is written for my colleagues and students in environmental sciences who know that attitudes are important but need a more fundamental understanding of the science behind them. Attitudes, as I will show, are essential for solving environmental problems. Rather than educating the public, we perhaps first need the public to educate us just a bit.

Okay, let's head for the river.

2

Reading Water and Minds

IN MY DEPARTMENT at the University of Wisconsin-Madison, we used to organize a canoe trip every spring for our environmental graduate students. Rich, who knew how to read water, was paired with Jordan, who—like most students—had little experience in a canoe. As they headed into a small rapids, Rich shouted, "Watch out for that rock dead ahead." A sarcastic, "Rich, *I see it*," came back.

Soon after, CRUNCH! And soon after that, a sheepish, "Oh, *that* rock." Jordan thought Rich was warning him about the obvious midriver boulder 50 yards downstream. Rich, however, was shouting about the rock just below the surface a canoe-length ahead. You could not see this dangerous rock. You had to infer it from a smooth boil as water slid over it. You had to read the water.

Much like spotting underwater rocks from their observable traces, social psychologists pinpoint attitudes by reading minds. Unlike psychics, who read minds through magic, we follow careful scientific procedures. We ask people to tell us what they think and how they feel. We read their minds by putting them in experimental situations and measuring their reactions. Even so, this sort of mind reading is tough. People often don't quite know what they think or how they feel. Sometimes they struggle telling us, and sometimes we struggle figuring out what should be obvious. That's because attitudes are invisible. They must be inferred like that submerged rock rather than directly observed. It takes time, systematic data collection, a body of theoretical principles, and a good bit of statistical analysis to be a decent mind reader.

"I Am in Love with Pines"

As a start in science-assisted mind-reading, let's ask Aldo Leopold to tell us about his attitude.[1] In the 1930s Leopold bought a worn-out piece of land in the Wisconsin River bottoms, converted an old chicken coop for weekend visits (he called it "the shack"), and started practicing restoration ecology. Leopold and his family planted white pines, about the only trees that would grow in the river bottoms' sandy, wind-blown soils. Year after year the seedlings died in those Dust-Bowl years, but the Leopold family kept replanting. Finally, some pines survived and grew, but here and there some were shaded by birches. One autumn day, a dozen years after planting the first pines, Leopold stepped outside his shack, ax in hand, to tend his pines. He began puzzling about his behavior, trying to read his own mind. Why cut birch to save pine? In *A Sand County Almanac*, he describes his attitude, thinking—as most of us do—that his attitude causes his behavior. He wrote:

> I find it disconcerting to analyze, *ex post facto*, the reasons behind my own axe in hand decisions. I find, first of all, that not all trees are created free and equal. Where a white pine and a red birch are crowding each other, I have an *a priori* bias; I always cut the birch to favor the pine. Why?
>
> Well, first of all, I planted the pine with my shovel, whereas the birch crawled in under the fence and planted itself. My bias is thus to some extent paternal . . . .[2]

At the base of Leopold's attitude—what he terms a "bias"—we locate a *value*. Values have inspired considerable study by social psychologists. Milton Rokeach identified 36 basic values held worldwide.[3] The first value Leopold mentions is paternalism. What Leopold called "a paternal bias," Rokeach would label "family security," or taking care of one's family, broadly defined. Leopold takes some paternal responsibility for the pine because he planted and cared for it. Values are the basis for many attitudes and play a major role in discussing pro-environmental behavior, as they should. Leopold was about to do something that affects the environment, cutting the birch, so it is fitting he told us how this fit his values. We must realize that for Leopold—like the rest of us—paternalism might be the source of his attitudes toward many things, from his five children to his scientific articles. We know it's at the base of his attitude toward pine trees because he tells us so. The important difference between an attitude and a value is that the value has no particular object, whereas the attitude does. Attitudes always have *objects*, something the attitude is about, and the object is important. In Leopold's case, the object is pine trees, or perhaps just the particular white pine he is admiring.

Sitting on top of the value is a component of attitude that social psychologists call *beliefs*. Beliefs also tie to the object. Leopold says he planted the pine, and the birch planted itself. These are specific beliefs. We call them the *cognitive component* of attitudes. One person might love pines and another person might hate them. But both can believe Leopold planted the pines and the birches planted themselves. The person who hates pines might think Leopold planted way too many, and the person who loves them might think he planted way too few, but they can both agree he planted them. These cognitions are sometimes called *knowledge*, but they are not knowledge in the sense we usually think of knowledge. A belief need not be correct. It can be inconsistent with scientific knowledge or the knowledge of an authority, but if people believe it, then it is true for them. What makes it a belief is the absence of emotion.

When you tie the belief to a value, you get a belief that says or implies something is better than something else.[4] This is called an *evaluative belief*. Leopold, sparing in his use of words, does not outline the structure of his values, beliefs, and attitude as I try to do here, but his prose implies the structure. The attitude sits on top of a value, two beliefs, and an evaluative belief that trees planted by themselves (or by natural processes) are better than trees planted by humans. (See Figure 2.1.) Daryl Bem, a well-known social psychologist, labeled this *vertical structure*.[5] Leopold's vertical structure in this example is consistent: value, belief, evaluative belief, and attitude, all logically following from one another.

The real driving force of attitudes is emotion, or as social psychologists call it, *affect*. This is the irrational part—the part not subject to reason—and the part that makes attitudes difficult for those trying to deal with them. Affect is what we see at public meetings over wolf restoration or when people discover their house sits on a toxic-waste site. This side of attitudes sends managers scurrying to social psychologists saying, "We seem to have a problem with attitudes." Affect or emotion engages the body as well as the mind. When you meet someone or something you hate, love, or fear, your heart pounds, your stomach ties itself in knots, your face gets red, and a clammy sweat covers your body. Attitudes differ from knowledge because they are driven by the love-hate, good-bad aspect of emotion. The summary statement of Leopold's attitude toward pines is full of affect: "The only conclusion I have ever reached is that I love all trees, but I am in love with pines."[6]

FIGURE 2.1 Vertical Structure Diagram of Leopold's Attitude toward Pines

This man does not just think trees are important. He loves all of them, but even more, he is in love with pines. This is different than saying, "I like pine trees." He is revealing a deep emotion tied to his attitude toward pines. In fact, less than six months after Leopold wrote this essay, he died fighting a fire that threatened these very pines.

So now we have beliefs, evaluative beliefs, affect, values, and vertical structure. However, there is more. Leopold runs down a set of beliefs and pegs the values underlying them. Attitudes are seldom based on single beliefs or single values. He wrote:

> The birch is an abundant tree in my township and becoming more so, whereas pine is scarce and becoming scarcer; perhaps my bias is for the underdog.
>
> The pine will live for a century, the birch for half that; do I fear that my signature will fade? My neighbors have planted no pines but all have many birches; am I snobbish about having a woodlot of distinction? The pine stays green all winter, the birch punches the clock in October; do I favor the tree that, like myself, braves the winter wind? The pine will shelter a grouse but the birch will feed him; do I consider bed more important than board? The pine will ultimately bring ten dollars a thousand, the birch two dollars; have I an eye on the bank?[7]

Leopold believes several things: (a) "the birch crawled in under the fence and planted itself"; (b) "birch is an abundant tree in my township"; (c) "the pine will live a century, the birch half that"; and several others. None of these beliefs is emotional. They all are beliefs that pine lovers and pine haters could share. Each belief, however, becomes evaluative when tied to values. At least five more Rokeach values are present in Leopold's cognitive-affect framework: equality (underdog bias), social recognition (woodlot of distinction), a comfortable life (eye on the bank), a sense of accomplishment (fear fading signature), and courage (braves the winter wind).

Leopold's belief system is based on more than one set of beliefs and more than one value. Social psychologists call this *horizontal structure*. Leopold's attitude, "I am in love with pines," is supported by seven separate belief systems, each based on an articulated value (see Figure 2.2). Think of the attitude being like a lintel, the part atop a door held up by the door sill, with beliefs being those supports. Each belief system holds up the attitude, "I am in love with pines." If you were to try changing Leopold's attitude, perhaps you could convince him birch is worth more than pine. Maybe the market changed. Would he change his attitude toward pines? Not likely, because the attitude is held up

I am in love with pines

Trees you plant yourself are better.		It is better to help trees that are less abundant.		It is better to take care of longer-living trees.		Having pines in a woodlot makes it better than the neighbors' woodlot.		Pine produces more income.		Better to withstand the elements than to provide shelter.		Indian pipes, pyrolas, and twin flowers are better than bottle gentians.	A pileated woodpecker is better than a hairy woodpecker.
I planted the pine.	The birch planted itself.	Birch is abundant.	Pine is scarce.	Pine will live a century.	Birch will live half as long.	Neighbors have no pines.	Neighbors have many birches.	Pine brings $10.	Birch brings $2.	Pine needles remain green in winter.	Pine needles provide winter shelter for grouse.	Bottle gentians grow under birches. Hairy woodpeckers are found in birches.	Indian pipe, pyrola, and twin flowers will grow under pines. Pileated woodpeckers will nest in pines.
Family security (paternalism)		Equality (underdog bias)		A sense of accomplishment (significance)		Social recognition (woodlot of distinction)		A comfortable life (eye on the bank)		Courage (braves the winter wind)		A world of beauty	Imagination (stimulates my imagination)

← Horizontal Structure →

FIGURE 2.2 Aldo Leopold's Complete Attitude toward Pine Trees

or bolstered by many other belief structures. We can say Leopold's attitude has a high degree of *horizontal structure*. This diagram shows the cognitive parts of the attitude, but the affective dimension is less apparent. It lies in evaluative beliefs and values themselves. How long a pine lives is a matter of fact, but people fight over values that ground an attitude.

There is more to it than that. Leopold's analysis of his own attitude shows another feature: *centrality*. Not all the belief structures underlying his attitude are equal. Some are more important to him or are more central to his attitude because they are linked to his self-concept or *identity*. Leopold wonders which beliefs are most important. After reflecting, he observes:

> All of these possible reasons for my bias seem to carry some weight, but none of them carries very much.
>
> So I try again, and here perhaps is something; under this pine will ultimately grow a trailing arbutus, an Indian pipe, a pyrola, or a twin flower, whereas under the birch a bottle gentian is about the best to be hoped for. In this pine a pileated woodpecker will ultimately chisel out a nest; in the birch a hairy will have to suffice. In this pine the wind will sing for me in April at which time the birch is only rattling naked twigs. These possible reasons for my bias carry weight, but why? Does the pine stimulate my imagination and my hopes more deeply than the birch does? If so, is the difference in the trees, or in me?[8]

If Leopold and I were sitting around the fireplace at his shack as he mused, I might respond: "They carry weight, Professor, because they tie to two important values: imagination and a world of beauty. These values are more important to you than the other values. Your whole life has been one of trying to be close to nature, to explore and innovate, and see things in new ways. The difference is not in the trees; it is, sir, in you. But there is more. You are a professional forester whose life has been tied to trees and reforestation. What tree fits this better than the white pine? It is fundamental to your *identity* as a forester, professor, and landowner. Your attitude about white pines is most central to who you are."

For most of us, our attitude toward pines is less central, has less affect, and is less well developed. Our attitude toward pines has limited horizontal structure and a long, spindly, vertical structure, at best. We neither love nor hate pines, but rather we like them a little or are mostly indifferent.

Leopold's description of his attitude toward pines is a textbook case because of its consistency and clarity with respect to attitude theory. It would be nice if all attitudes came so nicely packaged. To gain more perspective on real-world attitudes, let's look at some less iconic individuals: three students in my graduate seminar.

Snout Beetles and Singing the Blues

I asked my students to introduce themselves by giving a five-minute presentation on any topic important to them. The idea was to go beyond the usual name, rank, and department, and set the stage for challenging discussions throughout the semester. The students could not keep their stories to five minutes, and so these "introductions" took nearly two hours. At first I worried about the loss of instructional time, but soon I realized I could have scarcely found a better way to demonstrate the attitude concept.

One student, Margaret—a slender young woman with wire-rimmed glasses—spoke about the plumb curculio (*Conotrachelus nenuphar*), a snout beetle. What do you know about the plumb curculio? If you are like the rest of us in the seminar, nothing. Nevertheless, the plumb curculio was an exceptionally well-developed attitude object for Margaret. She had studied snout beetles and had written a scientific paper about them. The plumb curculio leaves marks on apples. The marks don't really hurt the apples, but because they make apples unattractive, apple-growers use poisons to kill the bugs. Margaret had worked several years trying to reduce poison applications, and she thought we should put up with some marked-up but edible apples rather than kill the plumb curculio.

Margaret's attitude could be classified as "environmental" because the plumb curculio is wildlife, albeit of the small kind, and was associated with poison in the environment. Her attitude was well developed, based on many beliefs, and tied to her identity and values. What about the rest of us? Margaret's talk could be viewed as an attempt to use information to create an attitude toward a new attitude object. She gave all sorts of facts about the plumb curculio, including its size, shape, and dispersion, and a little about what it does. Despite all this new information, a day later I doubt anyone could remember the name, "plumb curculio," let alone the details Margaret shared.

Because it was a new attitude object, our attitudes toward the plumb curculio were not stable. Our attitudes were so poorly developed they could easily be changed by bits of information. However, that wasn't going to happen because we did not care about the little critter nor would we likely seek, find, or analyze information about this attitude object.

I see many environmental attitudes like Margaret's, in which attitude objects are sources of well-developed belief systems for small, specialized groups. People who have such attitudes are often scientists or managers.

When scientists say they want to "educate the public," they usually mean they want the general public to know more about their own favorite attitude object, be it phytoplankton, the plumb curculio, or phosphorus in the water column. This focus on knowledge misses the key driver of attitude, which dominated the next two presentations.

Joe was an environmental historian who usually wore a coat and tie to class. Most of us pegged him as a guy who never left the library. We were wrong. Joe also described an attitude object that was new to us, but he filled his presentation with emotion. You might know of Koko Taylor if you listen to blues. I had not. Just as the plumb curculio was news to me, so was Koko, but Koko was no plumb curculio. She was Queen of the Blues. Not only did Joe know Koko's every recording and concert venue, he radiated such joy and excitement in her work that we could almost hear her raspy voice belting out songs. Beneath that quiet, collected exterior, Joe was a blues junkie. His enthusiasm was infectious. I wouldn't have been surprised if some of his classmates went out and bought Koko Taylor music after class.

Compared to Margaret's pitch about the plumb curculio, Joe delivered equal measures of love, awe, and information. Although we didn't learn much about Koko's life, we embraced her and her music. Joe's beliefs about Koko were mostly evaluative, whereas Margaret's beliefs about the plumb curculio were mostly emotion-free facts.

Cleaning Up Oil: The Exxon Valdez

The last student to talk was Howard, a tall guy from Alaska who was among the thousands of workers Exxon employed to clean up a huge oil spill after one of its tankers, the *Exxon Valdez*, ran aground on Bligh Reef in Prince William Sound in March 1989. This oil spill was the worst in U.S. history until it was eclipsed by the BP oil spill in the Gulf of Mexico 21 years later. The class hung on Howard's every word. This was a key environmental disaster only a few years before, and Howard *had been there*. However, from a teacher's point of view, the kindest thing to say was that his presentation rambled. What was the attitude object? Exxon? The ship? The cleanup? Or, according to Howard, the lack thereof? Joe and Margaret gave us nice, clear, textbook attitude objects. Howard, however, delivered a real beast, comprised of almost pure emotion, big and powerful, rampaging through his mind. Listeners could not detect any organization to Howard's system of values and beliefs (assuming they were organized enough to be called a system) underlying whatever attitude he was trying to share. Many of his beliefs were so negative and improbable they seemed outrageous, even for a pro-environmental audience. Negative affect overwhelmed Howard's attitude. To say Howard disliked Exxon was like saying Abel troubled Cain.

It was clear Howard's attitude toward Exxon would never change. Whenever a classmate said anything that could be construed as good about Exxon, Howard told more stories of damage or ineptitude. Furthermore, he argued from authority—he had direct experience. From his perspective, no one could have information he did not possess, so he could ignore whatever anyone said to the contrary. Even if one wished to try changing Howard's attitudes, one could never figure out his key beliefs. His attitude was so emotionally driven that causality went backward. Rather than being built up by beliefs stacked on values, Howard's immense hatred for Exxon allowed him to fit beliefs, even behaviors, to his attitude. This overwhelmingly emotional characteristic of some attitudes makes them resistant to change, even scary.

Lessons from Wolves

In 1990, Yale psychologist Stephen Kellert and I conducted a survey about public attitudes toward wolf restoration in Michigan's Upper Peninsula.[9] After answering 150 questions about wolves, 35% of respondents wrote comments at the end of the questionnaire. One man even wrote a long letter in Polish. I wasn't surprised. A proposal to reintroduce wolves into Yellowstone National Park spawned more than 8,500 letters from the public.[10] Biologists sometimes call wolves "charismatic megafauna," incorporating a sociological dimension into a biological classification because many people have strong emotions—positive and negative—about wolves. These deep feelings help separate "wolf" from millions of other attitude objects. Wolves generate not only passionate commentary, but also scientific studies. One of longest-lasting wildlife population studies (running over a half a century) in the world is on wolves, not the dull, blunt-nosed leopard lizard or the now well-known (at least to this book's readers) plumb curculio.

After getting the Polish gentleman's letter translated, we read terrible stories about wolves based on his experience in Russian POW camps. He had heard of wolves eating children, and he was afraid if wolves were introduced into Michigan, children would be attacked while waiting for school buses. His feelings were deep and strong.

The Upper Peninsula, Michigan's northernmost region, features vast forests and few people, about the same population density as Idaho, and less than half the density of Finland. This seemed an ideal place to restore wolves, so in Spring 1974, David Mech, a leading wolf scientist, released four wolves into the Upper Peninsula. By November, all four were dead at the hands of man: one by car, two by gunshot, and one by a trapper.[11] Fifteen years later, with wolves forcing the issue by migrating into Michigan, wildlife managers decided they must learn something about public attitudes if this natural colonization were to succeed.

The specific attitude object in the Michigan study was not wolves, but reestablishing wolves in the Upper Peninsula. Our survey showed 57% of the public supported restoration, 9% opposed it, and 34% were neutral. The vast majority believed that wolves (a) "have a right to exist," (b) "are important members of the ecological community," and (c) should be preserved "so that future generations can enjoy them." If we had been running the wolf for governor, those would be great numbers. Similar surveys produced similar results. In Colorado, in 1996, 66% of the population said they would vote yes on a referendum to restore wolves.[12] In Idaho, 72% of residents favored reintroducing wolves, as did 52% of Montana residents, and 44% of Wyoming residents.[13] Surveys in Minnesota and Wisconsin also showed strong support for wolves.[14] My students and I analyzed all studies between 1972 and 2000, and found an average of 60% of respondents supported wolf restoration.[15]

Kellert and I included knowledge questions to measure the cognitive component of attitudes. How big is a wolf pack? We asked: "True or False—Wolf packs generally average around 50 wolves." Of the respondents, 44% said they didn't know, 4% said, "True." Imagine packs of 50 ravenous wolves roaming the Upper Peninsula. No wonder my correspondent was worried about kids waiting for school buses. In actuality, wolf packs average 4–6 wolves. We also included open-ended questions like, "How many wolves do you think are in Michigan's Upper Peninsula?" The average response by people in the Lower Peninsula (Michigan's mainland, south of the U.P.) was more than 500 wolves. Upper Peninsula folks estimated about 80 wolves. The best scientific estimate at the time? No more than 20.

When the public gets such questions "wrong," natural scientists tend to dismiss their attitudes. Why, they wonder, should we bother asking the public its opinions about wolf restoration when its judgments are based on erroneous beliefs? Scientists must realize members of the public do not think they are wrong, any more than scientists think their data are wrong. It's a mistake to neglect "wrong" beliefs even if they differ from today's best scientific estimates. To understand why people support or oppose wolf restoration, you must know their beliefs about wolves. If someone thought a thousand wolves were running around in 50-wolf packs, and 50,000 wolves lived nearby in Minnesota, we might better understand why people were not big fans of restoring wolves in Michigan.

Three Principles: Consistency, Direct Experience, and Identity

To read water in rapids, rather than just staring at waves and trembling at the roar, we must understand how water, rocks, and chutes work. Likewise with attitudes, rather than wallowing in data, we need principles to guide our thinking. In my experience, three principles help me understand attitudes:

- Attitudes tend toward consistency, but they are not always consistent; assuming consistency in attitudes without data can be misleading.
- Attitudes based on direct experience have more beliefs and greater stability; direct experience can change attitudes.
- Attitudes tied to our identities tend to be more emotional and difficult to change; they can, however, change as our identities and roles change.

That's it. Three things to monitor as you head toward the rapids.

Most of us assume the parts of an attitude are consistent with each other. For instance, if you support wolf restoration, you should have positive evaluative beliefs about wolves. Our Michigan survey showed that. Among those who thought wolves symbolized nature's beauty, 9 out of 10 supported wolf restoration. Among those who didn't, support dropped to 3 in 10. Those favoring restoration generally did not think wolves were dangerous, cruel, or frightening. Those who opposed restoration were more likely to believe wolves were naturally cruel, a danger to people, and might attack people in the forest.

This principle does not assert that all components of an attitude are consistent. Consistency is probabilistic, not deterministic. Holding one belief is usually neither a necessary nor sufficient condition of holding another, or of having a positive attitude toward the object in question. One can have negative beliefs about wolves and still support restoration. Negative beliefs reduce the probability a person will support restoration, but not to zero. If one belief changes, that does not mean the rest will align like cogs in a gear assembly. Attitudes obey a psycho logic rather than a formal logic.

Although people in our sample were generally consistent, 1 in 10 who supported wolf recovery believed wolves were naturally cruel, but supported restoration anyway. Another 1 of 10 supporters (not necessarily the same people) did not consider wolves the symbol of beauty or nature. A third of those who supported restoration thought a wolf might attack them if they saw one in the forest. You can hold negative beliefs about wolves and still support wolf recovery. Attitude structures simply *tend* toward consistency. Perhaps the supporters who expected a wolf attack never planned to see one in the forest.

Perhaps they thought wolves would attack only people the supporters didn't like, not them. Attitudes simply have too many parts for them all to be consistent. However, we can say the more negative beliefs you hold about wolves, the lower the probability you will support wolf restoration.

Even Leopold, whose attitude toward pines seems to be the paragon of consistency, had inconsistency in his attitude. Indeed, that inconsistency made him think about his values and articulate the wide horizontal structure (Figure 2.2). He initially argues to himself that he must love the pine more because he planted it (paternal bias), but then wonders, "but this cannot be the whole story, for if the pine were a natural seedling like the birch, I would value it even more. So I must dig deeper for the logic, if any, behind my bias." The birch, after all, planted itself and he cut it down, so this seems inconsistent. Therefore, paternalism cannot be driving the attitude. This sends Leopold on his way, looking for other beliefs and values more central to his attitude and behavior.

This inconsistency in Leopold's well-organized attitude is good evidence that almost all attitudes, particularly the more complex ones, are inconsistent. His effort to explain or account suggests a general drive toward consistency. Dissonance between attitude parts or between beliefs and behavior is uncomfortable and has a motivational power. This idea was made famous by Leon Festinger with his "Theory of Cognitive Dissonance."[16] This theory is often cited, even outside of social psychology, because it's a wonderful post hoc explanation for attitude or behavioral change. Indeed, one can always point to dissonant cognitions, as Leopold did in his own attitude. Even so, people often have inconsistencies in their attitudes that inspire no effort to change attitudes or behavior. Many smokers, for instance, believe cigarettes are bad for their health. Dissonance effects have been shown in laboratory experiments, but this is when student subjects are put in situations in which they cannot avoid dissonant cognitions. However, in the real world, we can often avoid inconsistencies between our attitudes and behavior, and live with lots of dissonance. These kinds of explanations, as we will see, are often too simple. Human behavior and attitudes are considerably complex.

The consistency principle has a couple of more traps. Absent data, it is easy to assume consistencies that don't exist. Economists were shocked when my colleagues and I showed in another study that people who liked wolves *most* would pay *less* money to restore 500 wolves and more to restore 200 wolves. That seems inconsistent. In an economic world, $500 is always better than $200, so for wolf lovers—like money lovers—500 wolves should always be better than 200. In-depth interviews with respondents showed wolf lovers didn't believe they were inconsistent. They worried that too many wolves could create problems for wolf restoration, which could lead to wolf poaching and harassment, so they supported *fewer*, not *more*, wolves.[17] Likewise, it seemed inconsistent that Michigan hunters were among those with the most positive attitudes toward wolf restoration. If you think of hunters as *only* competitive with wolves, this might seem inconsistent, but if you think of hunters as people who spend lots of time in nature, and who are concerned about wildlife and support it, you might not be so surprised.[18] You cannot assume consistency based on guesses. Assumptions must be tested with data.

The cognitive fix takes the "wheels and gears" approach to attitudes. If you believe attitudes are consistent, all you have to do is add cognitions (also known as facts), and these will act as drivers to change attitudes in predictable ways. The cognitive fix usually assumes the greater the knowledge, the more positive the attitudes. However, Kellert and I found *no relationship* between knowledge and support for wolf restoration in Michigan. Those with the most accurate knowledge of wolves did not support or oppose restoration any more than those with less accurate knowledge. So, educating the public about wolves would not be expected to increase support. Even worse, in Sweden, Göran Ericsson and I found an inverse relationship.[19] Those groups who knew the *least* were *most* supportive of wolves. Would this mean we should "de-educate" the Swedish public to increase support for wolves?

Knowledge comes from experience, and an important characteristic of an attitude is where we get it in the first place. Farmers in the Upper Peninsula were the most likely people to have seen wolves, had animals killed by wolves, known people who had animals killed by wolves, and killed wolves themselves. Many had heard wolves howl. Their attitudes toward wolves were based on direct experience. In contrast, most Lower Peninsula residents had never seen, heard, or lived near wolves. Attitudes based on direct experience are better developed. They have more beliefs, they're more stable, and they have stronger affect.[20] When people "have been there and done that," their attitude is more horizontally structured.

Attitudes Leopold took many words to describe in *A Sand County Almanac* were based on direct experience planting and watering trees on his land. Margaret's attitudes were based on years of work and research on the plumb curculio, and trying to get farmers to apply less poison. And Howard? Well, he had worked on the scene of Alaska's huge oil cleanup, and knew everything.

However, farmers' negative attitudes toward wolves are caused by something more than direct experience. Even though they had personal experience with wolves, 95% of them had *never* lost an animal to a wolf, and only 1% had lost more than one animal. Losses to disease, weather, and even cars are clearly more serious to farmers than wolf damage, but there is more to farming than economics. People refer to farming as a "way of life" or a set of social behaviors, personal relationships, work patterns, attitudes, and even values. These forces, along with direct experience, drive farmers' and ranchers' attitudes toward wolves. For them, the wolf was more than just another forest animal. For many, it challenged their special way of life. It was a symbol of wildness, and part of a farmer's job is taming wildness.

Farmers, we found, were afraid wolf restoration would be used as an excuse to stop development, establish wilderness areas, and restrict timber harvests and farming practices. For many farmers, the wolf was a symbol of urban society's dominance. It embodied alien values about the use of animals and natural resources. Farmers hold strong utilitarian attitudes toward animals, in general.[21] They supported the wolf only if they thought it useful for providing fur. They were the most likely of any group to say, "If wolves had more practical value, I could get more interested in reestablishing them in Michigan."

When an attitude is part of who you are—your identity—it has many beliefs, considerable stability, substantial horizontal structure, and a strong emotional basis. Leopold was first a forester, so his identity in this role would be associated with his attitude about trees. He had become a "restoration ecologist" long before the term was coined, and he told us about his efforts in this role. Likewise, my students' assignment was to tell something about themselves. It was no surprise they described things they wanted others to use to identify them as a researcher, a fan, or an Alaskan.

These three characteristics—consistency, direct experience, and links to our identities—are components of what social psychologists often call attitude strength.[22] One way social psychologists measure attitude strength is to ask people how certain they are of their attitudes. We should—and do—feel more certain about things that inspire strong feelings.

However, even strong attitudes have uncertainty. Leopold wonders: "But what would I do if my farm were further north, where pine is abundant and red birch is scarce? I confess I do not know. My farm is here."[23] Leopold is admitting uncertainty in his attitude. Uncertainty, like inconsistency, is part of *all* attitudes, whether we recognize it or not. Social psychologists call this ambivalence. This is often our problem when, as scientists, we try to pin down attitudes. Our surveys and questionnaires, as well as our managers and the public, sometimes demand certainty when it does not exist.

Now let's practice these principles and try to navigate the Ozone-Hole Rapids, a class II rapids of moderate difficulty with clear passages; and further downstream, Climate-Change Falls, a class V rapids of extreme difficulty with violent currents and rock-strewn passages. Because they both deal with Earth's atmosphere, you might think they're the same. Beware! Assumptions like that will send you swimming.

Ozone Holes and Climate Change

Research that led to the ozone hole's discovery began in 1958 as part of the International Geophysical Year, when scientists began measuring ozone high above Antarctica. In the 1970s, three scientists who went on to win the Nobel Prize documented the chemistry and role that chlorofluorocarbonated (CFC) gases play in atmospheric changes. In 1985, other scientists identified a dramatic ozone depletion above Antarctica. This declaration of an "ozone hole" in the upper atmosphere[24] led to international treaties and CFC bans.

Have you ever seen an ozone hole? How about a ghost? Then why are you afraid of them? An ozone hole is an attitude object no one experiences directly, yet people have beliefs, feelings, and ideas about how to deal with it. How did this happen?

Our beliefs, knowledge, and affect toward this object were created by news media, based on information from scientists. This transfer of secondary information created an attitude about an ozone hole. Attitudes toward ozone holes are based on faith in science and what scientists say. In this case, the public has no direct experience to dispute the natural scientists who made the discoveries.

So why believe in ozone holes, even though we've never seen one? People might not know what an ozone hole is, but it's easy to say and sounds a little exotic. The concept is simple. Ozone hooks to something directly understandable, a hole; and we find holes in socks, roads, and arguments. Generally, holes are not good. An ozone hole lets ultraviolet light pass through Earth's protective atmosphere, making sunburns more likely. We all recognize sunlight, and many of us have direct experience with sunburn. This is where the affect comes in. We associate too much sunlight and sunburn with *cancer*. And now these damned ozone holes, which we never even knew about, are creating still another cancer risk. Ozone holes are a perfect attitude object for scientists who want to influence society, because we have nearly unchallenged authority over what the public believes about an object they cannot see, touch, or experience.

As complicated as the science might be, an ozone hole seems simple. What causes the ozone hole? Stuff we put into the air somehow eats ozone. Some of it came from spray-can propellants for deodorants. How do you save the environment and reduce cancer? Quit spraying your underarms. Most ozone-eating chemicals come from industrial processes, so it was easy to identify the responsible industries and work with them. Chlorofluorocarbonates were easy targets for a structural fix, much like zoning floodplains or eliminating plastic-foam cups. You could identify basic sources and change the context to change their behavior. The public didn't have to be educated to change their attitudes or consumer choices. When they bought deodorant in subsequent years, it no longer sprayed on. It rolled on. Problem solved.

However, because this attitude is not based on direct experience, it is not a strong attitude. It has simple parts and is loosely tied to other objects people feel strongly about. For most of us, the ozone hole is not tied to our identity. Only the most active environmentalists wear an ozone hole on their T-shirts. We have few beliefs about ozone, so new information can rapidly change our attitudes. Our attitude toward the intangible object, the ozone hole, is not stable, partly because of its simplicity and lack of horizontal structure. If we could knock out one belief, the whole thing would likely tumble. The attitude has an emotional component, but it is not strong. After all, lots of stuff causes cancer, and ultraviolet light is way down the list. It also lacks the stability and emotion we find in, say, farmers' attitudes toward wolves.

Ozone-hole debates raged in the 1970s and 1980s. When I ask students today about ozone holes, I get only vague responses. When I tell them we used to *spray* on deodorant, they roll their eyes, but ask them about climate change. Bingo! Up comes a well-developed attitude with many beliefs and lots of affect. This attitude object needs plenty of scouting and careful navigation.

One reason attitudes toward climate change are so dangerous is that most of us have direct experience, not just scientific reports. Climate change affects our lives. Why do I live in Sweden? One reason is that I can no longer be sure of skiing in Lodi, Wisconsin. In the good ol' days, it snowed all winter, and on weekends you could ski. When it snows in southern Wisconsin now, you better get out there and ski because the snow might be gone by the weekend. A limnologist friend, John Magnuson, has studied Wisconsin's Lake Mendota for years, and his trend data confirm my personal experience. The lake is now ice-covered fewer days than it was decades ago. Everybody who has lived a long time in Madison noticed the change, too. However, John can tie years with the fewest days of ice to *El Nino*, so he has a theory, or at least a correlation. He worked with other scholars to document declines in the number of days lakes worldwide are ice covered.[25] Frozen lakes pass the famous *"interocular traumatic test."* That is, they hit you right between the eyes. There's no fancy or complicated data here. Everyone understands ice and days as units of measure. Based on the direct experience principle, we should expect attitudes toward global climate change to be stronger and less likely to change than attitudes toward ozone holes.

Global warming is also based on strong visuals like pictures of receding glaciers, as well as complicated scientific evidence. Like ozone holes, it's the stuff of Nobel Prizes. However, it was the Peace prize that Al Gore shared—in part because of his movie, *An Inconvenient Truth*—that publicized the problem worldwide. In contrast, the Chemistry prize for ozone was only for its science, not the hype. The film stirred strong emotions. Global warming is more like Howard's rant about Exxon, whereas the ozone hole is more like Margaret's report about the plumb curculio.

Beliefs about global warming are closely tied to basic values. Dealing with this problem will require large-scale collective actions, which threaten core U.S. values like freedom. However, not taking action threatens health and welfare, not just of people but of the planet. How countries make such decisions and keep their word challenges our basic ideas about governance and autonomy. Many see efforts to address global warming as fundamental challenges to capitalism. The fight has moved to science as an institution, and scientists have had their e-mails stolen. Moreover, it is tied to growing identities, like "environmentalists." Worse, global warming cannot be reversed by simply applying structural or technological fixes, as we did with ozone holes. Carbon emission depends on how we live, work (jobs), play (relax and vacation), travel (cars, air planes), and heat our homes. Making such changes based on direct experience, ties to basic values and beliefs, strong affect, and ties to our identities makes global warming a huge challenge. That is, it's a class V rapids, worthy of this definition from the International Scale of River Difficulty: "Exceedingly difficult, long and violent rapids following each other almost without interruption; riverbed extremely obstructed; big drops; violent current; very steep gradient; close study essential but often difficult. Requires best person, boat, and outfit suited to the situation. All possible precautions must be taken."

Dirty Little Secrets

We will come back to these kinds of attitude objects in later chapters. First, though, I must clear up another point. On my commute to Madison one day I heard a distinguished pollster tell a radio reporter, "I have to reveal one of polling's dirty little secrets." I turned up my radio. Who, after all, can resist dirty secrets? Was someone taking bribes? Did computers make mistakes? Did one firm have sloppy procedures? The "secret" was about a question asked on two different surveys that produced a 7-point difference in the percent responding "yes." The reporter had noticed the difference and could not let it go unexplained. It was too large to be due to random error. Why such a difference in two polls? Now pushed into a corner, the pollster said:

We in the polling business all know it makes a difference where you place a question in a survey. We get one answer if a question is early in the survey and another answer if it is later. And these questions were in different places on the two surveys.

I smiled and shook my head. As a scientist, I would have thought it a "dirty little secret" or outright lie if the pollster had said question order made no difference. The physicist Werner Heisenberg identified this problem in the 1920s, and won the Nobel Prize for it a few years later at age thirty-one. He observed that we cannot determine the location and speed of an electron at the same time. To measure speed, one must bounce photons off the electron, and even though photons are small, they change the location of the even-smaller electron. In physical sciences, this is called the Heisenberg Uncertainty Principle. In polling, we call the same thing "*a dirty little secret*," but it's simply the observer's impact on the observed object.

We must estimate the "speed and location" of attitudes by bouncing crude questions off these ghosts. When attitudes have little cognitive structure, our survey questions influence attitudes like photons blowing away electrons. Weak attitudes can change quickly with new information in the survey. I call these opinions, not attitudes. Most of us have only opinions, not attitudes, toward pine trees, the plumb curculio, and Koko Taylor. However, Leopold's, Margaret's, Joe's, and Howard's were well-developed attitudes and unlikely to change with new information found in questions. Most definitions of attitudes describe attitudes as being "relatively enduring." They stay with us, but many of our opinions vanish in an instant, and thus do not fit these definitions.

The problem with most polls is that they ask only one question to measure the like-dislike, favor-oppose dimensions that opinions share with attitudes. When we get an answer to one question, it's much like a nibble on a fishing line. We don't know if we have an opinion (not worth taking home for dinner), a fairly specific attitude (a dinner-size fish), or a well-developed attitude, like Leopold's toward pines (something that might break your line). To determine what's nibbling our bait, and determine the attitude's size and heft, we must "set the hook" with many questions.

In our Michigan survey about wolves, we measured the emotional component of attitudes with five questions. When a person definitely agrees that wolf calls are nature's most frightening sound, wolves can be dangerous to people, wolves are naturally cruel, and wolves would attack; and the same person definitely disagrees that wolves symbolize nature's beauty and wonder, we have someone with a strong negative attitude toward wolves. At the other end of the scale is the person who strongly disagrees with the first four beliefs and strongly agrees with the last. Responses to questions using words like *fear, beauty, cruel,* and *attack* are clearly measures of affect—the emotional dimension of attitudes. The person at one end of the scale might be labeled a wolf hater, and the person at the other end a wolf-lover. Being at the far ends of this scale registers a strong attitude toward wolves, whereas those in the middle have only an opinion or possibly an ambivalent attitude toward wolves. This is why we must ask so many questions in attitude studies, and why the single-opinion question in a survey reveals so little. It takes lots of stout gear to haul in a real attitude.

Conclusion

Attitudes, as I understand them, are based on values and built on beliefs, some of which are knowledge and some of which contain an emotional component called evaluative beliefs. Attitudes have a horizontal structure, depending on the number of beliefs and values on which they are based. They have varying degrees of consistency and rationality. Strong attitudes resist change because they are based on direct experience, identities, and many beliefs and values. Some attitudes, like Howard's, are driven by affect, and every new fact is quickly tainted with a negative or positive slant.

Attitudes tend toward consistency, but the parts are not hooked together like a set of gears. Adding new information does not necessarily change them, but irrational attitudes cannot be ignored simply because they are "irrational." Indeed, the "irrational" part requires us to take them into account and carefully measure them to understand their dimensions as part of any environmental project.

Attitudes we see jutting from the water ahead are often only the peaks of large boulders. The boulders' great bulk is why, after years of endless effort, the river has not moved them. We, too, will fail to move them. Instead, we must navigate them, which requires understanding. Remember, beneath Leopold's observable behavior—cutting birches so his pines could grow better—was a huge structure of values, beliefs, and evaluative beliefs.

Those looking for a simple, clear definition of attitude might be frustrated. Indeed, social psychologists have defined it operationally in many different ways.[26] Along with the terms I noted, diagrams I drew, and principles I outlined, most conceptual definitions include these seven points:

- We cannot see attitudes; they must be inferred from something.
- Attitudes differ from behavior, which we can see.
- Attitudes have objects.

- Attitudes have cognitive (belief) and affective (emotion) components.
- Attitudes have a direction—positive or negative.
- Attitudes are relatively enduring.
- Attitudes are related to but differ from values and opinions.

Rather than debate elements of definitions, I tried in this chapter to discuss the attitude concept as a whole. You might not know everything about attitudes, but you now know enough to explore assumptions of the cognitive fix. In the next chapter we will examine how attitudes change, starting with Aldo Leopold, who went from wolf-hater to wolf-lover.

3

Attitude Change

ALDO LEOPOLD MEETS THE BENNINGTON WOMEN

"WE HAD NEVER heard of passing up a chance to kill a wolf," Aldo Leopold explained when writing that he and a companion emptied their guns at a mother wolf and six half-grown pups in "a mêlée of wagging tails and playful maulings."[1] Not only did Leopold report killing wolves, he clarified his anti-wolf attitude, advocating for "wise control" [extermination] of not just wolves, but also "mountain lions, coyotes, bears, bobcats, foxes and birds of prey." Ten years after the wolf massacre, his attitude persisted: "It is going to take patience and money to catch the last wolf or lion in New Mexico. But the last one must be caught before the job can be called successful."[2]

In technical terms, Leopold held a strong, stable, and well-developed negative attitude toward wolves. He even acted out his attitude in antiwolf behavior. He was a wolf hater and shot them whenever opportunities arose. Today, he would be seen as the worst of those who oppose wolf restoration. Yet despite this strong negative attitude, he changed his mind. Leopold's essay, "Thinking Like a Mountain," which he wrote almost three decades later for *A Sand County Almanac,* is an ode to the wolf. His epiphany encourages everyone that people can change. They can even shift their attitudes 180 degrees. As the heart and hope of the cognitive fix, attitude change needs closer scrutiny. In this chapter, we look at Leopold, Swedish hunters, Bennington College co-eds, the American public, upstate New Yorkers, Wisconsin residents, and more of my students to better understand how and when attitudes change.

These cases show attitude change often takes time, direct experience, and social influence. For Leopold and Swedish hunters, change was tied to their experiences. Leopold saw what happened when wolves were extirpated in America, and hunters saw what happened when wolves returned in Sweden. Leopold's attitude changed as he moved into a new social setting and acquired a new identity. Direct experience and identity principles help us understand these cases. The same processes went on in Bennington College, a small, liberal-arts school in New England where students acquired identity-based attitudes that persisted a lifetime.

I go on to show that less well-developed attitudes, those not tied to our identities or based on direct experience, can change quickly when a new attitude object is linked to stronger, more well-developed attitudes. That is what happened when a strange disease struck Wisconsin's deer herd, and when a supposedly popular proposal to restore wolves quickly derailed in New York State. Furthermore, an unplanned experience in my classroom showed how dissonance created by a guest speaker changed deeply held attitudes with limited horizontal structure. This case study illustrates the consistency principle. Finally, to understand societal rather than individual change, I explain how both cohort effects (changes in the population) and period effects (influence of specific events) alter attitudes.

Direct Experience and Identity Change

"How many psychiatrists does it take to change a light bulb?" The oft-repeated answer: "Only one, but the light bulb has to really want to change." Leopold's attitude, like the personified light bulb, changed from within. Nobody "educated" him or bombarded him with brochures telling him wolves were wonderful (the cognitive fix). Time and direct experience are key ingredients of attitude change. Opinions can change quickly, but deeply seated attitudes like Leopold's—which are close to basic values and are tied to identities—change slowly, if at all.

The key belief grounding Leopold's original attitude toward wolves weakened as he watched ecosystems change once wolves disappeared. "I thought that because fewer wolves meant more deer, that no wolves would mean hunters' paradise,"[3] Leopold observed in "Thinking Like a Mountain." However, that didn't happen when states extirpated wolves. Without predators, deer died of their "own too much," overgrazing and degrading mountain ecosystems.

Direct experience can turn attitudes against wolves, too. When Sweden had no wolves, surveys showed more than 60% of Swedish hunters supported wolves. After wolves returned and did wolf-like things like killing and eating beloved family pets and hunting dogs, surveys 20 years later showed support among hunters dropped to 40%.[4]

Roles influence experience, perspective, and attitudes. Leopold made a major shift from forester to wildlife scientist and teacher during the years his attitude changed. As a forester, Leopold valued production: more trees for human benefit. Leopold also thought beyond the trees to recreational benefits of more deer. He moved from management into science, and became a professor of game management. As part of this role change, he wrote the first textbook on game management and helped found the Wilderness Society. As he transformed from forester to scientist, Leopold took more holistic views of ecosystems. The wolf became a key species in the ecosystem and a symbol of nature and wilderness, not just a competitor for game.

This change did not come quickly or easily. It required at least a quarter-century of growth and experience for Leopold to shift his attitude toward wolves. Why, then, do we think it reasonable—or in any way possible—to "educate the public" in a few months, or even years, and expect ranchers, bear hunters, and Sami reindeer herders to quit shooting wolves? Note the metaphors we use for attitude change: "change of mind" or "change of heart." Such changes are like brain or heart transplants, but only the latter is doable, though not simple. Leopold's change required a long personal journey.

When Leopold changed reference groups, we would expect his attitude to change. Social psychologist Daryl Bem once observed that an attitude requires a "fact, a feeling and a following."[5] *Fact* and *feeling* refer to the cognitive and the affective parts of attitude, which we discussed in the previous chapter. To that, we now add "a following," people around you with similar attitudes. This is why we sometimes use the term "social" as a modifier to describe the attitude concept. Sometimes when people change roles, environments, and social settings, then like the light bulb, they are in a unique position to change their attitudes. One of the most famous studies on the effects of what sociologists call "reference groups" began at Bennington College. Although the Bennington story is not about a change in environmental attitudes, it demonstrates the power of others to influence what we think.

Isolation and Changing Reference Groups

About the time Leopold changed his attitudes toward wolves, a young social psychologist named Theodore Newcomb began teaching at Vermont's newly founded Bennington College. At Bennington, Newcomb collected data showing dramatic attitude changes among students during their four years of college. More important, he followed up with the students and showed that their attitude changes persisted for 25 and even 50 years.

Bennington College, established early in the Great Depression, lies three miles outside the small village of the same name in southern Vermont. The first class comprised eighty-seven female students and a handful of faculty. The college was a self-conscious experiment in liberal education. Students had considerable social freedom without externally imposed social rules: "Bennington regards education as a sensual and ethical, no less than an intellectual,

process . . . directed toward self-fulfillment and toward constructive social pur-
poses." (This statement has been read at every Bennington commencement
since 1936). Faculty members in those years were new, young, and eager to
build a college together. Given tuition costs, one would expect the students
were economically well off, and mostly from Republican, politically conservative families. Bennington's liberal faculty wanted students to understand the
struggles of those less well off.

As part of his research, Newcomb measured the political liberalism of students in each class with an attitude scale of 26 items.[6] During their years at
Bennington, the first class—which entered in 1932—became more liberal.
The same thing happened with students entering in 1933 and in 1934. (Table
3.1) There was something about being at Bennington—away from their families, but with liberal professors and more liberal upper-class women—that
changed their political attitudes.

Table 3.1   Increasing Liberal Attitudes of Bennington Students

Year Surveyed	Year Entered		
	1932	1933	1934
1932	65.8		
1933	68.6	60.1	
1934	66.5	62.3	58.9
1935	74.5	68.5	64.1
1936		78.8	72.3
1937			71.9

Newcomb found even more dramatic evidence of change when asking students how they would vote and how they thought their parents would vote in
the 1936 presidential election. The candidates were Alf Landon, a Republican;
Franklin Roosevelt, a Democrat; Norman Thomas, a Socialist; and Earl
Browser, a Communist. Freshmen, as you would expect, were much like their
parents, with 60% supporting the Republican, 30% supporting the Democrat,
and 10% supporting the Socialist or Communist candidate (Table 3.2). After
one year at Bennington, students showed nearly equal support for Republicans and Democrats, but their parents' preferences (without benefit of the
Bennington "treatment") were reported to be similar to the freshmen's parents. The most dramatic effect was among juniors and seniors, a majority of
whom supported Roosevelt and almost a third of whom supported Socialist or
Communist candidates. Only 15% supported the Republican.

Table 3.2 1936 Candidate Preferences of Students and
Student Reports of Parents

Candidate	Freshman		Sophomores		Juniors and Seniors	
	Students	Parents	Students	Parents	Students	Parents
Republican	62%	66%	43%	69%	15%	60%
Democrat	29%	26%	43%	22%	54%	35%
Socialist/ Communist	9%	7%	15%	8%	30%	4%

How did Bennington change attitudes? No doubt self-selection played a role. These were young, adventurous women willing to try something new. Given the college's free-spirited reputation, they were light bulbs desiring change. They came from families likely more liberal than the general public. Less than 1% of the nation's electorate supported Socialist and Communist candidates in 1936, but 7% of freshmen said their parents did. Thus, even Bennington's freshman class contained a core of students from families willing to endorse unconventional ideas.

College changes people. I went to the University of Chicago wearing a Goldwater pin in 1964. Over four years I shifted 180 degrees as I adapted to my new intellectual reference group far from my Wisconsin hometown. Hillary Clinton did the same. She carried a copy of Goldwater's *Conscience of a Conservative* to Wellesley College. Three years later she was working for liberal Democrat Eugene McCarthy in the 1968 presidential election.[7]

Based on the identity principle, we would hypothesize that attitudes acquired in college should be strong and persistent. Our understanding of the social psychology of attitude change comes largely from hour-long laboratory sessions. Few studies look at attitude change over even a couple of weeks. Newcomb's work is rare and noteworthy because he and his associates followed up the Bennington students over the next five decades. Social psychologists think attitudes are important, particularly because they *don't* change. The Bennington study provided the evidence.

Newcomb tracked down and resurveyed the Bennington women 25 years later in 1960 to determine if their political attitudes remained liberal. The presidential election that year between John F. Kennedy and Richard M. Nixon was a good test of liberal political attitudes. In the follow-up survey, about 60% of the Bennington women preferred Kennedy,[8] but 50% of the nation's electorate voted for Kennedy. These, however, were Bennington women and college graduates. Only about 30% of college-educated females reported support-ing Kennedy in 1960, so the Bennington women appeared twice as liberal as the comparison group. The Bennington effect had endured a quarter-century.

Before the 1964 election between Johnson and Goldwater, Newcomb sur-veyed the Bennington women again, and also asked whom their female rela-tives supported. This synthetic control group used people of the same gender, region, and socioeconomic status for a comparison. Bennington graduates were significantly more likely to prefer Johnson than were their female rela-tives who had not attended Bennington. The national survey in 1964 repli-cated the 1960 data: 90% of Bennington women said they voted for Johnson, compared to "about two-thirds of the total population of 'women like our grad-uates of the late 1930s.'"[9]

Twenty-five years later, Newcomb and younger colleagues followed up the Bennington women, then 50 years past college. They again showed these women stayed liberal over life's course. Just as new attitudes arose in the 1930s as the women changed their reference group, they maintained the atti-tudes by selecting friends and husbands sharing similar attitudes. As Bem reminds us, attitudes need a "following." Those who did not build this social network saw the "Bennington effect" diminish.[10]

Newcomb's work shows the power of attitudes. Once attitudes change and become part of new identities, they persist over time and affect voting behav-ior. This is why attitudes are important. Attitudes with well-developed cogni-tive structures and tied to our identities are stable and affect many things, including our policy choices. However, in thinking about the cognitive fix, we must realize the unique convergence of factors at Bennington:

1. Self-selection of women who were ready to change (attending Bennington rather than a more conventional school).
2. A time in life when young people form their identities.
3. An isolated college with a liberal normative climate. Our attitudes are influenced by those around us, not just by our own thoughts, and informa-tion we read in newspapers.
4. Time—four years.

Attitudes and the Media

Most people think the media change attitudes. However, with Leopold and the Bennington women, media had almost nothing to do with their attitude changes. Leopold changed his attitude based on direct experiences as a keen, scientific observer of nature. He watched what resulted from wolf-extermination policies he supported, and he learned from the events. The Bennington women learned from direct contact with professors and each other as part of their college experience.

In spite of our conventional wisdom that the media change attitudes, most research shows this is not true. What media do is set agendas.[11] As Bernard Cecil Cohen observed when identifying this function: "The press may not be successful much of the time in telling people what to think, but it is stunningly successful in telling its readers what to think about."[12] When Hurricane Katrina made the front pages of newspapers, we talked and thought about the disaster. Most of us read to gain information that supports our attitudes. We mentally refute inconsistent information. In my case, I thought this was another case in which the technical fix (like levees) failed. Meanwhile, my sister thought mostly about helping the victims. She made plans to travel to New Orleans to rebuild houses. Media reports didn't change our attitudes about floods, hurricanes, New Orleans, or our sense of self. My sister hoped this information would make her brother more compassionate. I hoped it would change her mind about nature. We were both disappointed.

The next two cases look at attitude changes that involved the media. We will see the attitudes did not change because of the media, but because the media framed the issues with new attitude objects linked to much stronger attitudes.

Attitude Change through Reframing: Wolves in the Adirondacks

From the wildlife manager's view, everybody seems to have strong attitudes about wolves. People love them or hate them, and their attitudes are strongly polarized. Or are they? Actually, attitudes toward wolves are not as strong as managers and wolf advocates think. One surprise in our analysis of 28 years of published studies was that about 25% of those filling out and returning surveys don't care much either way about wolves.[13] What about the 30 to 60% who don't return surveys? Our best guess is that nonrespondents *really* don't care about wolves. Most people know what a wolf is, but their attitudes have little affect or horizontal structure. Furthermore, their attitudes are not tied to their identity, which means the attitudes can change quickly if events change or new information surfaces.

That's what happened in New York State's Adirondack Mountains, a six-million-acre forest preserve currently without wolves. Researcher Mark Duda of Responsive Management surveyed this rural area and found 76% of residents supported wolf restoration.[14] Wildlife professionals, thrilled with this public support, announced they would soon reintroduce wolves. It made biological and sociological sense. The area had few people, plenty of room for wolves, and public support of landslide proportions.

Some locals disliked the idea and began reframing the debate. Rather than "restoring nature," they thought "people from Washington are telling us what to do" by "dumping wolves where we have hardly any deer." Thus, they linked wolves to attitudes toward deer hunting and local control. These attitudes were based on direct experience and tied to identities much stronger than attitudes toward wolves. "Local control" in rural areas is further linked to central values like independence and freedom. This framing of wolf reintroduction landed in local newspapers. Stories about wolves were really stories about local control, and wolves represented controlling outsiders. Therefore, weak attitudes can change, not so much by giving people information (the cognitive fix), but by setting the agenda and linking weak attitudes to stronger ones. Once wolf restoration was framed as an outsider-controlled issue and tied to values of freedom and independence, there was no going back. A Defenders of Wildlife member reported going into a 400-person public meeting and being pleased to see wolves on so many T-shirts until she looked closer and saw the wolves were in the crosshairs of riflescopes.[15]

Furthermore, community leaders challenged the survey and Duda's professional integrity. Local newspapers claimed his research must be flawed because "nobody" wanted wolves introduced. Although the survey followed normal scientific standards, Duda and his staff took this criticism personally and professionally. Even though the wolf-restoration project was annihilated by the attitude change, and biological scientists fled the scene, Duda wanted to know what happened. Using his own money, he conducted another survey the next year and found support had plunged by 30 percentage points. Who "changed" their attitudes? The Aldo Leopold wolf lovers? The wolf haters? Not likely. It was the great segment of the public who had not thought much about wolves and who had poorly developed attitudes. Because reframing the plan linked wolves to beliefs about local control and values such as independence, the new frame literally formed an attitude about wolf restoration where none had existed before. The new antiwolf attitudes had little horizontal structure (i.e., unlike Leopold's pine-tree attitude, they were not based on many beliefs and values), but they were tied closely to key values and community identity.

Because attitudes toward wolf restoration changed quickly, one might think they could easily change back. However, think about the attitudes' structure. They went from nonattitudes to an attitude linked to something much stronger. Such links are not easily undone, nor are the basic attitudes toward wolves likely to change. As the population changes over the years, we might see new migrants with different attitudes, but the locals' attitude will remain stable. In fact, two years later, another research group conducted a third survey and found the new attitudes remained negative.[16] I expect that a follow-up today would show similar results. More certainly, no wolves roam the Adirondacks today.

CWD and Wisconsin Deer

When a new attitude object enters the scene and is linked to far more well-established attitudes, we can see affect, beliefs, and even behavioral intentions change in days or weeks, rather than years or decades, especially if raw emotion charges the new object. This happened in Wisconsin. If you don't hunt deer or live in Wisconsin, you probably don't know what CWD means. Chronic wasting disease is mad cow disease in deer, a strange brain disease that causes animals to die long, horrible deaths. Similar diseases afflict various species and go by different names: in humans, Creutzfeldt-Jakob disease (CJD); in sheep, scrapie; and in cattle, bovine spongiform encephalopathy (BSE), which the media call mad cow disease.

In February 2002 in Wisconsin, three white-tailed deer tested positive for CWD. If such a strange disease had been found in the plumb curculio, the news would have been lucky to generate even one story on page 17, but CWD in Wisconsin's iconic wildlife species was something else. Deer and deer hunting is more than a big deal in Wisconsin. Surveys showed that more than two-thirds of Wisconsin deer hunters report: "If I had to give up deer hunting I would miss it more than all or almost all of the other activities I now enjoy."[17] Some schools, even factories, close during the nine-day hunting season as more than 600,000 hunters go afield. More than half these hunters leave home and go to a camp.[18] Signs hang in North Woods bars: "Hunting is not a matter of life and death. It is more important than that." With nearly one in three men and an increasing number of women in Wisconsin buying hunting licenses, it's safe to say that half the state's families are affected by the deer hunt. Therefore, Wisconsinites hold strong attitudes about deer. They are based on direct experience: deer hunting and venison eating. These attitudes also tie closely to identities, with hundreds of thousands of Wisconsin citizens describing themselves as deer hunters, and the state decreeing the whitetail its "wildlife animal." At the same time, few Wisconsinites knew anything about CWD or the human version, CJD, so we had a new attitude object suddenly hooked to deer and deer hunting.

In situations lacking direct experience, we look to others to see how they react. Wildlife managers acted terrified. Almost overnight, they proposed trying to wipe out the disease by killing every last deer in the region where sick deer were found. This was most remarkable in a state that had restored its deer herd over the past century through careful management. These wildlife stewards were now trying to kill off those deer in a large part of southwestern Wisconsin.

Richard Nelson, anthropologist and author of *Heart and Blood: Living with Deer in America,* described the event as the equivalent of a fire in the Sistine Chapel. Responsible officials used fires, tornados, war, and cancer as metaphors. "It was not a tornado or forest fire that hit a portion of deer management unit 70A . . . but state agencies responded as they would for any emergency," wrote Jerry Davis, a retired biology professor. Milton Friend, former head of the National Wildlife Health Center in Madison, likened chronic wasting disease hotspots to "a wind-whipped fire." Dave Weitz, a Wisconsin Department of Natural Resources information officer, said: "It's like a forest fire. You don't wait for it to get as big as it can get; you take care of it immediately." Wayne Cunningham, a Colorado veterinarian, used even stronger language: "I think it is time to treat this like cancer and cut deep and wide."[19]

Media reports suggested "most experts" believed meat from CWD-infected deer was safe to eat, implying other experts might disagree. The press started asking CWD experts if *they themselves* would eat infected venison. Simply asking the question increased the fear. Within a week, CWD—discovered in three deer—was being interpreted and managed as a statewide health risk. The state reinforced the risk's gravity by creating an interagency *Health* and Science Team (emphasis added). The science reporter for a statewide newspaper, writing under the headline, "Scientists are alarmed by chronic wasting disease," personalized the scientists rather than simply reporting their words: "It is striking to hear researchers talk about chronic wasting disease, or CWD and *hear the worry in their words*"[20] (emphasis added).

In these ways, the media campaign played to the affective, or emotional, side of the attitude rather than the cognitive, or knowledge, side. Daily media attention emphasizing scientific uncertainty, coupled with dramatic and reactive management by state agencies, simply increased fear. Thus, the press could not make the risk familiar, knowable, understandable, and manageable.[21]

The scope of the press coverage was amazing, especially for those of us who struggle to get even a single column inch of coverage for environmental issues. The *Wisconsin State Journal* and the *Capital Times,* the two major daily newspapers in the state capital, Madison, ran 746 stories on CWD (more than two a day) from March to December 2002. The *Milwaukee Journal-Sentinel* ran nearly 400, or more than one story a day those 10 months. The Gannett Newspaper chain, which owns 11 newspapers in northeastern Wisconsin, ran more than 500 stories, 149 of which were *on the front page*. Before CWD's discovery in the state, there were virtually no articles about it in Wisconsin newspapers.[22]

With this attention and lack of previous direct experience, a new attitude object (CWD) was created and hooked to other broader attitudes about food and recreation (venison and deer hunting). An Internet survey within three weeks of the discovery showed 39% of respondents were concerned about eating venison.[23] The first scientific study two months later showed 96% of the population had heard of CWD, and 42% had concerns about eating wild venison. Even the behavioral-intention component of the attitude construct was affected, with 36% of hunters reporting they would consider not hunting whitetails in November during the state's deer season.

In the case of wolves in the Adirondacks and CWD in Wisconsin, an attitude was created when a new object reached the public agenda and was hooked to broader, stronger attitudes by the mass media. This CWD attitude was based on almost no direct experience with deer infected with CWD. It carried high levels of emotion, both from its link with deer hunting and its ties to human health issues. A new attitude was created, and beliefs about deer changed within days or months.

The Consistency Principle in Action: The Case of the Exxon Mine

While trying to learn more about how media change attitudes, I received an unexpected lesson in attitude change inside my classroom. During the 1970s, Exxon found a huge concentrated ore deposit outside the North Woods community of Crandon, Wisconsin. Opponents from all quarters fought Exxon's efforts to develop this mine. Mining foes included the Wisconsin Department of Natural Resources, environmental groups, university professors, and students at UW-Madison (recall Howard and his anti-Exxon attitude in chapter 2). Exxon eventually gave up and sold the ore deposit to other mining companies, of which Nicolet Minerals was the latest. Nicolet tried turning the opposition around with a slick advertising campaign.

I did not expect scientific journals to carefully assess this advertising effort, nor did I expect Nicolet to divulge how much it spent on the ads or to rate their effectiveness, so I invited Dale Alberts, public-relations director for Nicolet Minerals, to visit the university and give a lecture about his experiences. I told him the class was examining "the role of attitudes and attitude change in natural resource management." Alberts did as I asked, and we learned something about the commercials, but he outfoxed me and the class and, in the process, taught an important lesson about attitude change.

To understand what happened, we need a little theory. William McGuire, a giant in attitude research, introduced the "inoculation theory" into social psychology.[24] The metaphor comes from vaccines. McGuire argued that many attitudes don't get tested much if they're tied closely to values that everybody agrees with. Although such attitudes look tough, they are paper tigers (his metaphor, not mine) and crumble easily. Why? Because they have little horizontal structure: You don't like something because, well, you don't like it. Furthermore, nobody around here likes it, either. They lack supporting beliefs because there's no need to develop them. McGuire and others have shown in laboratories that such attitudes collapse when confronted by new, inconsistent information. To bolster the attitudes, you "inoculate" them by giving both sides of the argument. Better yet, tell people someone is going to "try to change their attitudes." Not realizing that Alberts would try to change my students' attitudes, I failed to inoculate them against his challenges.

Although he wore a blue suit and tie, Alberts didn't fit our expectations of a slick, imposing lobbyist or boastful mining vice president. He was a slight man with an "aw shucks" approach. He started by quietly asking students questions about themselves, where they were from, and where they lived on campus. He then set the hook: Did they have computers? Well, they proudly said they did. Gosh, he said, do you know computers contain copper and other metals? Did they ever wonder where those metals came from? Well, no they hadn't. So he talked about that. Mines bore into the ground, mostly in third-world countries where they're operated under horrible social and environmental conditions. I could see where he was heading, but short of pulling the nearest fire alarm, I had no way out. So I sat back and pondered the next teachable moment.

"Of course," he went on, "if we use computers and metals, then we are responsible for these conditions—the social and environmental impacts." However, there wasn't much we could do about it because foreign governments can run their countries the way they want, and big companies will try to make as much money as they can. But here was a big lump of copper in Wisconsin. The state had spent more than 15 years reviewing and modifying plans, and, yes, the first proposal for the Crandon mine might have had some problems, but new technology had arrived and the state had beefed up its mining laws. In fact, Wisconsin might be the world's best place to mine with minimal environmental impacts while delivering clear social benefits.

The students KNEW Alberts was wrong, but they couldn't figure out why. They had never heard those arguments before, and they had no counterarguments. Their belief structure was simple: EXXON MINE BAD. It will pollute the North's waters, and that's bad. It's a big, rich mining company. That's bad, too. End of story. No subtlety or complexity, and only limited horizontal structure. Therefore, the students sat in stunned silence when Alberts said: "We are going to keep mining. That is what we do, and we can do it in Chile or Wisconsin where you live. Which do you want?" Alberts had linked the proposed mine in Wisconsin to social-justice values he correctly assumed they held. This forced them to confront obvious inconsistencies between their opposition to the mine and their support for the environment and third-world populations.

The consistency principle says parts of attitudes are generally consistent. Leon Festinger in 1957 proposed that dissonance (an uncomfortable motivation state) resulted when two parts of an attitude were inconsistent or if we behaved in a way inconsistent with our attitude and without much outside justification.[25] To avoid this discomfort, he argued that people would change their attitudes. The problems with Festinger's theory, as I noted in chapter 2, is that we all have inconsistencies in our attitudes. Even Leopold, when he asked himself if he would hold the same attitude if his farm were located where pines were abundant said, "I confess I don't know. My farm is here." We can ignore inconsistencies, but they don't go away.

In some cases (usually in laboratories) and in my classroom that day, we see a dissonance effect. In that context, the students couldn't ignore their environmental values and the inconsistency of allowing social injustice and pollution in the rest of the world because they opposed mining in Wisconsin. I could just about hear those inconsistencies grating in their brains. In our next discussion, that is all the students wished to discuss. Their minds had been changed, and it troubled them. They had no protection from these new ideas. They had not been inoculated. Attitudes are somewhat like muscles. The strongest grow from regular exercise, such as pushing against opposition. Had the mine enjoyed more support on campus, and had newspaper reports been more thorough by asking and explaining how these companies mined elsewhere, the students might have been better protected against Alberts's arguments.

The setting itself helped make Alberts's arguments effective. If he were writing an op-ed for a newspaper, my students could have skipped the article or dismissed it. But in the classroom, Alberts had their full attention. They couldn't escape. He further benefited from "academic authority" perceptions. Their esteemed professor (vis. me) had brought him in, which implied he had something worth saying. So they listened and could not ignore what he was saying. Their attitudes changed.

Cohort Effects: Old Attitudes Die Out

Another way attitudes change is when the population itself changes. This does not require individuals to change their attitude but for people with "bad attitudes" to leave the population and get replaced by people with better attitudes. To explain this, let's return to our wolf lessons. Our review of all the studies of attitudes toward wolves published over 28 years showed that, in *every* case, older people had more negative attitudes toward wolves.[26] Based on that, I tell my students they will become more negative toward wolves as they grow older. They tell me I am crazy. They will not become wolf haters. They are probably right.

Older people's more negative attitude toward wolves is most likely caused by what sociologists call a "cohort effect." Older people in these studies "learned" their attitudes while young during the 1930s, 1940s, and 1950s. During this period, more people lived in rural areas and on small farms, and they held negative attitudes toward wolves because they were considered threats to livestock, even to humans. As time goes on, older people die, and they're replaced by younger cohorts who acquire the more positive attitudes that grow in urban cultures where wolves are framed in more positive lights.

To see if cohort change influenced environmental attitudes more broadly, environmental sociologists Craig Humphrey and Conrad Kanagy teamed with demographer Glenn Firebaugh to examine attitude change after support for the environment increased from 51% to 74% in the decade of the 1980s. This increase was based on one question on the General Social Survey: "I'd like you to tell me whether you think we are spending too much money, too little money, or about the right amount on improving and protecting the environment." Part, maybe all, of this attitude change occurred because society changes. In this case, Reagan's election as president in 1980 perhaps got the public worried that environmental gains of the previous decade would be lost. Sociologists call such changes a "period effect." Everyone, regardless of age, was influenced by Reagan's presidency. The question is: Was any part of the change caused by a cohort effect? That is, were older people, with less favorable environmental attitudes, being replaced by younger, more pro-environmental cohorts who acquired their attitudes while growing up in the 1970s?

Their analysis showed that 17.9% of the observed change was caused by this period effect (which means "something happened," but we don't know what). The remainder (5.6%) was caused by cohort replacement.[27] So about one-fourth of the change observed during the Reagan years could be traced to young people entering adulthood with more pro-environmental attitudes than the older cohorts who were dying out. But don't forget about time. This change took a decade. Cohort replacement takes generations, so it's not an overnight solution to social problems.

This finding was good news for the future of environmentalism. Just as attitudes acquired by the young women at Bennington College persisted, we expect the pro-environmental attitudes of this young cohort will also persist over five decades until younger cohorts replace them.

Period Effects and Measurement Challenges

Unfortunately, our understanding of environmental attitudes is limited because the attitude object "the environment" is, alas, especially slippery. The wolf, by contrast, is an attitude object that can be captured, tagged, and collared. An ozone hole, even though it comes from the most indirect of measurements and the say-so of scientists, is relatively simple and specific. "The environment," as we commonly refer to it, was a social construction of the 1960s,[28] and a broad, general, and abstract attitude object.

In 1965, the Gallup and Opinion Research Corporation thought there was enough interest to ask about the environment for the first time.[29] These surveys had no questions about ozone holes, biodiversity, or wolf restoration. Nor were the questions about the environment in general. Rather, they asked about air and water pollution.

A serious problem for assessing attitude change is that the pollsters started changing the questions as environmental attitudes grew stronger, belief systems filled out, and new attitude objects emerged. Although modifying questions to accommodate better environmental awareness might seem reasonable, it makes it nearly impossible to track change over time. Imagine trying to track changes in CO_2 if scientists replaced it with measures of CO and then again with measures of H_2O just because they had an O in the molecule.

In the early years of environmental polling, the attitude object was a belief that pollution was a serious problem where you lived, or that government should not cut spending for pollution control. After the first Earth Day in 1970, open-ended "most important problem" (MIP) questions were asked. The attitude object changed from pollution to the environment's rank among national problems. In fixed-response questions, the attitude object changed from "pollution" to "the environment." Roper asked people if they were more on the side of "protecting the *environment*," and how they felt about "*environmental* protection laws." The National Opinion Research Center (NORC) asked if the United States was spending too much or too little on "improving and protecting the *environment*." Cambridge Reports asked how people felt about "sacrificing environmental quality." Only Roper continued asking people if they felt that severe air pollution, water pollution, or a shortage of water supplies would be a serious problem. But then Roper added "25 to 50 years from now" to the question, again changing the attitude object by adding a time dimension.[30]

With Ronald Reagan's election, and particularly his appointment of James Watt as Secretary of the Interior, some thought the environment was going to be ignored. Roper even quit asking questions on protecting the environment in 1984 and didn't resume until 1989. In the 1980s the attitude object was laws; it was not pollution, most important problems, or the environment. Trade-off questions asking people to choose between the environment and energy, and environment and jobs added still other attitude objects.

What we can say for sure is that, between 1965 and 1970, there was a sea change in attitudes. The percentage of people who believed reducing air and water pollution was one of three problems the government should address jumped from 17% to 53%;[31] the percentage viewing air pollution as a serious problem leaped from 28% to 69%; and the percentage viewing water pollution as a serious problem soared from 35% to 74%.[32] Such dramatic change is at the base of the cognitive fix, but let's not overlook an important point: *Nobody set out to change these attitudes.* Not even the most dedicated conspiracy theorists claim that a cabal of environmentalists planned how to change America's environmental views. The social sciences frequently discuss why these changes occurred, but they find no definitive agreement.[33] Indeed, as opinion started shifting back from those high levels in the early 1970s, policy scholar and economist Anthony Downs offered the environment as an example of how issues go through attention cycles, and how declining support is inevitable.[34]

However, Downs was wrong. The public did not tire of the environment. Support remained stable, increased slightly in the 1970s, and took off during the Reagan years. In terms of attitude change, Reagan might have been the great environmental president, but no one would have predicted that, either. This chart from Riley Dunlap[35] (Figure 3.1) shows that the belief that "environmental regulations have not gone far enough" increased when the anti-environmental Reagan was elected, dropped when the pro-environmental Clinton/Gore team took office, and stabilized after an anti-environmental Republican Congress gained control in 1995 until the turn of the century. What happened next? We

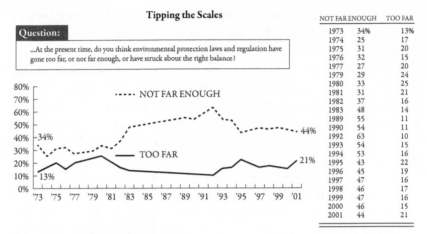

Tipping the Scales

Question:

...At the present time, do you think environmental protection laws and regulation have gone too far, or not far enough, or have struck about the right balance?

	NOT FAR ENOUGH	TOO FAR
1973	34%	13%
1974	25	17
1975	31	20
1976	32	15
1977	27	20
1979	29	24
1980	33	25
1981	31	21
1982	37	16
1983	48	14
1989	55	11
1990	54	11
1992	63	10
1993	54	15
1994	53	16
1995	43	22
1996	45	19
1997	47	16
1998	46	17
1999	47	16
2000	46	15
2001	44	21

FIGURE 3.1 **Attitude Change 1973–2001**

don't know, because Roper quit asking the question. In any case, we can be certain environmental concern did not disappear as predicted, and that period events like the election of certain presidents can change environmental beliefs.

Most important is that attitudes of the broader population ebb and flow in ways we cannot predict or control, and that is the problem. Thus, hoping that naturally occurring attitude change will solve environmental problems is like a canoeist hoping the river will somehow clear out the rapids roaring around the next bend.

Conclusion

Rocks don't wash downstream overnight. Many attitudes change, but slowly. Leopold's attitudes toward wolves, the attitudes of the general public toward the environment, and the attitudes of Swedish hunters toward wolves took decades to change. For the Bennington women, the change took only years. Environmental attitudes in America changed when younger cohorts slowly replaced older citizens in a process taking decades. Cognitive fixes usually hope for more rapid change—that is, "Get through the rapids right now!" They wish to solve immediate environmental problem by educating the public today.

The cognitive fix also demands that we plan to change attitudes and that we go out and do so. Most of the cases I discussed involved naturally occurring change. They were neither planned nor predictable, and in some cases were undesirable. No one set out to change Aldo Leopold or the Swedish hunters, but their attitudes changed as they got experience with wolves. The Wisconsin DNR did not want the public to fear venison and consider not hunting, but that's what happened as the agency struggled to deal with CWD. Conservation biologists who hoped to relocate wolves to the Adirondacks were shocked and disappointed at the almost overnight change to antiwolf attitudes, but they were helpless to reverse it. No secret cabal met at some military base in Nevada in the 1960s to make Americans more receptive to environmental protections during the next four decades, but it happened anyway. So while rocks do shift their position, it is not canoeists who move them.

There were two cases in which people set out to change attitudes and succeeded. It's not surprising that both were in college settings. The Bennington faculty hoped to change their students' political attitudes, and in a near total-immersion setting lasting four years, they succeeded. Mr. Alberts, the mining company's spokesman, walked into my classroom and changed the students' attitudes by giving information inconsistent with their more central attitudes and values, knowing they could not ignore it. Students change because it's a time in their lives when they are processing new information and ideas while forming their identities. Many of my colleagues in environmental studies think their courses change attitudes. I expect they are right. These self-selected populations, at this time in their lives, are particularly susceptible to information from their teachers. However, for solving most environmental problems, the cognitive fix requires we change the attitudes of homeowners, automobile drivers, and the general public, not students in our classes.

Attitudes based on direct experience are stronger, change more slowly, and tend to be stable. Leopold gained experience over the years by watching what happened to ecosystems in which wolves were extirpated. Wisconsinites with no direct experience with CWD had to invent their attitude based almost exclusively on secondary sources. Such change can happen quickly when linked to stronger attitudes.

Leopold's and the Bennington students' attitudes changed as they changed their identities. There was something special about being a Bennington woman, and this played out in their increasingly liberal attitudes and the stability of those attitudes over time. Leopold changed identity as a forester and his attitudes toward wolves changed accordingly, but getting people to change their identities is neither simple nor fast. In fact, it's usually impossible. Identity change is but a siren song for the cognitive fix. It's possible and powerful, but generally out of reach.

Inconsistent information changed my students' attitudes, but again, it was a unique case. Mr. Alberts had the floor and artfully juxtaposed inconsistent cognitions in ways my students could not dismiss. They had not been inoculated.

When that happens, attitudes change. However, it's easy to ignore inconsistencies when the cognitive fix plays out in the department coffee room or in the realtor's office when someone is making a down payment on a spiffy riverside house with a great view.

When attitudes have little horizontal or vertical structure, they can change quickly by linking them to more central, well-developed attitudes, which resemble basic values. Thus, we saw quick-change attitudes toward CWD in Wisconsin, wolf restoration in New York, and the Crandon mine in my classroom.

So attitudes do change under some circumstances, but that is not enough to make the cognitive fix an effective solution to environmental problems. Two further assumptions must be explored. First, our environmental attitudes influence our pro-environmental actions. Second, we can plan and carry out strategies to change attitudes and change behaviors through the "education process." In the next chapter, I explore that first assumption. What did Leopold, once equipped with positive attitudes toward wolves, do when the chips were really down?

4

Attitudes Are *Not* Everything

IN 1943 ALDO Leopold was appointed to the Wisconsin Conservation Commission, the body that approved the state's hunting and fishing rules. Soon after the appointment, Leopold wrote "Thinking like a Mountain," his famous essay reporting his changed attitude toward wolves.[1] Less than a year after penning this essay, the Commission took a vote that tested his attitude. Deer hunters were demanding bounties be reinstated on coyotes and the state's remaining wolves. On a cold January day, the commission met and voted to pay people to kill Wisconsin's last few wolves.[2] Aldo Leopold, the man with the changed attitude, voted affirmatively.

If attitudes mean anything, how could Leopold say one thing and do another? How could he honor wolves in his words but vote to pay people to kill them? Voting is a clear, observable behavior that—better than most behaviors—represents attitudes. Leopold's vote contradicted the attitude in his essay. As we shall see, Leopold is neither alone, nor unique, in failing to act consistently with his attitude. The struggle in social psychology and in everyday life is to reconcile this divide between attitudes and behavior. This gap is the fundamental problem with the cognitive fix or "educate the public" solution to environmental problems. What does it matter if attitudes change if they have so little to do with behavior? This chapter examines how and when attitudes influence behavior and, more important, when they do not.

The Strange Case of LaPiere and the Chinese Couple

To begin this journey, we must learn something about a 10,000-mile road trip Richard LaPiere took with a couple of friends. The original report, published in a prestigious academic journal in 1934, was all but ignored for 30 years until it was "rediscovered" in the mid 1960s[3] and would be listed as one of the four most influential articles in social psychology 80 years later.[4] Years after LaPiere retired, my student Bob Baumgartner and I sat in his living room and asked him to tell us more about that road trip.[5]

LaPiere had befriended a Chinese couple who were in graduate school with him at Stanford University, and they gave him an excuse to engage in his passion for driving. The three made several trips exploring the West Coast, and they even drove all the way to New York. Like any good host, LaPiere worried how his guests would be treated. As he recalled 50 years later: "We know people hate . . . the Chinese. . . . There is prejudice against them." Despite his fears, they had no problems at the first few places they stopped for lunch or overnight stays. Like a good social scientist, LaPiere turned this into a research opportunity and recorded what happened at 67 "hotels, auto camps and 'Tourist Homes,'" and at 184 "restaurants and cafes" during their travels. Among these 251 establishments, only one refused service. Six months later, LaPiere sent a questionnaire to each establishment, asking, "Will you accept members of the Chinese race as guests in your establishment?"[6] He received responses from 128, but only one said *it WOULD accept Chinese people as guests.*

That is a serious problem for those who think attitudes and behaviors are virtually the same. Not only is there inconsistency between attitude and behavior, but behavior can be *opposite* of attitude. The problem gets worse. The common failure of attitude to predict behavior is often explained away because the wrong component of attitude is being measured.[7] If LaPiere had simply assessed the affective component of attitudes (e.g., How do you feel about people of the Chinese race?), we could have "explained away" the inconsistency by saying, "Well, you can dislike Chinese [attitude] but still think you ought to serve them in your hotel." Or if we had measured knowledge and beliefs about Chinese (e.g., Chinese helped build the transcontinental railroad, agree or disagree; or many Chinese live in San Francisco, agree or disagree), we could have said these beliefs were irrelevant to the action of serving lunch.

However, LaPiere cleverly measured a component of attitudes we call "behavioral intention" (BI). This is the element of attitude that is supposed to be the precursor of behavior in popular theories of reasoned action or planned behavior.[8] What you say you intend to do (BI), in this case, refuse to serve Chinese, is supposed to be virtually the same as what you eventually do (B). However, that did not happen. LaPiere showed that, in the world outside the laboratory, people act inconsistently with their behavioral intentions. This study defies how most people—even some social psychologists—think attitudes work. So, why do people say one thing and do another?

Situations versus Attitudes

Social psychologists have gone out of their way to dismiss LaPiere's findings on methodological grounds. One such critic, who must have taken a class from LaPiere or met him in the 1960s, claimed the Chinese couple were served in deference to their white companion, a distinguished, powerful, white-haired gentleman. Many others—including Fishbein and Ajzen, even as late as 2005[9]—suggest someone other than the desk clerk or waitress who served the couple (who really liked Chinese?) could have filled out the questionnaire, and this unknown person had negative behavioral intentions. When Baumgartner and I reviewed these possibilities with LaPiere, he laughed again. He was barely 30, with a newly minted PhD, when the study began, hardly the distinguished, white-haired professor he became. As he discussed in his original article (which few seem to have read carefully), he made major efforts to stay out of the situation. Because the couple was served every time except once, whether LaPiere was present or not, the possible effects of his presence can be dismissed. He also reminded us this trip occurred long before Holiday Inns and even a national highway system. LaPiere said all these hotels, restaurants, and guest houses were small, locally owned places where the person serving you almost certainly would have also filled out the questionnaire.

In spite of their pickiness, these critiques make us think about the situation, physically and socially. These are all examples of things other than attitudes toward Chinese channeling action in specific settings. Behaviors are specific, observable events influenced by elements of the situation and "other factors." In this case, the attitude or behavioral intention is *but one* factor. So consider the situation: It's the early days of the Depression and you're running a restaurant in a small Nebraska town. In walk two well-dressed customers who speak excellent English, but they're Chinese. You would just as soon not serve them, but they are strangers and unlikely to return. Besides, turning them away—throwing them out—would be disruptive and uncomfortable. So, you take their money and perhaps hope they won't return. Six months later, you receive a short questionnaire from some faceless professor at Stanford asking if you would serve Chinese. You say no. In general, maybe those in LaPiere's study preferred not to serve Chinese, but as we now know, they will do so under the right circumstances. Donald Campbell long ago explained LaPiere's findings by describing thresholds.[10] The people disliked Chinese, Campbell argued, but not enough to decline money and create an incident by refusing a customer, when they're essentially following a script as server or hotel clerk.

It takes a powerful attitude to overcome situational and social constraints that serve as thresholds. However, when these constraints are absent, even a relatively weak attitude can guide behavior. If the negative attitude were stronger, with more beliefs and emotion underlying it, we would expect the unwitting subjects in LaPiere's experiment to have acted more consistently with their subsequently expressed behavioral intentions. "What if your friends had been black?" we asked LaPiere. "Oh," he said, "I am sure we would have been turned away. People really hated blacks."[11] Besides having a stronger negative attitude, the threshold for turning away blacks might have also been lower because they were routinely denied service in the South and other places.

Given the situation described by LaPiere, do we know how these establishments' owners would have reacted if LaPiere and his friends had returned daily? How about if a busload of Chinese tourists had pulled up to the cafe? In these specific situations, the costs of serving the Chinese might have been higher, and the owners might have acted consistently with their behavioral intention to refuse service. But we don't know. All we know is what happened once, a single event with surrounding characteristics. An attitude, even a behavioral intention, seldom includes all the characteristics of a specific situation. That is an important difference between attitudes and behaviors. Attitudes are abstract; behaviors are concrete.

So Why *Did* Leopold Vote to Place Bounties on Wolves?

This analysis of LaPiere's study helps us understand Leopold's vote favoring predator bounties. It was a specific vote, at a specific meeting, after a specific deer season, with a strong negative response by hunters. That's what faced Leopold as he weighed a public either-or decision: to pay or not pay people to kill wolves. Why did he vote for the bounty? In spite of environmental literature touting Leopold's prowolf attitude change, we must consider the possibility that Leopold's attitude was not sufficiently strong, even in 1945, to overcome other factors influencing his vote.

It is easy to find antiwolf quotes in Leopold's early writings. In his later writings, it's not so easy to find a simple statement of prowolf attitudes comparable to his "I love all trees but I am in love with pines" vow. Despite repeatedly combing "Thinking like a Mountain" and other essays, I was hard-pressed to find a solid statement of clear support for wolves. Even as Leopold watches the green fire fade in the dying wolf's eyes, he doesn't say he changed his attitude. He simply said the "wolf didn't agree with me." Furthermore, the ultimate positive attitude about the wolf is not Leopold's but, rather, the mountain's. Leopold never said in so many words that he had changed his mind. Realize, also, that he did not volunteer to write this essay. Only after former student H. A. Hochbaum badgered and cajoled him did Leopold finally write about wolves.[12] No one had to persuade him to declare his love of pines. He had little ambivalence about it. His attitude toward pines was well worked out, and he was proud of it.

Just before the vote about bounties, Leopold, the Conservation Commissioner, wrote, "No one seriously advocates more than a sprinkling of wolves."[13] Granted, wanting a few wolves was a big change from wanting to kill every last one of them. However, under pressure from hunters, his new attitude wasn't strong enough to keep bounties off Wisconsin's last few wolves. After the vote, Leopold rationalized that the bounty was more for coyotes and wouldn't hurt wolves.[14] It is hard to believe anyone with a glimmer of a prowolf attitude today would vote to restore bounties on wolves. I think we environmentalists may have socially reconstructed Leopold's prowolf attitude as stronger than it actually was in the 1940s.

Situational constraints might have also disconnected Leopold's vote from his attitude. Susan Flader argues there was "a good deal of legislative pressure on Leopold and commissioners around this time," and on a deer-related issue, "Leopold claimed, moreover, that he was told in person that a raise in the department director's salary depended on his silence."[15] Knowing the bounty would pass anyway, Leopold might have gained political capital by going with the crowd.

Leopold's behavior, like the actions of hotel and restaurant owners in LaPiere's study, was influenced by the interplay between attitude strength and the thresholds of a specific situation. It takes a powerful attitude to overcome high barriers, although a weak attitude will be expressed in behavior if the barriers are lower. Cognitive fixes focus on the attitude component, and structural fixes focus on context or setting. Situation trumped attitude in Leopold's vote and in business owners serving the Chinese.

Saving the Saiga Antelope

Conservation biologists are learning these lessons about attitudes and behaviors.[16] For example, let's go to Russia's steppes, a big, empty place where the saiga antelope population is fast declining. After the Ice Age, the saigas ranged from the British Isles, across Europe and Asia, and into North America, including the Yukon. However, having lots of saigas did not ensure their survival, and the population was nearly wiped out by the 1920s. Under a careful restoration effort, the saigas were brought back to a population of about two million in the 1950s. Then it declined again, by 95% during the 1990s.

The assumed cause? Poaching. The proposed solution? The cognitive fix, of course. "Change attitudes" and "educate the public." To better understand the situation, an international research team visited parts of the Russian Federation, Kazakhstan, and Uzbekistan, where saiga declines were dramatic. The group spent four years on site and conducted in-depth analyses of six communities. All researchers learned local languages so they could conduct interviews without interpreters. Using focus groups and household surveys to measure attitudes, they found the region's knowledge of saiga ecology and population decline was remarkably high. "Local people valued saigas highly, partly because they are viewed as the flagship species of the steppe . . . but also because of their perceived importance for the ecosystem."[17] Nine of 10 knew saiga populations were declining. They further believed poaching caused it. So they valued the species and understood its biological needs.

The research team then asked three knowledgeable individuals in each community separately and anonymously to list households that regularly poach saiga. Only names appearing on all three lists were considered poachers. How did attitudes predict poachers? The study team unequivocally found "no association between attitudes and poaching involvement."[18] They further noted their "findings support an increasing number of studies suggesting that positive attitudes toward a resource are not necessarily linked to positive conservation action."[19] Conservation biologists are discovering on their own what social psychologists have long known about attitudes and behaviors.

What separated poaching families from nonpoaching families? Poverty and unemployment—factors other than attitudes. The Soviet Union's breakup had had huge economic and social impacts in these communities. With the loss of state-transferred income, people turned to any means to survive. The poorest families poached saiga even though they held its symbolic meaning in high regard and realized the animals were on the brink of extinction. As the saiga antelope research team put it: "While positive attitudes toward conservation are argued to be essential for conservation success, positive attitudes do not necessarily imply positive actions in terms of changes in resource use behavior."[20]

Attitudes: Necessary but Not Sufficient

A half-century after Leopold voted to restore wolf bounties, the animal's likeness appeared on 21,000 Wisconsin license plates. These special plates cost $25 more than regular plates and provide nearly $500,000 annually for the state's Endangered Resources Program. Do folks driving around with a wolf picture and the words "Endangered Resources" emblazoned on their plates have positive attitudes toward wolves and wildlife?

Of course, they do. We don't expect wolf-haters to cough up cash to fund wolf restoration. Ninety percent of those with wolf plates supported efforts to "increase the number of wolves living in Wisconsin." Ninety-eight percent agreed that "protecting rare plants and animals helps maintain the integrity of

the natural environment," and 97% thought it important to "protect rare predators like the wolf, the barn owl and the lynx in Wisconsin."[21]

So, attitudes are important for behavior, right? Yes, but if deeds are supposed to reflect attitudes, the environmental movement's power is greatly
overrated. First, only 0.5% of Wisconsin motorists buys wolf plates. Second,
what about the 99.6% who don't buy wolf plates? Do they hate wolves? Not
according to Matt Wilson's surveys for the Wisconsin Department of Natural
Resources. He found that millions of Wisconsinites have positive attitudes
toward wolves and wildlife but don't buy wolf plates. Because millions have
strong positive attitudes toward endangered species and wolf restoration but
don't pay to put a wolf on their license plates, the correlation between attitudes
and behavior was low. These data are consistent with social psychological
studies: Attitudes and behavior are different things. A positive attitude toward
wolves is a necessary condition for the prowolf behavior (buying the plate) but
not sufficient by itself to inspire wolf-plate purchases.

So why don't people with positive attitudes toward wolves buy wolf plates?
Outside constraints play a role. If you don't own a car, you can't buy a plate, no
matter how positive your attitudes. (However, you can go to the Web site for
the Wisconsin DNR's Endangered Resources Fund and contribute money.)[22]
Or you might not have an extra $25 for a special plate. Indeed, those who did
not buy wolf plates had slightly lower incomes. But the problem with attitudes
is that many, sometimes conflicting, attitudes affect a particular behavior.

Registering a car is just that: a state-mandated registration. It's not a mech-
anism for funding environmental research. Therefore, owners' minds might
be far removed from environmental issues when they send money to the
Department of Motor Vehicles. Perhaps their feelings about endangered resources are irrelevant, and they bought other special plates instead. Maybe
they prefer the University of Wisconsin, the hallowed Green Bay Packers, or
one of the other 28 special plates Wisconsin offers. Still others might have
positive attitudes toward wolves but negative attitudes toward the Department
of Natural Resources (DNR). Others might think general-tax revenues, not
donations, should fund endangered resources.

The point is, as we saw earlier, all behavior is specific, based on a single act
in a single setting, complete with a set of meanings. The question, "Do you
think protecting rare plants and animals helps maintain the integrity of the
natural environment?" renders answers that are too broad and general. It also
says nothing about license plates or research funding for the DNR. That's one
reason such attitudes might have little to do with those specific behaviors.

What about Leopold? Would he have bought a wolf plate for his car? We
don't know, of course, although we would expect he would—as always—be

ahead of the curve. Instead, consider Stanley Temple, the former Beers-Bascom Professor of Conservation in Leopold's own Department of Wildlife Ecology at UW-Madison. Temple helped found, and was president of, the Society for Conservation Biology, so we would expect he has positive attitudes toward wolves. A recent film on Leopold's life, *Green Fire,* showed Temple sitting by Leopold's shack while praising the late professor. Then Temple got into his car with a Wisconsin license plate reading "GRN FIRE," but no wolf.[23] I wrote to Stan, a friend and former colleague, and asked about his attitudes toward wolves and why he didn't have a wolf plate. He replied, "I do, indeed, have a 'pro-wolf attitude.'"[24] But he also has reasons (other beliefs and attitudes) that keep him from buying a plate:

1. He gives money directly to the Endangered Resources Program through a tax check-off.
2. He doesn't want to give money to the Department of Transportation to administrate a plate.
3. He views a plate as "passive symbolism for endangered resources" and devotes his professional life to active engagement.
4. He has been critical of the "now-recovered wolf as the emblem of endangered species in Wisconsin." Therefore, he considers it an inappropriate symbol.

His old license plate had the university's abbreviation for the Wildlife Ecology Department. When the dean changed the department's name, Temple changed his plate to "GRN FIRE," which seemed "more in keeping with my post-academic career as a senior fellow at the Aldo Leopold Foundation." So, of course, attitudes are important for what we do. However, in this case, as in every case, complex beliefs, identities, and prior behaviors drive specific acts in specific situations.

We found the same kind of gap between positive attitudes toward hunting and actual hunting behavior.[25] A Swedish survey showed none of the 84 people in our sample who held a negative attitude toward hunting actually hunted, and none of the 31 hunters in the sample had a negative attitude toward hunting. When you present data this way, it looks like attitudes strongly influence hunting behavior (see Table 4.1). Hunters like hunting and non-hunters don't hunt, in *every* case. The problem was the remaining 337 people who answered the survey. They had positive attitudes toward hunting *but none of them hunted.* Scores from the attitude scale explained slightly less than 10% of the variance in hunting participation.[26]

This "low" correlation is common in attitude-behavior studies, and it doesn't mean something is wrong with the study. It simply means attitudes

Table 4.1 **Attitudes toward Hunting and Hunting Behavior among a Random Sample of the Swedish Population between the Ages of 16 and 65.**

Reported behavior	Attitude	
	Antihunting	Prohunting
Hunt	0	31
Do not hunt	84	337

and behaviors are different things. It's easy to say "I like hunting" on a survey, but it's much harder to receive hunter training, find a place to hunt, buy and train a dog, become part of a hunting team, and do all the other things associated with hunting behavior. And not all attitudes on a survey imply one must engage in the behavior. Many nonhunters in the study ate and enjoyed game meat, and had friends who hunt. Liking hunting is an attitude. Hunting is a behavior. They are related, as expected from the consistency principle, but these cogs don't always mesh. The positive attitude is a necessary but not a sufficient condition for hunting participation. Increasing the already favorable attitude toward hunting is unlikely to increase the number of hunters, and certainly trying to get antihunters to like hunting will do no good. Even if we could change antihunters' attitudes, only 1 in 10 people with positive attitudes toward hunting actually hunt—so getting all 84 to like hunting would give us only 8 more hunters. That does not mean hunters should disregard public attitudes toward hunting, because these attitudes (opposition to trophy hunting, for example) can lead to structural fixes, like banning hunts for certain species. However, trying to increase hunter numbers through efforts to change attitudes will not work.

Behaviors Are Not Consistent Either

One thing we know about attitudes and behavior is that the best predictor of behavior is behavior. If you see people do something, the best guess is that they will do it again, like recycling garbage, voting Democratic, or hunting deer. Attitudes and behavior should influence each other. If you engage in a behavior, you are supposed to reflect on it and change your attitude to be consistent. Then, as your attitude becomes stronger, you engage in more attitude-consistent behaviors.[27]

Even behaviors that look similar to outside observers can differ in meaning to the actor as I once discovered the hard way. Given what we learned about the wolf plates, I thought we had a sure-fire opportunity to help wolves while showing the importance of environmental attitudes. The Timber Wolf Alliance (TWA), the major supporter of wolf awareness and restoration in Wisconsin, obtained the names and addresses of wolf-license-plate owners to invite them to join their organization.

I figured many of these people would buy the $25 membership. After all, they were the self-selected 0.5% of people with the *most* positive attitudes toward wolves, and they had demonstrated this commitment by paying $25 annually for a wolf plate. This prior behavior demonstrated they had the cash and they were willing to spend it for a wolf symbol on their car. Capitalizing on this identity-based attitude seemed a sure bet.

Like many social psychologists, I had no experience as a fund-raiser, so based on theory only, I expected about 40% of this dream group to join the TWA. The actual response shocked me: Only 1.7% of wolf-license-plate owners bought a membership. I was crushed. Fortunately, the Timber Wolf Alliance wasn't. By mailing nearly 15,000 letters to this group, the TWA netted $8,025 in donations and enrolled 253 new members. That not only covered the mailings' costs, but many of the new members renewed to provide even more support.[28]

When I complained to my colleague—an economist—about this select group's poor participation, he shook his head as if I were an idiot. "Tom," he said, "*they already gave money.*" Economists track this sort of thing. From his viewpoint, if you give money once, you might believe you've paid your share and aren't about to give more. By focusing on the plate's monetary cost, I forgot people were buying a plate and an identity while giving money to a government organization. The TWA provided no sign for their car and no visible identity. The money would be used for education and activism. Money sent to the DNR would pay for science and management. In short, many attitudes—not just attitudes toward wolves—factor into a supposedly simple behavior corresponding to a prowolf attitude and consistent with prior prowolf behavior. I got caught in the trap of the consistency principle. Just because something seemed consistent to me, I considered it consistent for other people. You can never assume. As I learned the hard way, you must always test.

The Specificity Principle

The argument I make to explain the attitude-behavior gap is that attitudes are usually general and every behavior is specific. As in the wolf case, a broad belief—"Protecting rare plants and animals helps maintain the integrity of the natural environment"—poorly predicts single specific behaviors. However, one would expect more specific beliefs to better predict observed behavior.

Stan Black and I tested this by studying people who bought lead-free gasoline. In the 1970s, lead-free gasoline reached America's pumps, but it cost two cents more per gallon than leaded. This might not sound like much, but on a percentage basis, it's about 15–20 cents more in today's prices. So consider: Would you pay two or three bucks extra per fill-up for a product that polluted less?

By working with gasoline dealers, we obtained a sample of people who purchased lead-free gasoline and those who did not.[29] The results supported our hypotheses: People with positive attitudes toward the environment (general attitudes) were no more likely to buy lead-free gasoline (a specific behavior). We then measured more specific beliefs. People who believed air pollution (something lead-free gasoline might influence) was a problem were slightly more likely to buy lead-free gasoline. When we examined beliefs about lead-free gasoline (closer to what Fishbein and Ajzen call "attitude toward the act") by asking if they thought lead-free gas reduces pollution, our data showed people holding this belief were more likely to buy lead-free gas. Finally, drivers with a sense of obligation (a "personal norm"), along with internal sanctions of guilt and shame for not buying lead-free gas, and pride for buying it, were much more likely to buy lead-free gas. The more specific an attitude is to a behavior, the better it predicts the behavior.[30] When an attitude measures the time, action, context, and target of the behavior, it better predicts the corresponding action. This specificity principle has had strong empirical support and is now well established in social psychology. More than 30 years ago, Ajzen and Fishbein reviewed 109 attitude behavior studies that showed those with high correspondence (generally more specific attitude measures) showed higher correlations with observed behavior.[31]

The Specificity Principle: Attitude measures more specific to the attitude object and the act itself show higher correlations with observed behaviors. More general attitudes influence a greater variety of relevant behaviors but at weaker levels. Attitudes measured at very general levels should not be expected to be associated with a specific behavior.

According to the specificity principle, general attitudes should predict general behavior, but our lead-free study only had a specific action: buying one kind of gasoline. Most of our tests of the attitude-behavior relationship looked at a single act, like serving one Chinese couple, poaching a saiga, or buying a wolf license plate—all specific behaviors. Russell Weigel, a psychologist at Amherst College, advanced the case by measuring a general behavior.[32] He argued that we measure general attitudes with multiple items, so why not measure pro-environmental behavior with multiple environmental actions? First he got a traditional measure of general environmental attitudes of residents in a small community. Over the next six months, researchers posing as environmentalists knocked on doors and gave people who filled out the attitude survey opportunities to engage in pro-environmental actions. Thus, multiple indicators of actual behavior (not reports of past behavior or behavioral intentions) were observed and recorded.

If householders signed all the pro-environmental petitions, agreed to take them to a friend, showed up with a friend at the roadside litter pick-up, and recycled all eight weeks, they received the fourteen-points maximum on the general pro-environmental behavior scale. Householders refusing all these opportunities scored zero on the general behavioral scale. As predicted, the general pro-environmental attitude correlated better with this general behavior scale than with any single behavior. The reason general attitudes toward the environment, such as the widely used New Environmental Paradigm Scale (NEP) scale,[33] seldom predict specific behaviors very well is that attitude measures are too broad and general, whereas behaviors are specific. However, Weigel's work showed general environmental attitudes predict general environmental behavior, and this bodes well for broad pro-environmental actions.

The problem for the cognitive fix, however, is that we're most often interested in changing specific behaviors, like littering, poaching, or getting people to buy wolf license plates or lead-free gasoline, or donating to the Timber Wolf Alliance. General pro-environmental attitudes everyone wants to promote have little to do with those specific actions. General attitudes toward Chinese people and saiga antelope had virtually no effect on specific behaviors implied by those attitudes.

We can also find evidence that the specificity principle works in both directions. In the previous chapter, we examined cohort and period effects on general environmental attitude change. The attitudes measurement was a broad gauge of environmental attitudes from the General Social Survey.[34] In following the specificity principle, we would not expect this general attitude to be influenced by specific events because it summarizes many beliefs and experiences. To test this assumption, the authors examined the influence of three "big" specific environmental effects in the 1980s: the discovery and report of the ozone hole in 1985; Chernobyl in 1986; and the "resignation," or firing, of the anti-environmental secretary of the Department of Interior (James Watt) in 1983. Their analysis showed these specific events did not make people change their general attitude toward spending money on the environment in general.

Aldo Leopold, LaPiere, and the Goose Hunting Permits

One fine autumn day my colleague Rich Bishop and I mailed $11,000 of University of Wisconsin checks to a group of unsuspecting goose hunters. Bishop, an economist, was trying to estimate environmental values by using surveys, and I was trying to demonstrate the gap between attitudes and behaviors.[35]

Aldo Leopold had tried to establish an economic value of geese long before we mailed these checks. Leopold began by estimating the value of a single bird, a big gander he missed during a morning hunt.[36] "All thumbs," he said. (Like the typical hunter, even Leopold excused his misses.)[37] He guessed this bird was worth about as much as he would pay for a symphony ticket. Then, like many economists, he extrapolated: "I doubt not that this very gander has given ten other men two dollars' worth of thrills. Therefore I say he is worth at least twenty dollars to the human race."[38] Suddenly we had a monetary value for an environmental good to compare with other goods and services.

The problem in Leopold's reasoning, from a social psychological point of view, is that he did not have to pay cash to see and miss the gander. He expresses a behavioral intention: what he *thinks* he would be willing to pay beyond the cost of shells, travel, and equipment. Remember, Leopold had positive attitudes toward wolves, too, but voted to put bounties on them. The merchants who served the Chinese couple said they would not serve Chinese people, but they did. So how do we *know* Leopold or anyone would *really* pay two dollars to see that gander unless someone collected the money? That was what Bishop and I were doing.[39]

To test the validity of such behavioral intentions against observed behavior, we sent checks to 237 goose hunters who had just received a free permit to kill one goose during a one-week season. The offers ranged from one dollar to $200, which amounted to a take-it-or-leave-it offer: Return the check or send us the permit (behavior[B]). At the same time, we sent letters to an independent sample of goose hunters who also received the free permits. This letter included only a survey, no check. The survey's first question measured a behavioral intention (BI): "*Suppose* we sent you a check for $5.00 and asked you to send back your goose hunting permit in return, would you do it?" Other people received higher offers all the way to $200 in the same take-it-or-leave-it format as those who received checks. Each person was offered only one amount.

The LaPiere study showed a gap between what people did and what they said they would do. We attributed this inconsistency to three things:

1. Specificity: The BI was about members of the Chinese race in general, but the refusal was for a specific Chinese couple traveling with an American in a specific situation (B).
2. Situational Thresholds: It was easier to say on a questionnaire that they would refuse hypothetical Chinese guests (BI) than turn them away in person (B).
3. Attitude Strength: Although they disliked Chinese, their attitudes might not have been strong enough to overcome the thresholds.

The design of our goose-permit study—randomly assigning goose hunters who received the permits to the cash (B) or survey (BI) test, and making the behavior and behavioral intention as similar as possible—should have eliminated the factors that led proprietors in LaPiere's study to do one thing and say another. The BI and B were at the same specificity level. Both groups had applied for the permit and received it in the mail the day before we mailed our checks and questionnaire. The BI was not about a general hunting permit but the same specific permit, so the BI and B corresponded. Situational constraints were minimized and equalized. Hunters receiving the cash offer had only to put their permit or check in the self-addressed stamped envelope and send it to us, whereas the behavioral intention group had only to put a mark on a questionnaire and return it. Of course, some people had weak attitudes and didn't care much about goose hunting, and others might have needed the money more. However, randomly assigning hunters to the cash versus survey groups should make the groups equal except for chance.

So what happened? Drum roll here. The permits cost us, on average, sixty-three dollars. Not bad for the value of what the Wisconsin DNR gave away for free. However, when hunters simply estimated what they would take for the permit, *supposing* we had sent them a check, they said it would take $102. The estimated value based on behavioral intentions was more than 60% higher than the value determined by behavior. That's why I'm skeptical when psychologists and other researchers say BI's are good stand-ins for behavior. Even when we rule out factors creating the gap, a big gap remains.

So why the difference? I believe the explanation lies with the direct experience principle, at least in part. Attitudes based on direct experience are stronger and less likely to change, and we are more certain of attitudes based on experiences. For instance, most of us buy things more often than we sell them. Only rarely do we sell cars, houses, or personal possessions. Furthermore, it is unlikely that any Wisconsin goose hunter ever sold a free hunting permit before. In fact, it is illegal to sell permits, so hunters have little or no experience with what they would take when they received our checks or surveys.[40] Hunters were giving us their best guess about something they had never experienced. Likewise, after trying to figure out if he would cut pine trees if his farm were farther north where pines were common, Leopold concluded: "I confess I do not know. My farm is here."[41] He dodged the hypothetical question.

Like Leopold, these hunters could not precisely estimate what they would actually do. However, being helpful respondents, they obligingly answered our survey despite their uncertainty. Those in the cash group, on the other hand, had direct experience that was unavailable to the survey group. Having a check up to $200 in hand made members of this group think long and hard (some in this group even called to thank us for the money) about the choice. In the process, they did the cognitive work to begin building an attitude. Remember those "dirty little secrets" revealed in chapter 1? A person's attitude, as expressed on a survey, can be influenced by a question's placement, where simply answering lots of questions first influences the attitude. For those with a check in hand, the question was not hypothetical. In contrast, hunters with the survey might have mulled it a minute or so, but because it wasn't real, they made a quick judgment without similar careful thought. Years later we repeated this study, asking deer hunters to pay for a free (but hard to get) deer-hunting permit. Hunters have more direct experience buying than selling permits, and we found no significant difference between the cash and survey groups under these conditions, which we would expect, based on the direct experience principle.[42]

The Invisible Constraints

One interesting thing about human behavior is that, when we try to understand why we or others do something, we rely on internal explanations and discount situational factors. In social psychology this is called the "fundamental attribution error."[43] Malcom Gladwell, in his popular book *The Tipping Point*, notes in a section called "The Power of Context" that "human beings invariably make the mistake of overestimating the importance of fundamental character traits and underestimating the importance of situation and context."[44] This tendency keeps us thinking that attitudes must be vital to behavior when they are not.

Leopold is no different from the rest of us. Let's take a quick visit back to Leopold's shack, where, in chapter 2, he was cutting birches to save pines. He tries to figure out why he is doing this by examining his attitude. It looks like Leopold's attitude toward pines is the sole driver of his behavior, but it is not. It only seems important because, as Leopold tells it, he has virtually removed all situational factors from his analysis. Leopold limited the boundaries to a dichotomous choice (cut the birch or not) only on his land, and then only when a birch is crowding out a pine that he and his family planted. Even with his propine attitude, he does not cut birch trees wherever they stand. Should he visit Umeå, Sweden, the City of Birches, we would not expect him to ax birch trees on Umeå's main street. All these situational factors disconnect his attitude (propine and antibirch) from behavior in most settings. Attitude is but one factor, and, in many cases, it might be one of the *least* important factors affecting behavior. So, to save pines, wolves, or saiga antelope, we must think beyond attitudes.

Conclusion

The gap between environmental behaviors and attitudes is caused by physical and social constraints that limit our action, the strength of the attitude to overcome these thresholds, and the lack of correspondence between attitudes usually measured at the general level and behaviors that are usually single specific acts.

This doesn't mean that attitudes are irrelevant to pro-environmental actions. It's clear that positive environmental attitudes are necessary conditions for behavior. However, they are not sufficient. If Wisconsinites hated wolves, they would not have the opportunity to buy wolf license plates, and $500,000 a year from those plates is nothing to sneeze at. As noted in chapter 1, structural fixes require public support. The structural fix to fund the Wisconsin Endangered Resources Program with wolf plates would never have been proposed without a strong base in positive attitudes among millions of citizens. So even though *individual* attitudes have little to do with *individual* behavior, they are necessary to support collective actions to change the structure or context of human behavior. That's why it's important to monitor and understand them even if they tell little about what one person, even Aldo Leopold, would do in specific situations.

The cognitive fix is based on the assumption that not only are attitudes of individuals closely related to their behavior, but also that we can change these attitudes. Chapter 3 showed attitudes *can* change, but it's usually slow and unpredictable (The Wisconsin DNR certainly didn't want to scare hunters about CWD anymore than I wanted my students to change their antimining attitudes). However, this analysis gave us little guidance about how we actually change attitudes short of total immersion (Bennington College and my classroom), enormous media efforts with new attitude objects (CWD and wolf restoration), or broad-scale social change (cohort replacement) over long time periods.

So we have doubts, based on good theory and past evidence, and unknowns that must be explored, but we can still be surprised, as I was when I believed wolf-license-plate holders would join the Timber Wolf Alliance. Science requires us to test even improbable assumptions. This is especially true when assumptions are widely held outside scientific circles. In the next chapter, I will report on my own and others' efforts to inspire pro-environmental behavior by educating the public and changing attitudes—an experience that changed my attitudes for sure.

5

Educating the Public . . . and Other Disasters

AS AN UNDERGRADUATE at the University of Chicago, I discovered "attitude" was a scientific concept, subject to experimental inquiry. I soon had
hopes that, based on the best available science, one could change attitudes,
educate the public, and save the environment. I wasn't alone, then or now. A
colleague teaching in environmental studies recently wrote to say that, when
it comes to environmental problems, "The students are just SURE, with all
the earnestness you can imagine, that 'educating the public' is the solution."[1]
This chapter, unfortunately, is not about my success in changing the attitudes
and behavior of others. Rather, it's about a long journey of my own education
as I learned the limits of attitude change for solving environmental problems.

As with Aldo Leopold, this took a long time and was based on direct experience, starting with grad school at Madison. Irwin Deutscher's new paper on
"Words and Deeds"[2] shook my initial faith about changing attitudes and
behavior. He cited LaPiere's study, which you now know, and Leon Festinger,
the man who gave us the term *cognitive dissonance*. In an address to the American Psychological Association, Festinger said he had found only three studies
that seriously examined the relationship between attitudes and behavior
change, and *all* showed that efforts to change behavior by changing attitudes
were unsuccessful.[3] Pronouncements by these giants in social psychology
were hard to ignore. Why study attitudes if we can't change them and they
have little to do with behavior?[4] Well, recall Leopold's attitude toward wolves.
We know attitudes can change (albeit slowly), so I continued believing we
could educate the public. If only we could figure out how to do it right.

Lesson from the Energy Crisis

After I returned to Wisconsin as a professor in 1973, two students, Mike Prouty
and Keith Hansen, showed up in my office, hoping to do independent study.
Mike was hard to miss. He sat near the front of my class, wore a red stocking

cap, and nodded in agreement when I made good points. I suggested Mike and Keith try to test my claims that utilities were increasing demand for electricity through advertising. My activist self "knew" that was why we were building power plants, whereas my scientific self wanted to test the hypothesis that advertising changed attitudes, and therefore, behavior.

A nice thing about electricity consumption is that it's an observed behavior, unlike behavioral reports or intentions that often have little to do with what people really do. With my help, Mike and Keith selected six apartment buildings and read their electric meters daily. After 12 readings, we sent residents in two buildings a letter asking them to use less energy, and we gave good reasons for doing so. We sent a different letter to residents in two other buildings, encouraging them to use *more* energy. This letter emphasized electricity costs were low (only two cents to keep a safety light on all night), and that off-peak electricity consumption reduced power-plant pollution. We had two control groups: One building got "education" through a standard utility brochure listing how much electricity specific appliances used, with no encouragement to use more or less energy. The second control building got nothing in the mail.

An obvious, necessary, but often-ignored condition for attitude change is that the information must reach the sensory organs of people you're trying to change. If they don't read the letter, we surely could not expect change. So, we telephoned reminders to residents to read the letter. Mike and Keith then read the electric meters for the next 12 days. We found a 6% increase in electricity consumption (about one-half kilowatt-hour a day) for the group we encouraged to use more. However, the group we asked to use less electricity *also* *increased* its usage by 6%. Even the control group receiving the utility message used about 6% more energy. The only group that didn't increase was the one receiving no mail. Before you jump to the conclusion that mailing electricity information gets people to use more of it, you should know that our statistical analysis showed all these differences could have occurred by chance. Taken together, the data were consistent with the hypothesis that information makes no difference either way. "Educating the public doesn't work."

The standard explanation for such failures is that the information campaign was not powerful enough. We all hope that if we simply provide *more* and *better* information, the "educated public" will change their behavior. We are like the farmer who thinks he can beat the weather and the markets if he just uses a bigger tractor. For us, the bigger tractor arrived in autumn 1973 when world oil prices jumped from $2 per barrel to $10! In 2012 dollars, that would be like oil prices jumping from $100 a barrel to $500 a barrel. This caused the energy crisis, the biggest educational campaign to change people's attitudes and behavior that anyone could have conceived. America's attention turned to energy as never before in the 20th century. Gasoline prices more than doubled from less than 50 cents a gallon to more than a $1 a gallon. This caused shortages, long lines, and fisticuffs at gas stations.[5] The government imposed two structural fixes: It extended daylight savings time and set a 55 mph speed limit. President Nixon himself ramped up the cognitive fix by speaking to us on TV to encourage energy savings. Public-opinion polls showed substantial changes in reported behavior: 68% of Wisconsinites reported using less electricity, 29% reported using their appliances less, 82% reported lowering the temperature in their homes, and 69% said they used less gasoline. National surveys showed similar declines.[6] However, remember, this was reported behavior. Were they really doing it?

This was what I had been waiting for. Surely this mega-treatment would affect electricity consumption. Surely the public was "educated" as well as it ever could be about energy. I could now simply measure the effects. Unfortunately, electric meters get read only once a month, so there were not yet enough post-energy-crisis observations to measure an effect. We needed daily data on residences, and because of the student project, I had daily measures of energy consumption for nearly 100 apartments *before* the autumn energy crisis. I hired Mike to return to those apartments and read the meters for specific days in March and April so we could compare them to our earlier data. I could finally show that "education" changes behavior (even if it required a huge "treatment"). No one could stage an energy crisis to get people to conserve energy in a few apartments, but it would be nice to show how effective it was for changing people's behavior. After all, people told pollsters they were saving energy.

The data were easy to analyze but disappointing to read. Before the energy crisis, the average apartment used 8.42 kilowatt hours of electricity daily. After a year of "energy conservation education," the same apartments used 8.39 kilowatt hours daily. In other words, there was no statistically reliable or noticeable reduction in electricity use. The public might have "been educated" about something, but for this small group—apartments for which we had precise data on actual (not reported) behavior—the biggest education treatment one could hope for brought no change.[7]

The energy crisis, however, affected energy consumption, but not for people in those apartments. Because of the government's structural fixes, the University of Wisconsin decreased its electrical use by 15%, Madison reduced its commercial electrical use by nearly 7%, and Madison's general residential population reduced its electrical use by 1%. Furthermore, motorists reduced their average highway speeds by 10% with the new 55 mph speed limit.[8]

What happened in "our" apartments? Maybe they used so little energy that even with changed attitudes and attempts to conserve electricity, there was nothing more to cut. This wasn't the case. What always surprised us were the consumption differences among apartments. Day after day some apartments used 2–3 kwh, whereas others used 16 kwh. Why did some people use so much more electricity than others? They were roughly of the same social class and living in same-size apartments, but some were electricity hogs. If those using 8 times more than others could be convinced, or coerced, to use even 25% less power, we could save bundles of energy. The potential was there. We just had to find the right fix.

The Structural Fix: Time-of-Use Pricing

At about the same time, there was an effort to quit building power plants and to use those we had more efficiently. A big power plant is like driving around a small town in an 8-cylinder gas-guzzler at 25 mph just because you like going 70 on the freeway once a year. It is not efficient. With declining production costs and a serious dedication to keeping steady energy supplies "on demand," the utilities had overbuilt capacity. Therefore, lots of power plants sat around for those few days each year when demands peaked. Daily peaks also occurred. The question became: Could the public "be educated" to change their behavior and use less energy during peak times?

Economists proposed a structural fix: Change electricity prices, they argued, and behavioral change would follow. Avoid the whole muddy business of attitudes. Wisconsin's Public Service Commission told utilities to consider charging people more for on-peak electricity. Utility executives asked a simple question: "Will this work?" On the third hot, stinking, sweltering, humid day—when even cornstalks curl their leaves to escape the sun—won't people say: "The hell with it. I don't care what it costs. I'm using the air conditioner"? And if everyone does that, won't the peak be higher than before, and won't we have real problems?

So, they proposed research. University scientists, commission staff, and utility personnel worked together for a year to design what we hoped would be the nation's best time-of-use experiment. I was excited. We would answer some questions raised in the apartment study (my science side) and, if time-of-use rates worked, Wisconsin could put off building power plants (my activist side). I hadn't forgotten my unsuccessful fight as a graduate student to keep a power plant from being built near my hometown. I hoped time-of-use pricing would eliminate the need for new power plants.

We selected a random sample from 217,000 residential customers in northeastern Wisconsin. Participation was to be mandatory. There would be no volunteers because volunteers were expected to be more favorable to conserving electricity or saving money. We needed to know for sure if time-of-use pricing would work for everyone. For a year we would gather baseline data by recording, every 15 minutes, household energy consumption. Then for 3 years customers would be on the time-of-use rate. This would give people more time to change their behavior, buy new appliances, and adjust to the rate. We would survey the customers to see what happened to their attitudes. These were all big improvements over Mike and Keith's "pilot" study of 100 apartments before and after the energy crisis.

Our experiment tested 3 peak periods: a 6-hour peak, the shortest peak time the utility could handle; a 9-hour peak; and a 12-hour peak, the longest peak we figured the public would tolerate. We also tested price ratios: 2:1, where on-peak electricity costs twice as much; 4:1; and 8:1, where on-peak electricity during the 6-hour peak cost almost 14 cents per kwh, and off-peak electricity cost less than 2 cents per kwh. This, we thought, was bound to get people's attention.

The experiment was not as Draconian as it might sound. In spite of high peak prices, the rates were designed to be "revenue neutral." The average customer would pay the same monthly amount under standard or time-of-use rates. The experimental rate gave customers a choice. Unlike the rest of us, they could shift some consumption to off-peak and save money. The only way a regular customer could save money was to turn off the appliance. However, for time-of-use customers, weekends were always off-peak. So a person with experimental rates could enjoy air-conditioning all weekend for a fraction of its cost to regular customers. By paying higher prices for electricity for, at most, 60 hours a week, the customer got cheap electricity during the remaining hours. Freezers, dehumidifiers, and other high-use appliances could easily be set to run during off-peak hours and save people money. For smart householders, these rates could be a great deal.

Moreover, time-of-day rates are fairer than standard rates. If you want to use electricity during peak periods, you are "demanding" an expensive piece of a power plant. Many argue that those wanting peak electricity should pay more. Movies, telephone calls, and airplane tickets are all priced differently depending on the time of day or day of the week. That's why cheap flights that pop up on Internet searches mostly have 6 A.M. departures. If time-of-use meters had been used from the start, electricity rates probably would have always been based on the time of day.

When the dust settled 5 years later, things looked good for attitudes.[9] The data showed people generally like time-of-use rates and, surprisingly, those with the longer peaks and higher ratios liked them better because they could shift more activities off-peak to save more money. People responded to price. The structural fix worked. Those in the 8:1 group shifted more than the 2:1 group, and all time-of-use groups used less on-peak electricity than did the control group. Even during heat waves, people did not backslide and use more energy, which was what utility people had feared. Best of all, the measure of the effect of behavioral intention on behavior was 2–3 times *larger* than the price-ratios variable. If people felt committed to using less on-peak electricity and believed it was important, sure enough, they used less on-peak electricity. The behavioral-intention component was also linked to the cognitive component: The more people knew about time-of-use prices (peak periods, price ratios, etc.), the more committed they were and the more they shifted. So our data showed attitudes were related to behavior, which is not always the case. However, we did not know if it was possible to increase the knowledge level and commitment of people to shifting. Testing the effect of education required a second experiment.

Time-of-Use with Education

Wisconsin Electric Power Company (WEPCO)–the state's biggest utility, serving Milwaukee and southeastern Wisconsin—was proposing time-of-use pricing based on this first experiment's success. When WEPCO planners and utility executives presented this proposal to a citizens advisory committee (CAC), they hit some snags. Sure, the CAC said, time-of-use rates might work in northeastern Wisconsin, where people live on farms and in small towns, but it gets real hot in Milwaukee. What about people in apartments? Could they shift their consumption? That was a good question. Because apartment residents were mostly excluded from the first study, we didn't know. The CAC finally asked, What about "educating the public"? You can't just put people on the rate without giving them information about how to live with it. WEPCO agreed these were good questions, and approached the team that did the first time-of-use experiment. Thus began another 5-year effort.

I argued we should subject any communications program to the same rigorous scientific tests we did for rates. Our communications assessment had to be built into the experimental design. Finally, it looked like I would get to *really* educate the public about energy conservation. Half the households in each rate would get "standard information," a notice that they were on the new rate, bills showing the amount of electricity used during on-peak and off-peak periods, a general booklet on how to adapt to time-of-use rates, and notices of daylight savings times and other changes affecting rates. This information, the usual kind of dull stuff people get from utilities, was included in 10 mailings over a 2-year period.

The other half of the households, the "accelerated communications" group, received the same 10 and 27 additional contacts over the 2 years. We sent 5 special information brochures, complete with colors and pictures. One mailing focused on "winter" appliances and another on "summer" appliances. Another told about water heaters. Still another discussed electric space heaters. We sent a refrigerator magnet, which showed stacks of coins to illustrate peak times and peak rates. Another magnet listed high-use appliances. Customers got special brochures, written in clear language, telling them how to read a bill. During the first summer, we hand-pasted a special "can't miss this" florescent notice on the bills so residents knew the on-and off-peak prices and peak hours. The CAC sent letters encouraging them to shift, and telling them how shifting helped the energy situation. During a hot period in summer, we sent a "third-hot-day notice" encouraging them to keep on-peak use low during the hot period.

Some of these materials got customers actively involved. Research showed that if you could get people to track how much energy they used—called "self monitoring"—they would use less.[10] We sent the accelerated communications group a chart to record the amount they used on and off peak. We sent an energy quiz and gave prizes to all who returned it (more than 60% did). Another study showed people used less energy if they could self-identify themselves as energy savers with a decal and feedback.[11] So, we crafted stickers for the 50% of customers who used the least on-peak electricity.

Besides learning from information, we learn from observing what others do. If time-of-use rates were system-wide, we could expect newspapers to report how others adapted. However, because we had only a random sample of customers scattered around the service territory, we created a newspaper, *The Time of Use Times,* which we printed on newspaper stock and published three times during the experiment. Its first edition had photos and 24 stories, which totaled about 10,000 words. Later editions listed people with the lowest on-peak usage.

It sounds like we really pushed these people, but over those two years, the contacts were less than 2 per month; that was enough to get their attention but not enough to be a bother. The utility put these communications together with our help. This was about the most one could do to "educate the public" about time-of-use rates.

So what happened? In plain, heartbreaking words, *it didn't work.*

During the last summer, people in the accelerated communications group used 29% of their electricity during on-peak hours and the basic communications group used 30%.[12] The 1% difference could have occurred by chance. The communications program did not improve basic understanding of the rate. Nine of 10 customers in both the accelerated and standard-information groups knew that electricity cost *more* during on-peak hours. They had gotten the basic message of the structural fix (electricity costs MORE during on-peak hours) without help from our education program. Fewer than half of either group could accurately cite actual charges or peak ratios. All they knew is that it cost more. Perhaps this is all they needed to know. Basic communication was sufficient.

Households that got more information recalled details of peak hours more accurately, but these specifics didn't seem to shift behavior. The information, however, changed some evaluative beliefs. Those who got additional communication were more likely to believe time-of-use rates provided social and household benefits. They also had more positive attitudes toward time-of-use rates. So, there is *something* to be said for education. *Our program did "educate the public," but it didn't much change their behavior.*

Those in the accelerated program had a 9% stronger commitment level to shifting. Those with a higher commitment used significantly less energy on peak. So attitudes work as we expect: We could change commitment through information, and commitment affects behavior, but the two taken together were still too weak to show an overall effect. In other words, the accelerated communications program didn't influence attitudes enough to make a difference.

We did find some good news. People in the accelerated communications program used 13% less energy during on-peak summer hours than those in the control group (167 kwh per month on peak versus 192 for the low communications group). They also used 8% less off peak. That's why the percent on peak did not differ between the two groups. Those in the accelerated program used less energy both times, so the ratio was the same. It seems the communications campaign "generalized" to cover all energy, persuading people to use less energy both on and off peak.

However, the goal of the communications program was to get people to shift and respond to the price signal. In that, it failed. It's hard to get excited about this general reduction. It's like shooting at one duck and trying to be happy when a different duck falls. If programs to "educate the public" are to be useful, we must hit the target. True, we got people to save energy, but that looked good only until we calculated the costs of running the communications campaign for all customers if everyone were on time-of-use rates. In that case, the utility's costs to prepare and mail all the accelerated information would barely be worth the energy savings.[13] Although we were among the first to study energy conservation and time-of-use pricing, others have found essentially the same results.[14] Time-of-use experiments continue, and another one that tried to "educate the public" 20 years after our disaster reached the same conclusion: There was "little evidence of significant changes in load in response to these information interventions."[15]

If you want people to reduce on-peak electricity consumption, charge higher on-peak prices and give them reasonable amounts of information. You will get a 3–5 percent decline in on-peak electricity use.[16] As I've said repeatedly, the structural fix works. The cognitive fix, as I tried to implement it in more than 15 years of studies, failed. That's why I sink beneath my desk when people enter my office and say, "All we have to do is educate the public."

Of course, that research examined only electricity consumption. The public can certainly be educated in other areas, right? What about advertising, where we spend fortunes trying to change attitudes and behavior? How well does that work?

Changing Attitudes about the Exxon Mine

A decade or so after the energy studies, I met Sara Johnson, a former student, for lunch on Madison's State Street. She was mad as hell. Promining ads had saturated TV for weeks. "Exxon Minerals[17] says they have never run such an ad campaign for any mine," she ranted. That didn't surprise me a bit. Exxon was in big trouble. The company had proposed a technological fix that collided with deeply held identity-based attitudes, and now it was trying with all its might to "educate the public."

The ads were good, and they ran night after night on TV news. More than 75% of my students remembered them when I asked the next day. The ads tied mining to basic values, created new beliefs, and jacked up emotion, but their effectiveness *and* saturation actually worked against the company.

The first ad showed the Wisconsin flag with its two prominent figures: a miner and a sailor. Those occupations, important in the 19th century, still wave atop our capitol. As we watched the flag, the narrator's warm voice reminded us of the early days of Wisconsin mining. Miners were called badgers, named after the fierce animal that burrows beneath prairies. What happened after these terrible, polluting mines closed? We built farms, and mining villages became quaint tourist centers. Everything was wonderful. Exxon tied mining to farms, state history, our flag, the badger, small towns, and community identity. It might be hard to imagine, but I struggled to avoid warm, fuzzy feelings about mines after watching the ad.

Another ad showed geese flying over a lake, a sparkling stream, and school kids boarding a yellow bus. The scenes generated a warm feeling for North Woods communities, where the mine would be located. That's where honest, hard-working Wisconsinites were scrambling for the forest's last few jobs. A mine would provide these good people respectable, high-paying work. No longer would sons and daughters have to leave their families for jobs in distant cities. How could anyone oppose economic opportunities and all the good they would do the northern part of the state?

Not forgetting where most Wisconsinites live, the last ad featured Dennis Bosanac, president of Milwaukee Local 1114 of the United Steelworkers. With the union seal in the background, Mr. Bosanac said: "Some legislators in Madison want to stop mining. That's like asking over 10,000 working people to stop breathing. Don't they know that thousands and thousands of us work in jobs that depend on mining? Don't they know how important mining has been and will be to Wisconsin? We want to be part of it. Those high-paying jobs belong in Wisconsin, not someplace else."

The story behind the ads began in the 1970s with slow-flying planes coursing back and forth over the North Woods. Using a new search technology, Exxon Minerals discovered a big, concentrated deposit of copper and zinc under a couple of hundred feet of glacial till south of Crandon, one of those small towns in the ad. Besides logging, Crandon had a seasonal tourist industry, but that was about it. If God had wanted to help a depressed area of Wisconsin, he couldn't have put a clump of minerals in a better place.

Environmental work to secure mining permits began soon after. The process was long, with many steps and stumbles, and finally snagged on where to put wastewater. Exxon first proposed putting it in Swamp Creek. What better place for dirty water than an old swampy creek? Unfortunately for Exxon, Swamp Creek ran into the Wolf River, one of Wisconsin's prime trout waters. The Wolf is a river you see on glossy calendars: blue water, frothy white rapids, and some guy or gal with a fly rod netting a brown trout. (In fact, Sara and her boyfriend, Steve, were noted trout anglers.) Twenty-four miles of it are designated a National Scenic Riverway. On hot summer afternoons, hundreds of people paddle the Wolf's rapids. It also runs through the Menominee Indian Reservation, where it's central to their spiritual heritage. Finally, the Wolf provides spawning grounds for lake sturgeon, an ancient species covered in bony, shell-shaped plates and coveted by anglers. Department of Natural Resources fish managers weighed in. Swamp Creek and the Wolf River were ruled out as places to dump mining waste.

Undaunted, Exxon engineers devised a technological fix: a 40-mile pipeline to dump waste into the Wisconsin River. This probably made perfect sense from an engineering point of view. The Wisconsin River, with 25 dams to provide electricity and regulate water flow, had been the dumping ground for paper mills and municipal-waste systems for decades. Exxon, however, missed the substantial and successful effort to clean up the Wisconsin. People could now catch, and *even eat,* fish from the river whereas there were none before, but now Exxon was proposing to dump mining waste in a recently restored river.

Although the Wolf River is special to Indians, locals, and recreation elites, it's remote and touches relatively few people.[18] The world abounds with Wolf rivers, but there's only one Wisconsin River and it flows for almost 500 miles through the state's core. One in five Wisconsinites lives in the 15 counties along its banks. The main highway to the North Woods' vacation country crosses the river a half-dozen times. Reservoirs behind Wisconsin River dams are lined with thousands of summer cottages and year-round homes. The river was the icon of Portage, my hometown, and I swam from its sandbars while growing up. Leopold's shack still sits along its shore, and my Uncle Bernard hunted geese in its backwaters. Millions have taken boat trips through the Wisconsin Dells.

Now Exxon was proposing to dump mining waste into the Wisconsin River, something that generates direct experiences for millions of people. According to the direct-experience principle, their attitudes should be strong. The identity principle also comes into play, because this is the *Wisconsin* River. I doubt most Wisconsinites could point out Crandon on a blank map, but they sure know where to find the Wisconsin River. Although the mine's wastewater would have been pretty clean and the river probably had the capacity to handle it, a new cognitive-affective link was forming: MINE WASTE IN THE WISCON-SIN RIVER! The *Mauston Star-Times*—one of those newspapers with no reason to comment on the mine before learning Exxon planned to pipe waste to the Wisconsin River—captured the mood in an editorial titled, "Only Crandon Wins in Gamble with the River." Its opening lines read: "Imagine a pristine river, ambling its way through farmlands, valleys and towns across Wisconsin. That is the Wisconsin today. Imagine again the same river, only this one choked with oxygen-depleting chemicals which liter the shoreline with dead and dying animals and vegetation."[19]

Although the Exxon mine had been a big issue for environmentalists (it was easy for them to get upset), most folks in Wisconsin had ignored the controversy for years. Instead, they went about their business, raising kids, following the Green Bay Packers, and visiting local bars for a Friday night fish fry. However, this proposal to dump mining waste into the Wisconsin River fired up the entire state. A Republican state legislator, representing an area far from the mine, introduced a bill to ban mine waste from being dumped into the Wisconsin River. Up and down the river, more than 40 communities, townships, and counties passed resolutions opposing the Exxon mine, not just the waste dumping, but the mine itself.[20] In my Lodi township, bound by the Wisconsin River, the public trooped into Town Hall to demand an anti-Exxon mine resolution. The protesters were retirees, business people, and regular folks living along the river. Many of these citizens had never before been active in environmental issues, and their vocal opposition got local governments statewide, including the town of Lodi, to oppose Exxon's mine.

Exxon's ad campaign started several months after these actions. The company realized it had made a mistake and played catch-up to educate the public about the mine. It was too late. The media set agendas. They tell us what to think about, not what to think. The Exxon ads, day after day, simply got people thinking about the mine again. And Wisconsin knew what it thought about a mine that intended to pollute the Wisconsin River. If the ads had been fewer and less moving, they would have been easy to miss or ignore. Instead, they broadened the opposition from environmentalists, Indians, kayakers, canoeists, trout anglers, and fish managers to the broad, solid core of Wisconsin's citizenry.

The result was dramatic. After a couple of months of advertisements, and spending more than $400,000 lobbying against a mining moratorium bill, Exxon could only watch as the Wisconsin Legislature voted on the bill. It was widely agreed the bill's mining standards were the toughest of any in the union. Wisconsin's Assembly voted 91–6 in favor for the bill and in the Senate, 29–3 in favor. The state's popular Republican governor, Tommy Thompson, signed it into law. The Legislature's champion environmentalist, Representative Spencer Black, crowed: "This issue has energized people more than any other issue I've seen in my time in the Legislature. We do not want Exxon experimenting with our North Woods."[21] The Exxon mine had suffered a deathblow. Such is the power of advertising when it confronts attitudes steeped in emotion, tied to identities, and based on direct experience.

Why, after media saturation and the best ads Madison Avenue had to offer, did Exxon drown in the Wisconsin River while trying to change attitudes? I asked Sara if the ads changed her attitude. Did they make her like the mine? I thought she was going to dump her cup of steaming coffee into my lap. "No, of course not!" she snapped.

"Well, what did they do?" I continued.

"They made me really, really mad!" she replied. Thankfully, she put her coffee cup back down.

The ads had turned on her feelings, but her emotion wasn't positive about the mine. It was the opposite. Sara's existing strong, negative attitude—built on many beliefs and tied to her basic values—was probably similar to Leopold's attitude toward pines. Then along came Exxon, which blatantly tied the mine to state symbols—the flag and the badger, and made Sara angrier. I suspect it had the same effect on other environmentalists. Daily, during the evening news, they watched at least three Exxon ads telling them how good mining was for Wisconsin. Not only did this ad campaign mobilize Sara and other environmentalists, it also mobilized average folks who lived in little towns along the Wisconsin River. Exxon's canoe had T-boned the huge rock in the river. The rock wasn't going anywhere, and efforts to dislodge it only worsened the damage.

The next day I asked the 28 students in my class if they had seen Exxon's ads. Of the 17 who had, 16, like Sara, said the ads made them feel more negative about the mine. Only one felt more positive. Sara and my class are hardly representative, of course. That's why, after the dust settled, I invited Dale Alberts, the mine's public relations director, to speak to my class. You remember Mr. Alberts from chapter 3. He gave us an unexpected lesson in attitude change. When he got around to discussing the ads, he conceded his company had spent about $500,000 and—based on surveys they had done—it looked like attitudes had, well, "actually become slightly more negative." This was not surprising, but I was glad to hear it from the source. Public survey data showed the same decline: 43% of the public opposed the mine in 1994, and in March 1997 (two months into the ad campaign), a statewide telephone survey found 48% opposition.[22] So the ad campaign not only failed to change attitudes, but also deepened people's negative opinions and raised the mining issue on the public agenda.

Disaster in Nevada: Advertising Fails Again

Exxon in Wisconsin wasn't the only powerful group with nearly unlimited funds to waste trying to educate the public. In Nevada, the American Nuclear Energy Council (ANEC) wrapped its canoe around a large rock, too.[23] A proposal to put the entire country's nuclear waste inside Yucca Mountain, 100 miles north of Las Vegas, had generated much controversy and scientific study. Paul Slovic, one of the world's leading risk researchers, had conducted surveys *before* the advertising campaign began. This provided an unusual case of baseline data to evaluate the advertising's effectiveness. Their surveys showed four of five people in Nevada opposed the Yucca Mountain Repository. Their opposition was based on "perceptions of risk, a profound lack of trust, and a concern for issues of equity . . . and a deep social and cultural skepticism about things nuclear."[24]

To change public attitudes and build support for the repository, ANEC hired a Las Vegas advertising and consulting firm, and launched a set of ads narrated by a popular local sportscaster. To demonstrate the safety of transporting nuclear waste, the ads showed a high-speed locomotive ramming a truck and trailer carrying waste. The announcer indicated the cask that would hold nuclear waste survived the devastating crash. In another ad, scientists claimed nuclear waste could not explode. In a third ad, a different scientist asserted the waste could not cause cancer.

QUESTION: What happens when you go all-out to change a strong, well-developed, identity-based, emotional attitude?

ANSWER: Slovic and his colleagues: "Despite the barrage of pro-repository messages, almost three-quarters of the respondents (73.8%) said they would oppose the repository if they were to vote on whether it should be built—almost exactly the same proportion as before the ad campaign."[25]

Besides missing the mark, the ads inflicted substantial collateral damage for ANEC, just as Exxon's ad campaign had done. Although more than 70% of the public saw the ads the first few weeks, more than half said the message did not change their attitudes. Worse, 32% said the message made them *less supportive*. Just as the Exxon ads turned off Sara and my Wisconsin students, the Nevada ads backfired, too.

Furthermore, the Nevada ads generated an outcry about attempts to manipulate public opinion. Nevada's U.S. senator demanded explanations from the Department of Energy, and Nevada's governor wrote to other states calling for investigations into the use of electricity ratepayer money to try changing attitudes in Nevada. Local businesses turned the ads on their heads in their own advertising with parodies. Eight months after the Decision Research survey, Arizona State University conducted a second survey. It showed 41% of the public was less trusting after seeing the ads, and opposition to the repository remained unchanged at about 75%.

Seldom do we see such clear evidence of an advertising-campaign failure, because we seldom have good baseline data or funding for impartial scientific study of the effects. How did the American Nuclear Energy Council respond? You got it. More advertisements. However, in 2011, twenty years after these ad campaigns, Nevada still has no nuclear repository and Wisconsin has no mine. Is my message about the cognitive fix getting through?

So Why Do We Spend So Much on Advertising?

If those two cases of failed advertising campaigns and my experience reducing energy consumption through "education" are typical, why do companies spend billions of dollars advertising consumer products? In 1982, $33 million was spent advertising toilet paper.[26] Twenty-five years later, three companies alone spent more than $141 million advertising the same product.[27] That's more than the combined operating budgets for Yellowstone, Yosemite, Grand Canyon, Rocky Mountain, Great Smoky Mountains, and Mount Rainier national parks. You would think toilet paper would sell itself. Who must be convinced toilet paper is a good, useful thing? Try getting along without it for a couple of days.

What if there were only *one brand* of toilet paper on America's store shelves? Would *anyone* spend $140 million trying to get you to buy it? That's exactly the point.

Advertising does not change behavior. It mostly shapes and directs behaviors that take place anyway, and that's why it's sometimes worth the expense. If you already have a positive attitude toward a product and engage in a behavior—such as using toilet paper, drinking beer, or driving a car—small attitude changes can make big differences in market share. When you stand before 30 feet of shelves loaded with several brands of toilet paper, which do you choose? If you remember a commercial the night before gave you a slightly warmer feeling about one product, it might influence your choice. Good ads get people to shift from one brand to another in what is essentially the same product, whether it's beer, cars, soft drinks or toilet paper. Those shifts can make companies millions of dollars. Good advertising gets consumers to buy a different brand of something they would buy anyway.

When we restore trout streams, we study the current and build wing dams so the flowing water diverts slightly to clean gravel bars or carve deeper holes for trout to hide in. Likewise, advertising diverts the forces of consumer desires to create sales. In contrast, Exxon and ANEC tried to use advertising to turn the stream and make it run uphill. And that, as we have seen, doesn't work.

Even with such undifferentiated products, structural fixes have more of an effect than advertising. The study of toilet paper concluded: "Advertising seems to reinforce preferences for current brands rather than stimulating brand switching. However, features, displays, and especially price have a stronger impact on response than does advertising. The effect of brand loyalty dominates that of other variables."[28] In short, advertising is partly a defensive effort to keep you buying the same brand. When you stand before the shelf, it's price, features (softness), the way it's displayed (I'll bet the toilet paper with the most shelf space wins), and packaging (one roll per package or the multiple-roll "economy size")–all structural fixes—that determine what you buy.

Turn the toilet paper example around. How much advertising money do you think it would cost to get Americans to quit using toilet paper? Try using only your bare left hand instead, like many people in the world do. This would save many trees. Would paid celebrities extolling the virtues of a toilet-paper-free world convince you? Or would such TV ads just look stupid?

You would think hard-nosed captains of industry would demand facts and figures proving that ads make a difference, but if you're the junior vice president who just committed your company to $100 million of advertising, do you want to carefully evaluate how the program worked? Of course, it succeeded. If sales go up, the program worked. If sales go down, the VP can say, "Thank god we advertised, or they would have crashed." Even though empirical evidence shows, at best, negligible effects of advertising, powerful forces keep us all believing in the Myth of Massive Media Impact.[29]

Another reason companies spend so much money on advertising and promotion despite their lack of demonstrated effectiveness is that corporations have much to spend. In the first two months of the 2010 oil spill in the Gulf of Mexico, BP hired a political advertising agency and committed to more than $50 million in advertising.[30] This sounds huge, but it was less than one-half of one percent of the $10.5 billion BP expected to pay shareholders the next *quarter* alone. Who cares if it did any good? It didn't cost much anyway. The U.S. National Science Foundation's budget for social psychology, which funds research for the whole nation, received $3.6 million the same year.

Some advertising failures are famous. Advertising didn't get people to like Ford's Edsel, a car that went nowhere except into the dictionary, where it became defined as "a product, project, that fails to gain public acceptance despite high expectations, [and] costly promotional efforts."[31] Nor did advertising inspire people with strong attitudes based on decades of behavior and personal identification with "The Real Thing" to drink the "New Coke." Nor did Steve Forbes, who spent $17 million of his own money to promote his candidacy, win the presidential nomination.[32] People got to know Forbes quickly, didn't like him compared to other candidates, and didn't vote for him.

There's a saying in the advertising world that nothing kills bad products faster than advertising. But don't take it from me; listen to an ad agency. After a couple of devastating antihunting TV specials, concerned hunters who mistakenly thought this changed attitudes toward hunting wanted to reestablish positive attitudes toward by "educating the public." (Is this getting tiresome?) They went to an experienced, well-known advertising agency, which conducted focus groups, ran surveys, and came back to the hunters with hard data. With the candidness of real professionals they said: "There is not much that we can do to help, unless you seriously change hunting. If you start to require all hunters to take tests or do something significant to change hunting, then we can help you 'sell' the new hunting. But running pro-hunting advertisements without such a change will do no good."[33]

Fish Stories

The media can shift the behavior of a few people, which made Wisconsin fish managers believe in its power, at least for a year or two. The Escanaba Chain of Lakes in northern Wisconsin's Vilas County is set aside for research, and all anglers must stop at a check station for an access permit. After their trip, they again report in, and their fish are weighed and counted. Among the more than 1,300 lakes in Vilas County, these five little research lakes are largely unknown. At least they were until *Outdoor Life*, a magazine with a circulation of about 1.5 million, published "The Secret Lakes of the North Woods," where "you are almost guaranteed to catch a fish on every cast."[34] It is true, as writer Jack Kulpa told his *Outdoor Life* readers, that there are no bag limits. It was probably less true that "a relative handful of anglers have been catching fish here by the bushel." In what is excessive for even outdoor magazines, Kulpa reported that a named state biologist "will be the first to tell you that on some days, you can literally catch a fish on every cast" and that "when the bass action peaks in the North, catches of 50 and even 100 fish per angler are common." A fishing Eldorado!

QUESTION: What year did *Outdoor Life* publish this article?
ANSWER: See Figure 5.1, which shows anglers' trips to Pallette Lake, a lake in the Escanaba Chain. Researchers thought this was such an anomaly they didn't publish 1984 data in one of their scientific papers.[35] The biologists were glad when "things went back to normal" after three years.

Although we don't have a control lake to see if angler numbers went up as much, nor any survey data on why anglers came to the Escanaba Chain (fish biologists are lots more interested in fish than in why people fish), nothing besides the *Outdoor Life* article offers a plausible explanation for the big jump in anglers. But whose behavior changed? Did skiers, backpackers, skydivers, and couch potatoes head to the Escanaba Lakes? Not likely. To have your attitude and behavior changed, you first had to be an *Outdoor Life* reader. Even among this group, many people don't fish. So, we wouldn't expect even an article that claimed fish were leaping into boats to turn nonanglers into anglers. *Outdoor Life* circulates across the United States, so we would expect few who live in California, no matter how much they like fishing, to show up in Wisconsin. More than likely, the article shaped the behavior of anglers

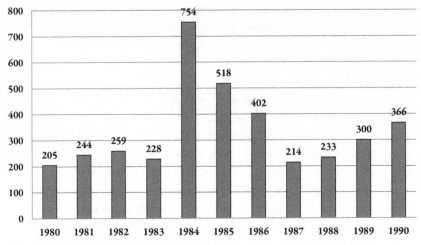

FIGURE 5.1 Anglers' Visits to Pallette Lake

already fishing in the North Woods. The article simply suggested a new spot and got North Woods anglers to try the Escanaba Lakes. If we count every additional 1984 trip as new anglers, the 536 people affected by the article would be far less than one out of 1,000 readers.

These anglers headed to the Escanaba Lakes with high hopes, and from years of research, we have a good idea what they experienced. The research data show that rather than a fish on every cast, anglers average almost four hours per fish, and seven of ten anglers catch *no* fish.[36] This was nothing like *Outdoor Life's* fish story. Given this experience, even the most optimistic anglers changed their weak attitude based on the article to a much stronger attitude based on direct experience ("There ain't no fish in this crummy lake"). As we can see from the graph, they presumably didn't come back. That's one reason advertising can kill a bad product: People discover it more quickly, and once they try it, they don't like it.

When the Irresistible Force Meets the Immovable Object

Since we're out and about in Wisconsin, let's go back to deer hunting. To refresh: Attitudes among Wisconsin deer hunters are based on direct experience, tied to identities, filled with emotion, and grounded in friendship and family reference groups. From an attitude point of view, this is the immovable object. No anti-hunting advertisements will make deer hunters turn in their guns, any more than Exxon and ANEC ads changed attitudes about mining and nuclear wastes.

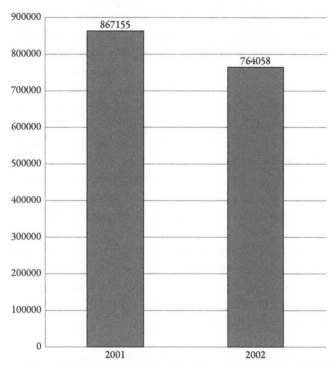

FIGURE 5.2 **Deer Hunting Licenses Sold in Wisconsin Before and After the Discovery of Chronic Wasting Disease**

Sometimes, however, streams run uphill, at least for a little while. In February 2002, this immovable object (deer hunting) met an irresistible force when the Wisconsin DNR discovered chronic wasting disease (CWD, or mad cow disease in deer) in three deer, and wildlife managers inadvertently "scared the stuffing" out of hunters. The two major daily newspapers in the capital city, Madison, ran 746 stories on CWD (more than two daily) during the last 10 months of 2002. The *Milwaukee Journal-Sentinel* ran nearly 400, or more than one a day. The Gannett Newspaper chain, which owns 11 newspapers in northeastern Wisconsin, ran more than 500 stories, 149 of which were *on the front page.*[37] Compared to this, one *Outdoor Life* story on the Escanaba Lakes was virtually nothing. And that's far more coverage than Exxon and ANEC bought for millions of dollars. Every day the press amplified worries from the scientific community and managers of Wisconsin's treasured deer herd. Attitudes and behavioral intentions changed (see chapter 3), with 36% of hunters reporting in May 2002 they would consider not hunting white-tailed deer in November.

What happened in the gray days of autumn when Wisconsin's annual ritual of deer-hunting season played out and families prepared to hunt? What did hunters really do? (See Figure 5.2) The day before the firearms deer season opened in 2002, hunters finally decided, and the DNR sold more licenses that day than ever before. The final data showed only a 12% decline in deer-license sales. In spite of having their socks scared off by threats of deadly venison trumpeted in the press day after day after day, more than 750,000 deer hunters bought licenses for the gun and/or archery seasons.[38] To the chagrin of anti-hunters (who saw an opportunity here) and the great relief of the Wisconsin DNR (which funds most of its wildlife programs from deer-hunting license sales), the state's deer hunt went on almost as normal. Such is the power of the press to change behavior against strong attitudes. Even in the most re-markable efforts to "educate the public," scarcely 10% of hunters were suffi-ciently influenced to change their behavior. After no one died from venison in subsequent years, hunter numbers rebounded some.[39] So the answer to the age-old question—at least for attitudes—is clear: When the irresistible force meets the immovable attitude object, even if the attitude changes, 9 out of 10 times the behavior remains stable.

Conclusion

Long before CWD arrived in Wisconsin, however, my faith in the cognitive fix had pretty much dissolved, thanks largely to 15+ years of work on energy studies. I learned the hard way that educating the public did not conserve electricity in Madison apartments. Nor did increasing information get Mil-waukee households to shift electricity use from on-peak to off-peak hours. For me, these lessons were disasters. The good news, although it took time to ap-preciate, was that structural fixes did work during the energy crisis (e.g., speed limits) and in both time-of-use experiments. There was a future in well-designed structural fixes.

Educating the public was also disastrous for Exxon Minerals in Wisconsin. There's little doubt its hope for a technological fix of dumping mine waste into the Wisconsin River hit an impassable rock garden of attitudes based on iden-tities and direct experience. Technological fixes must be designed to be consis-tent with attitudes, and this one was not. Exxon's advertising campaign threw gasoline on the fire by reminding people repeatedly about the mine. The media did what it does so well, set the agenda, not change attitudes. Likewise, advertising was disastrous in Nevada, where ANEC spent millions of dollars trying to change attitudes that, because of the emotional load, were as solid as those casks designed to protect nuclear waste from speeding locomotives.

We saw, too, that advertising is overrated, even in the marketplace. It seldom creates new behaviors although it can sometimes shape ongoing behaviors. This might justify the expenses, but usually advertising does not get examined closely because it's in no one's interest to show it doesn't work.[40] The fishing story gives some insight into why managers and the public think media hype works. One article doubled the number of anglers on the Escanaba Lakes, but that was no more than one in 1,000 readers who showed up. The fact that few anglers returned shows how direct experience trumps media hype. The CWD adventure showed that, if you can generate hundreds and hundreds of news stories in 8 months, you can change attitudes and shift behavior (in this case in the wrong direction) in about 1 of 10 people, but that's as far as it goes.

I realize this chapter challenges conventional wisdom with just a few stories of my own field experiments, experiences of two large corporations, and observations on fishing and deer hunting in Wisconsin, but don't simply take my word on this. William McGuire, whom the *American Psychologist* called "the field's premier researcher in the psychology of persuasion,"[41] makes much the same point with more than 450 references in his classic "The Myth of Massive Media Impact."[42] Sharon Dunwoody, my UW-Madison colleague and chaired professor in Environmental Communication, makes the same point about media campaigns, noting: "The goals are often noble ones, the dollars spent gargantuan, and the outcomes all too predictable: Messages seem to change the behaviors of some people some of the time but have almost no discernible impact on most people most of the its time."[43]

Like it or not, this is the way it is. But if educating the public doesn't work, what should we do instead? A big sign high on a bluff over the Mississippi River pointed me in the right direction.

6

NORMS

HIGH ON A bluff over the Mississippi River, a giant sign shouting "NORMS" welcomed me back to Wisconsin as I drove to Madison to continue my research on norms. But rather than being a message from my new colleagues, as I first thought, it was just a guy named Norm, who, in his enthusiasm to sell house-trailers, forgot the apostrophe. Norms, however, deserve such notice as one of the most useful, powerful concepts in the social psychologist's toolkit for understanding human behavior. They are the key to changing environmental behaviors. Norms direct our actions and carry us along like the river's current. When we flow with the current, we don't really notice and understand their power—until we strike rocks or try swimming upstream.

Norms at *Handelsbanken*

I've been schooled regularly in going against the flow since moving to Stockholm. What you do normally in Sweden is what you do *normally* in America: drive on the right side of the road, go into McDonalds, and order a Big Mac. But not always! On my first visit to a Swedish bank, I noticed people sitting in chairs like at a barbershop while others stood around reading signs on the wall. One person was standing in front of the teller, so I stood behind her. When she left, I moved to the window. Immediately, another person jumped up from a chair and rudely pushed in front of me without saying "ursäkta mig" (excuse me). The teller took care of him. I heard a "bing," and another old Swede pushed me aside.

I quit assuming I knew what was going on. I left my self-made line and started looking around. I noticed people holding little pieces of paper, and when the next person came in the door, she went to a machine, pressed a button, and took one, too. Trying to look nonchalant, I strolled over and punched the button. My piece of paper said "96." The next time I heard a bing, I looked toward the sound and saw a big sign reading "89." Oh, I finally got it. These people were taking turns, and the number system acted like a big line.[1] Now that I had my number and knew what I was doing, I no longer felt stupid, guilty, and nervous—what social psychologists call "internal negative sanctions." Rather, I felt clever and proud ("internal positive sanctions") because I figured out another small mystery of Swedish society. I further escaped the informal negative sanctions of dirty looks and people pushing past me . . . and the more formal sanction of having the teller not serve me because I did not have a "nummerlapp." My behavior had changed with no effort to change my attitude. I was simply motivated to comply with the "norm."

Norms and the Chinese Couple

Social norms, not attitudes, drove the behaviors of restaurant and hotel personnel in LaPiere's study. Whenever behavior is regular—remember that more than 99% of those personnel served the Chinese—you can be sure something *other* than attitudes is the influence. Attitudes tend to show differences between people. Some who answered LaPiere's survey might have hated Chinese, others might have disliked them, and a few might have even liked them. If attitude was the key driver in locations LaPiere studied, we would have expected more behavior variability by hotel and restaurant personnel. Because the behavior was the same (and opposite of the expressed attitude), some outside force must have determined it. The sign over the Mississippi shouted the answer: NORMS.

Norms are associated with roles. Picture LaPiere and his Chinese friends as they finish lunch. A restaurant employee approaches. What will she do? Ask Professor LaPiere to dance? Dump their leftovers on their laps? Crawl under the table? Of course not. This worker, as we know, is a waitress. She will politely ask if they are finished or want anything else. If they're full, she will give them the check and clear the table after they leave. If the person approaching their table were a stocky, six-foot tall male stuffed into a button-popping blue uniform with a big star on his chest and carrying a Tommy gun (remember this was the Bonnie and Clyde era), the LaPiere party would have expected he wasn't there to fill their water glasses. These behavioral regularities, which are associated with roles, most often drive our behaviors and expectations. Cops with pro-environmental attitudes behave much like cops who hate the environment. Waiters and waitresses generally carry out their roles whether they like or dislike the customers.[2] Role behaviors in the restaurant trumped attitudes toward Chinese.

NORMS 101

The big difference between norms and attitudes is that you can *see* norms. Attitudes are invisible. We must guess at them by reading minds. In contrast, we can get lots of traction understanding norms because we *can* see them expressed in behavior. For those of us wishing to save the environment, it's what people do rather than what they say that's crucial, and that makes norms especially interesting.

Norms are *behavioral* regularities. When everybody does the same thing, we call it the "norm." It's a norm to be right-handed. Heights and weights have "norms." No humans stand three meters tall or weigh 1,000 pounds. We also have statistical norms for the number of children borne by couples. These things can all be seen. Cialdini and his associates called behavioral regularities a "descriptive norm."[3]

However, there's more to social norms than simple behavioral regularity. Norms come with sanctions: rewards or punishments administered by others. They have an "ought" component: what we should do. This is called an "injunctive norm." It's what people say we should do, even if they don't always do it.

Is being right-handed or brown-eyed really a social norm? Both are descriptive or statistical norms, just as having two children is currently a statistical norm in the United States. Lefties claim many "punishments" for being different: inoperable scissors, a phone booth's design, a wine glass's place on tables, and even how to kiss. These punishments are not planned to hurt or even change anyone (although left-handed children were once forced to shift to using their right hand); they just result from trying to swim against the current. So even when norms have small injunctive components (people thinking it's what they *should* do), they still influence behavior.

Social norms exist when the social group—whether as large as an entire society or as small as two friends—sanctions behaviors. Sanctions in small groups are usually informal, that is, unwritten; given face to face, sometimes verbally; and sometimes unspoken, as when Swedes pushed me aside at the teller's window. However, for society to function, some norms must be written, as in signs restricting where we park and laws demanding we stop at red lights. We call these "formal norms," and they come with formal societal sanctions, like parking and speeding tickets. Some even impose prison for violating other laws.

Of course, social norms have psychological dimensions, which are represented by individuals' belief systems. These norms are a special kind of attitude because they have a behavioral referent (that is, the attitude object is often the behavior itself). Most important, they come with internal sanctions.

If you follow the norm, you feel positive about yourself; if you don't, you feel negative. Individual representations of norms include guesses about other people's behaviors: "Mom, *everybody* is going to the dance." They include expectations about the probability of sanctions and a loss of esteem from others: "He will hate me if I don't." We form our idea of the norm most often by watching the behavior of others, as I did at the bank. And when you're in a foreign country where you don't speak the language, you spend lots of time watching, as I discovered.

Thus, for a group or social system, we can speak of formal norms, something in writing with formal sanctions; and of informal norms, something unwritten with informal sanctions. We can also think of norms at the individual level. Personal norms carry an individual sense of obligation with internal sanctions. It's important to realize personal norms might not be the same as social norms. Social norms are like downstream current in the river's main channel, but along its banks or behind its rocks are places called "eddies," where water actually goes upstream. Likewise, some people in society hold personal norms that differ and go against the currents of social norms. Conflicts between personal and social norms sow seeds for social change.

Within individuals, norms also exist as "perceptions" of social norms. For example, what percentage of people would shoot a wolf? A person might know it's illegal to kill a wolf and hold a personal norm to not kill a wolf, but still believe "most people around here would shoot a wolf if they saw one." That's their perception of the social norm, and it might differ from the collectivity's actual normative behavior. To summarize, we have statistical norms, formal norms, informal norms, personal norms, and perceived norms. To clarify, let's take another lesson from Aldo Leopold, and return to those pesky birch trees.

Aldo Leopold and Tree-Cutting Norms

Along with his positive attitude— "I am in love with pines"—Leopold also had a "personal norm" about cutting birches that crowded out young pines at his shack. Leopold said he had a personal obligation to engage in this specific behavior, and we expect this obligation came with internal sanctions. After a morning of cutting those "invasive" pine-shading birches, Aldo presumably returned to his shack feeling proud and self-satisfied from a good morning's work. That's an internal positive sanction, much as I felt after deciphering the Swedish bank's "nummerlapp" system.

However, suppose Leopold went for a walk, noticed a birch shading a pine, but brought no ax. We would expect, because of his personal norm, that he might have worried, and felt a bit guilty that he wasn't taking good care of his beloved pines. This guilt and worry is an internal negative sanction, and people act to reduce guilt, so we presume Leopold would form a behavioral intention to cut the birch during his next visit to the shack. This is all inside Leopold's head, so we call it a personal norm.

Now suppose that while returning to Madison in the family's 1935 Chevy, one of Leopold's kids recalled seeing a birch that had dodged the ax, and asked, "Say, Dad, how come you didn't cut that birch that's shading the pine I planted?" That question suggests the birch-cutting norm exists outside of Leopold's head, and is a norm in the small social system of his family. Aldo is now getting a negative informal sanction from his offspring, and would likely feel guilty as he drove his family down Highway 12.

However, the birch-cutting norm is *not* a formal norm in the larger society, for no laws in Wisconsin or Sauk County demand you cut birches that shade pines. Furthermore, violating this norm brings no formal sanctions, fines, or prison sentences. Because it's unlikely this was a behavioral regularity outside Leopold's family, it wasn't a societal norm at all. Norms can exist within and outside individuals. Sometimes individuals' personal norms—their sense of obligation coupled with internal sanctions—can differ from the social norm, but both are usually congruent.

The Anti-litter Norm

Rather than speculating further about Leopold's family, let's consider a more widely held norm that affects the environment: littering. We know antilittering is a norm for four reasons:

1. It is a behavioral regularity.
2. If our behavior is consistent or inconsistent with the norm, internal sanctions result.
3. We expect the possibility of informal sanctions for violations of the norm.
4. The larger society imposes formal sanctions for littering.

We all carry the anti-littering norm within us. At least I haven't met people who say that it's good to litter and that not littering makes them proud and not littering makes them feel guilty.[4]

To learn more about littering as part of my dissertation work, I handed out 7,409 voter-registration notices to pedestrians in Wisconsin Dells, a tourist community.[5] My goal was to spot and interview litterers. Two surprises resulted. We think people litter all the time because we attribute all trash on the ground to litterers. I was no different. I expected about half the people accepting my useless handbills to litter. However, during my many weeks distributing handbills, only 138 people dropped them on the street. That's barely a large enough sample to study. The unpredicted, but most important, finding of my research was that more than 98% of those who took the handbill *did not litter.* The perceived norm that "almost everybody (except me, of course) litters" is out of sync with the statistical or descriptive norm, for only 1.9% littered.[6]

The second surprise—although by now most readers won't be shocked—was that the litterers' attitudes toward littering were just as negative as the nonlitterers' attitudes. Thus, people with strong negative attitudes toward littering were just as likely to litter as people with weaker negative attitudes. So, there was zero correlation between the degree of the negative attitude and the behavior. The point I again missed, however, was that no one had positive attitudes toward littering and almost no one littered. This is one reason people think attitudes and behavior are essentially the same. *In aggregate*, people oppose littering, and in aggregate, 98.1% of those who took my handbills *did not litter.* That is a powerful consistency, but it exists only because our attitudes about littering had reached normative status, with no one holding positive attitudes.

However, if almost nobody litters, why do we see so much litter around? Littering leaves traces of norm violations, and this visibility makes us overestimate littering rates. Most norm violations leave no trace. That Swedish bank did not post a sign reading, "Heberlein acted like a dork here." When litter builds up, we associate each piece with a litterer, almost a "one person, one vote" view of the world. The norm violation's irrefutable proof is the trash lying around. In fact, at least half the litter we see comes from other sources. It blows out of trucks and spills from overflowing or blown-over litter barrels.[7] In those cases, nonlitterers are producing litter. The pieces of litter we see are bad measures of a norm violation, but because we have no other way to explain them, we attribute their presence to litterers. This tendency to overestimate the role of character traits (blaming litterers) and underestimate the effects of situation (overturned trash cans) is well known in social psychology as the "Fundamental Attribution Error," which we discussed in chapter 4. It's another reason we persist in thinking attitudes are related to behavior.[8]

The anti-littering norm is also a mild norm. You shouldn't litter, but it's not so bad if you do. I can (and do) ask students to go out and litter in the name of science and education. I cannot ask them to go out, rob a bank, and write a report on what happens. Apropos of its status as a weak norm, few places enforce anti-littering laws (formal sanctions). Oklahoma once launched an anti-litter campaign with threats of $1,000 fines and possible 30-day imprisonment.

What happened? "The courts have refused to enforce this law, maintaining that they have more important things to do."[9] The trivial nature of litter violations was immortalized in the 1960s by Arlo Guthrie's ironic saga "Alice's Restaurant," in which a littering conviction made him unfit to be drafted and fight in Vietnam.[10]

Internal Sanctions

Because police officers and our mothers can't be everywhere, internal sanctions enforce most norms. For years, my students were especially upset when I assigned them to go out and litter, and then write a report about what happened and how they felt. Those internal sanctions kicked in, even with the imprimatur of Professor Heberlein saying it was OK to litter. According to the students' reports, what really got them was *having to litter in front of somebody*. They expected the other person to say something negative, holler at them, or pick up the litter (an informal external negative sanction), which would make them feel bad. They didn't seem to worry much about external formal sanctions, that is, somebody calling the cops to arrest them.

After mustering the courage to litter—which some never did, if their reports are accurate—they were amazed that even when tossing a soft-drink can that almost hit someone, they suffered no direct sanctions. Occasionally, when walking with someone, the target person would say something about littering loudly enough for the litterer to hear. The person who saw my student litter was probably influenced by what we might call the "mind your own business" norm. Giving people informal sanctions makes those delivering the message feel uncomfortable.

Focusing and Deactivating Norms

Norms can powerfully influence behavior, but not always. In spite of the norm, some people in some circumstances litter. Indeed, litter was a symbol of environmental irresponsibility on the first Earth Day. John Lindsay, the charismatic mayor of New York at the time, claimed on TV that he picked up litter dropped by people on the street. An award-winning advertisement sponsored by Keep America Beautiful tried to persuade people not to litter by showing huge litter piles. The mayor's words and the advertising visuals suggested the norm was violated frequently. Robert Cialdini refers to such suggestions as a gap between the injunctive norm (what people should do) and the descriptive norm (what they actually do.)[11]

When do norms fail? Why do people litter? To influence behavior, norms must be focused. There may be many programs in your computer, but they do nothing until you click to activate them. The role we are in often "focuses" us on the norm. The script that comes with being a waiter or waitress implies many behaviors that the actors consider when performing the role.

Littering is not associated with a particular role, so the norm sits somewhere in the background like those computer programs. The littering norm doesn't kick in until you have something you want to toss and you consider what to do. Thinking about the "litter-able" material is a first step in the process of activating the norm. In the study in which I distributed handbills, we found that litterers were more likely to report they "did not think about what to do with the handbill." Cialdini and his colleagues who introduced focus theory to the study of norms (particularly the anti-littering norm) found that having another person litter in front of a research subject decreased littering under certain circumstances.[12] The researchers argued that seeing a person litter in a clean environment makes the subject think about littering (probably thinking "what a slob"), and "focuses" the anti-littering norm when the subjects are soon confronted with a littering opportunity.[13] Those who had the norm "focused" are less likely to litter. Other researchers have shown that attractive, imaginative litter barrels get more use, presumably because they attract attention, which focuses the anti-littering norm to make people consider what to do with the junk they're carrying.[14]

However, even when we focus on norms, they can be deactivated and fail to influence behavior. This process has been used to explain why people fail to help others in distress. This was a popular area of psychological research when I first thought about litter. Shalom Schwartz argued that a two-step process can deactivate universally held helping norms that apply for someone in need. First, we can deny negative consequences for the person in distress.[15] If we think no one will be hurt, the norm doesn't apply and we don't have to do anything. Second, we can deny personal responsibility. Bystanders in helping situations can ignore the victim by saying they are not responsible: It is not my job. I can't do what's needed. Someone else will help, and so on.

A behavioral regularity in littering studies is that prelittered areas always have higher littering rates. For instance, I passed out handbills to students leaving a classroom. When the hallway was clean, four percent littered. When the hallway was a mess, including some similar (marked) handbills, the littering rate was four times higher.[16] Compliance with the anti-littering norm is influenced by the type of litter, the setting (city streets, parking lots, grocery stores), the presence of litter barrels, and the amount of litter in the areas. These features make not littering more or less costly, and deactivate the norm.

William Finnie, an Anheuser-Bush researcher, watched what people did with waxed-paper hotdog wrappers in downtown Philadelphia. Unlike those Wisconsin Dells tourists who, to my dismay, hung onto their handbills, one-third of Finnie's hotdog eaters littered. He found that, if the streets were clean and trash cans were around, the littering rate fell to 15%. When the streets were dirty and no trash cans were present—thus making it more costly to obey the norm and to deactivate it by reducing negative consequences—more than half the people dropped wrappers on the street.[17]

Scott Geller, a behavioral psychologist, had hundreds of his students hand out (and then track) handbills featuring daily specials at grocery stores in Blacksburg, Virginia. When store floors were clean, only 1% of customers littered. When stores were prelittered with 140 marked handbills, the littering rate increased, but only to 5%.[18] The huge number on the floor didn't seem to create a descriptive norm sufficient to overcome the existing norm of shoppers not dropping paper on the floor. In an attempt to boost the new (littering) behavior in a second study, they wrote on the handbill, "Please litter. Dispose of on the *floor*." Still, shoppers dropped only 14% of handbills with those instructions.[19] So much for educating the public to engage in anti-environmental and anti-normative behavior.

To explore focus theory, Cialdini and his associates put legal size (8½ by 14 inch) orange handbills under the windshield wipers of parked cars. When the parking lot was clean, 14% of parkers littered, but when it was prelittered with similar handbills, candy wrappers, cigarette butts and paper cups, more than twice as many (32%) littered.[20] In a second trial, they found 18% of people headed to an amusement park littered when the area was clean, and more than 40% littered when the areas were prelittered.

Research in the Netherlands showed that violating another norm appeared to deactivate the anti-littering norm. They put big white fliers on the handle-bars of parked bikes. Riders couldn't steer their bikes without ditching the handbill, so they had to do something if they wanted to pedal home. With no trashcans in sight, 33% of the Dutch bicyclists littered. When the wall in front of the bikes was covered with graffiti, the littering rate roared to 69%. A second study found a 30% increase in littering when firecrackers (illegal in the Netherlands) were shot off nearby.[21]

Why do people litter more when settings are prelittered? It seemed to me that this fits Schwartz's theory about norms, even though this norm concerned littering the environment, not helping others. A littered environment reduces negative consequences. One more scrap of litter won't hurt. The environment is already a mess. A prelittered environment also lifts individual responsibility. You might think littering brings negative consequences, but you aren't responsible. The people who littered before you caused the problem. Or the mass of litter might cue you that "someone" will come to pick it up. This makes *them,* not you, responsible. So, littered floors might help people deny personal responsibility.

Good theories must be tested, which is why I passed out thousands of handbills and pasted "fake" litter to sidewalks to increase dismally low littering rates. When spotting litterers, we asked them for short, on-the-street interviews about tourism, including some measures of awareness of consequences and responsibility denial. After a litterer was interviewed, a control nonlitterer was stopped and asked the same questions. This allowed us to test Schwartz's theory and see if it could be extended from interpersonal helping to a pro-environmental behavior.

The resulting data were remarkably consistent with the theory. For those aware of consequences and who did not deny responsibility, only 11% were litterers. As predicted, they were less likely to deactivate the norm. Of those less aware of consequences and who denied responsibility, 74% littered. Deactivation was not a stepwise process for littering in this situation. Being unaware of consequences and denying responsibility were equally effective at leading non-normative behavior. Furthermore, focus theory and norm-activation theory seem to work together. Those who said they thought about how to dispose of the paper were less likely to litter independent of the deactivation variables.

Of course, because people had just littered, they might be justifying their act by saying nobody was hurt (low awareness of consequences), and it wasn't their fault (responsibility denial) because somebody handed them a junk handbill. Schwartz argued that people can have general tendencies to be aware of consequences and to feel responsible for their actions across settings. He developed a general measure of the latter. This measure, which had nothing to do with littering, was included in a mailed survey completed later. This showed litterers were more likely to deny responsibility for various actions and less likely to believe there were negative consequences for littering. So it's fair to say that litters are less responsible people. Just remember that, in this setting, less than 2% of people fit this label.

Consequences, Responsibility, and Environmental Norms

Because responsibility and consequences are important in deactivating an existing norm like littering, I wondered if they might be important in creating a new norm. In the 1970s, few people were buying lead-free gasoline. It cost more, and cost is one factor that keeps us from acting consistently with our pro-environmental attitudes. However, some people were buying lead-free. Stan Black and I hypothesized that this was because they held a personal norm or sense of obligation. This norm should be related to believing that using leaded gasoline had negative consequences for humans and the environment. We further argued that people who felt more responsible for these consequences would be more likely to hold the norm. So, we enlisted gas-station attendants to get us a sample of lead-free buyers and a matched sample of regular-gas buyers.

We sent a questionnaire to both groups, asking if they felt responsible for causing and reducing air pollution.[22] We measured their awareness of consequences by whether they thought using lead-free gasoline reduced air pollution. We also asked if they perceived a social norm to buy lead-free gasoline. That is, did they . . .

1. Think others would approve of their buying lead-free gasoline?
2. Think others had a feeling of obligation to buy lead-free gasoline?
3. Know others who purchased lead-free gasoline?

All three variables influenced personal norms to buy lead-free. Those holding a personal norm were more likely to believe using lead-free helped reduce air pollution, that they were responsible for reducing air pollution, and that there was some kind of informal social norm to using lead-free gasoline. Most important, those holding the personal norm were much more likely to be observed buying lead-free gasoline. Note: This isn't saying they would (behavior intention-BI) or they did (behavior report) buy it, but they were seen by another person filling up with lead-free (an observed behavior), and thus it was not a component of attitude (BI) nor subject to self-reporting bias. To us, it looked like increasing the awareness of consequences and feelings of responsibility might lead to new norms and to behavior consistent with these norms.[23]

I also examined the role of these variables in a stronger emergent norm of saving energy during the 1970s energy crisis.[24] A survey in March 1974, about the same time we were reading meters in that apartment complex, showed that awareness of consequences, feelings of responsibility, and measures of a perceived social norm led to a sense of a personal obligation to use less energy just as a personal norm emerged to buy lead-free gasoline.

Several years after those studies, environmental sociologists Riley Dunlap and Kent Van Liere examined feelings of responsibility and awareness of interpersonal negative consequences as determinants of reported yard-waste burning in Spokane, Washington.[25] They found those who believed there were few alternatives to yard burning were more likely to burn waste than were those who denied negative consequences of yard burning (i.e., said that the resulting air pollution was modest and burning did not make "it difficult for people with respiratory problems to breathe"). They included no measure of a personal norm in their analysis, but the norm-activation variables influenced reported behavior.

Stan Black and Paul Stern applied an expanded version of the activation model with multiple causal levels to explain reported energy conservation among Massachusetts households in the mid-1980s.[26] They included a perceived social norm, ascription of responsibility, and awareness of social consequences. Measures of these three variables were more consistent with Schwartz's theory than with the yard-waste burning study. Their analysis showed, as predicted, a strong and consistent effect of holding a personal norm. Holding this personal norm, in turn, had the strongest direct effect on reported energy conservation behavior in all the models.

Stern and his associates went on to make major strides in exploring and testing this model, and generalized it to what they call the "Values-Beliefs-Norm Model."[27] In this model, values and general orientations—much as I described in chapter 2 in our analysis of Leopold's attitude—are at the base. Atop these come beliefs about negative consequences for the valued object, and the ability to reduce those threats. In turn, these lead to a personal norm to engage in pro-environmental acts that generally influence reported and even observed behavior.

Creating New Norms

To understand how norms change, we return to Aldo Leopold. Each spring at his shack, Leopold recorded when plants bloomed and when geese and cranes arrived. These baseline data, followed up a half-century later, showed clear evidence of climate change.[28] Although Leopold didn't intend to document social change any more than he was trying to demonstrate climate change, he left a marker for a change in environmental norms through a cleverly disguised fish story.

On a hot day in June, Leopold drove 200 miles north of his home to fish the "Alder Fork." While wading through a tag-alder thicket, he was attacked by hordes of mosquitoes before a trout finally took his fly "with a great gulp . . . shortly I could hear him kicking in the bed of wet alder leaves at the bottom of the creel." Spotting a larger trout in the next pool, Leopold sneaked in and reported, "For the duration of a cigarette I sit on a rock midstream—and watch my trout rise under his guardian bush."[29]

Although the environmental community rightfully sees Aldo Leopold as the paragon of environmental responsibility, in one paragraph he violated two norms that emerged since his death. The first is catch-and-release fishing. These days, many trout fisherman feel a strong personal obligation to throw back fish. They rarely keep, kill, and eat trout they catch. Second, in the United States and much of Europe, laws now limit smoking, and guilt-ridden smokers are sometimes ostracized.

An oil painting of Leopold covers a wall in his old department at the University of Wisconsin-Madison. This rendering came from a photograph of the professor standing among admiring students at the shack. Instead of holding an ax, Leopold holds a cigarette. I asked Leopold's biographer, Curt Meine, to look for pictures of Leopold with cigarettes. In his responding e-mail, Meine said, "I was surprised at the number."[30] The university itself provides evidence that antismoking has become a norm since that picture was taken: After choosing that Leopold pose for another publication, editors cropped the photo so Leopold stood alone. The cigarette? It disappeared with the students.

Although it might be sad to see Leopold as a latter-day environmental scofflaw, the overall message is positive. It shows norms governing environmental behavior can change, and that even Leopold is out of step with the times six decades later. The bad news is that norms change slowly. Decades, not years, measure their change.

Nor do we have good ideas for creating new norms. It's like starting a flood to collect insurance money. Fires are easier. However, as a step forward, let's see how three environmental norms—the two Leopold violated and the recycling norm—grew and changed, and ask what happened.

The Catch-and-Release Norm

When Leopold was alive, my dad and uncles never considered throwing back a trout unless it was too small to eat. Every May, the Heberlein patriarchs met at the family cabin on the banks of the Big Spring Creek for the season opener. They ate huge meals cooked by Uncle Earl, told bad jokes, and killed fish— lots of them. Yellowed photos from my uncle's box camera show proud, smiling anglers holding stringers of 20–30 trout.

It's no longer appropriate to kill trout. The sure signs are informal external sanctions from other anglers. Just try sporting a creel, which Leopold used to carry home dead fish. Somebody is sure to say something. Even if no one is around, guilt keeps many anglers from using a creel or even thinking about keeping a fish.

What changed during those 60 years, and how can we change other behaviors affecting the environment? Norms usually grow from common practice. For hundreds of years, sportsmen threw *some* fish back. Most of those were fish too small to justify cooking, but others were spared because anglers had enough fish or were pursuing other species. Occasionally they released them out of respect for the fish.[31] So, it wasn't unthinkable to catch and release a fish.

In the 19th century, laws emerged with formal sanctions (fines and presumably even jail sentences) mandating fish be released under certain circumstances. Several U.S. states closed or limited seasons, and they established size limits and bag limits to conserve fish stocks.[32] Fish caught outside the season or measuring shorter than the size limit had to be released. Fishing wardens were hired privately and later by governments to enforce the laws.

The extension of catch-and-release regulations, with anglers informally agreeing and urging each other to release their catch, grew from an orientation change in managing fisheries. To meet demands for fish during the 19th century, the primary solution was growing fish in hatcheries and dumping them in lakes and streams.[33] A new idea emerged in mid-20th century, after Leopold's death. It emphasized sustainability and preserving ecosystems rather than dumping tame trout into waterways. A growing number of anglers preferred certain kinds of ecosystems with wild fish. This preference required wild stock be conserved through recycling—even if the law said you could keep some. A private organization, Trout Unlimited (TU) in Michigan, formalized this approach to trout management with its founding.[34]

When my friend Steve Born joined TU two decades after its start, it had 50,000 members. He recalls his first meeting, at which members wore pins reading, "Limit your take, don't take your limit." (Note that we don't wear pins for established norms like "I drive on the right side.") This was clear evidence of an emerging norm, and opposite that of the Heberlein patriarchs. My forebears viewed limits as suggested goals. If you exceeded them, it was simply a sign of good fishing that day. Releasing fish under the limit was unthinkable, and keeping a few beyond your limit wasn't such a bad idea.

Changing the value from stocked to wild trout and forming an organization based on the new value began capturing sportsmen's hearts and minds. It helped that trout fishermen write, and several great writers (e.g., Hemingway, Maclean, E. B. White) fished trout. Furthermore, highly educated trout anglers read and proselytize.[35] Angling stories spread the norm and gave it high status. Increasing demand and competition in fishing further drove the catch-and-release idea.

As income and leisure time increased and baby boomers matured, the number of anglers—particularly trout anglers—skyrocketed. As they put enormous pressure on trophy streams, the anglers became more ecologically sensitive. They understood the environmental consequences of fishing. Taking a 5-pound, 25-inch native cutthroat from a Montana river meant killing one of the last survivors of a hatch from bygone years. Short of quitting angling, the only solution was recycling trout.

An awareness of consequences played a big role in growing this norm: environmental consequences, that is, reducing population of certain age-class trout; consequences to other humans, that is, fewer fish to catch; and consequences to yourself, that is, fewer fish next time. The environmental effect on fish populations leads directly to human consequences: If you keep trout, kill them, and eat them, there are fewer trout for other people. People like Leopold, my dad, and my uncles—who caught and killed fish—were hurting other humans in a clear way. That seems to be a necessary condition for norm emergence.

However, there's more to it. Early one morning I caught a monster bass while casting from a rickety pier on Parker Lake. My proud dad took me to the hardware store in the nearby village to enter my fish in the big-bass contest.[36] Angling's competitive element, amplified by market and media forces, soon took catch-and-release beyond elite fly-fishers.

Bass fishermen—blue-collar, salt-of-the-earth anglers—received a big lesson in catch-and-release when bass fishing became a competitive sport. Bass-fishing contests are fun to watch and seem to provide local short-term economic benefits. A small navy of professional fishermen in high-powered boats with sonar, lots of know-how, and the latest tackle put lots of pressure on Billy Bob's lake. The number and/or weight of fish determine the winners. After early contests, fish were sometimes left in piles to rot, causing locals to wonder if it was a good idea to hold tournaments on their prized lakes.

To deal with this, the Bass Anglers Sportsman Society (BASS) that sponsored contests imposed catch-and-release formats. BASS tournaments became the model for a different class of angler. In 2011 there were three times as many BASS members than college-educated TU members. More important, BASS fishing contests are televised by ESPN, so hundreds of thousands see professional anglers working hard to bring live bass to the weigh-in. The technology of keeping fish alive also grew, creating new products that 60 giant (the smallest is 40,000 square feet) Bass Pro Shops and other mega-outdoor retail stores gladly promote and sell.

So if Leopold were alive today, I expect he would toss trout back in or at least explain the fish he kept. The norm is present and powerful. Just how powerful? A while back I started fishing for Wisconsin's state fish, the muskellunge, near my North Woods cabin. Muskies are hard to catch, and for several years I caught none. My dad and uncles also fished for muskies. These fish are so big and mean that when old-timers brought them alongside the boat, they shot them with a.22 pistol rather than net them. That pretty much ruled out catch-and-release. The musky's white meat was especially prized in camp, and I can remember eating beer-battered musky fillets as a boy.

Therefore, I told fishing buddies and anyone else who would listen that when I caught *my* first legal musky, I would kill it and eat it as a sacrament to honor my father and uncles. Then, on a windy November day on the blue waters of a nameless lake in Ashland County, it happened. I held my first legal musky for a quick picture—and released it. I stood there a little amazed, maybe like those restaurant owners who served the Chinese couple but told LaPiere they "would not serve members of the Chinese Race." Such is the power of NORMS.

The Antismoking Norm

Smoking norms have changed dramatically since Leopold sat on that rock, cigarette in hand, contemplating a wily trout, but that change took a half-century, with virtually no progress for the first 20 years. When Leopold died in 1948, about 40% of Americans smoked. In 1970, 40% still smoked, despite three major attempts at a cognitive fix:

1. Physicians were banned from cigarette advertising (1953).[37]
2. The Surgeon's General report announced significant health effects (1964).
3. Warning labels were required on cigarette packs (1965).

Even by 1991, the number of cigarettes smoked per capita in the United States was about what it was in 1946 when Professor Leopold smoked amid his admiring students.[38] Since 1991, something dramatic happened. In response to cognitive fix failures, structural fixes consistent with widespread negative attitudes toward smoking were implemented with some success.

My own smoking tale reflects this historic change and the principles discussed in earlier chapters. I started smoking at the University of Chicago the same year warnings were required on cigarette packs. My father had shifted from smoking cigarettes to smoking a pipe, and I thought pipes smelled good (positive beliefs and denial of consequences, i.e., cigarettes might cause cancer, but pipes don't because you don't inhale). More important, my social psychology professor smoked a pipe in class. (Like the Bennington women, I was ready to change and I had a high-status role model.) Lighting a pipe in the wood-paneled classroom seemed like an academic thing to do (change in identity). No one complained. Later that year I even smoked a pipe on an airplane with the permission of my seatmates (lack of negative sanctions). As a professor, I smoked in my classrooms until the early 1980s, when a student complained (awareness of negative interpersonal consequences). A decade later, in 1991, Chancellor Donna Shalala restricted smoking for the entire UW campus (a structural fix), and my pipe was reserved for home or around the campfire. In 2003 I finally quit, a personal change that took almost 40 years.

The new antismoking norm was taking hold. Surveys showed that although a majority of physicians smoked in Leopold's day, that group plummeted to 4% by 1990.[39] Structural fixes, like the ban on my own campus, were being implemented elsewhere. California banned smoking in bars in 1998, and Ireland followed in 2004. Even legendary Irish pubs could not stand against the new norm. Structural fixes give people experience, and direct experience can change or create new attitudes. Employees of California bars surveyed four years after the smoking ban were much more positive about working in a smoke-free environment than a comparable sample surveyed during the ban's first six months.[40]

Today we have formal sanctions against smoking in the form of laws, informal sanctions in the form of complaining friends and family, and even internal sanctions in the form of nicotine addicts losing self-esteem and feeling guilty about their weakness. By 2011, 35 of 50 U.S. states had some kind of smoking ban, and all but two were implemented in the 21st century, more than 50 years after Leopold's death.[41] Behavior was finally changing. By 2007, less than 20% of the U.S. population smoked.[42]

The most dramatic finding is the amount of time needed to create a new norm around a simple public health behavior. Such changes in health-related behaviors not only take decades to implement, they take repeated information from many sources. Norms can change, but it takes a combination of cognitive and structural fixes, and lots of time for the new behavior to take hold.

The Recycling Norm

Much like my American banking norms, my recycling norms didn't travel well. On a hot afternoon sailing among the Australian Whitsunday Islands, I finished off a "tinny," the local term for a can of beer. I asked where I should recycle it. "Just toss 'er in the dustbin [the local term for garbage can], mate."

I declined. "No, this is an aluminum can. It needs to go to the recyclables." Of course, the can had no needs. These existed only in the mind of a social psychologist. Again, I was urged to throw it in the dustbin. Again, I refused. Finally—when discovering that even if I sorted out every recyclable, they would go into the same trash when we returned—I gave in. I felt almost as bad putting it into the regular trash as I would have if I had chucked it overboard. For me, the recycling norm had become as strong as the anti-littering norm. Forsaking recycling brought feelings of guilt and shame that were hard to overcome, even with a Whitsunday Islands cruise to distract me. Internal sanctions, of course, are why norms are so powerful.

The recycling norm appears to have grown with increasing environmental awareness. The United States had about 1,000 recycling programs in 1988. By 1999, the number exceeded 9,000.[43] The idea of recycling, like the idea of releasing some fish, was not new. Certainly our pioneer ancestors reused what they could, and the generations who lived through the Great Depression were reluctant to discard anything. During WWII, paper drives and scrap-metal collections became major patriotic efforts, but during the prosperous 1950s and turbulent 1960s, I think many felt too rich or too busy to recycle.[44]

The real issue with recycling is that you need some sort of structural fix. That is what stymied me in the Whitsundays. Without large-scale recycling programs to turn goods into something else, individual behavior is meaningless. Citywide programs started in the 1970s, and social psychologists began studying them.[45] By the late 1990s, about a third of the U.S. population had access to curbside recycling programs.[46] Participation rates were not high in the early years, and even the best interventions seldom boosted participation rates above 15%.[47] Although those with more knowledge were more likely to recycle, simply giving people more information—the now well-known cognitive fix—did not seem to increase participation.[48] The most successful programs were those that grew the norm rather than those that tried to educate the public.

In a widely cited field experiment, Joyce Nielsen and her associates at the University of Colorado showed that city blocks with a "leader" more than doubled participation rates, up to 27%.[49] Block leaders simply went around informing people about pickup days. In doing so, they helped create or activate a norm by showing that someone else was recycling, that someone cared (and hence, might be hurt) if they did not recycle, and that someone was watching and might administer informal sanctions. Of course, those participation rates are low compared to the 98% who hung onto my handbills. Recycling, however, is a combination of many behaviors, some of which are messy, whereas not littering was no real chore for the 30 seconds it took tourists to walk that Wisconsin Dells street. Therefore, we would expect the anti-littering norm to be much more influential than the recycling norm.

A statistical assessment of a new recycling program in Portugal showed the personal norm, a perceived social norm (what you thought significant others thought you should do), and a measure of personal responsibility for recycling all had strong positive associations with participation. General attitudes toward the environment and even attitudes toward recycling did not influence behavior.[50] Norms trump attitudes again.

People now have positive attitudes toward recycling, and many hold personal norms to recycle. However, effects of the situation and the influences of other attitudes make it hard to behave consistently with weak norms. One way to lower these barriers is to pick up recyclables rather than make people take them to recycling centers. This structural fix increased recycling.[51] Giving people a special pickup bin also appears to focus the norm. When controlling for beliefs about personal costs, surveys showed people with bins were more aware of the positive consequences of recycling than those without bins. A measure of personal responsibility affected the reported behavior *only* for those without bins and roadside pickup. With the structural fix in place, feelings of personal responsibility had no additional effect on reported recycling. Structural fixes can, at least in this case, promote behavior independent of activation variables.

The Grandson Test

These three emergent norms seem to pass the grandson test: They are simple enough to explain to young boys. Smoking is probably the easiest to explain. The behavior is clear and public, and schools work hard to inculcate the antismoking norm. I can tell my grandson Henry that smoking makes you cough, smell bad, and die young. Someday he might not buy that, but the logic, at least, is simple.

Recycling can be more difficult, but recycling stations are easy to find and often list what they accept. Sometimes, however, I stand puzzling a long time while trying to decide if a greasy pizza box is really recyclable. (According to a recycling station I visited with Henry's class during a field trip, it isn't.) However, cans and bottles are easy to count and find, and our three grandsons enthusiastically collected and carried them to a Stockholm grocery store for recycling, especially when finding the payment was three times what they receive at home in California.

Catch-and-release usually passes the grandson test. "Put 'em back," I say when Peter and I fish Spring Creek. "But Papa Tom, what if I catch a really big one?"

"We'll take a picture and toss it back. If we kill fish, they won't be here for us to catch on your next trip." That will hold him, unless and until he lands a lunker . . . in which case I will probably hide it inside my waders and invite it home for dinner. Peter and I will feel guilty, but at the same time a bit self-satisfied, as I show him how Uncle Earl fried trout.

Not littering is a harder behavior to observe and explain. Although we all know litter when we see it, we don't always see it that way when we litter. Stuff blows out of the car or off the picnic table. Litter or not? You can't find a recycling spot when traveling, so you leave your aluminum cans for others so they can get the refund. Litter or not? The popcorn box stays on the movie theater's floor because, after all, somebody is paid to clean up. The apple core goes out the car window, because it will biodegrade and birds might eat it. Litter is a matter of definition and who gets hurt and who benefits. I once found a ten-dollar bill while picking up roadside trash. Explaining to David that this valuable find is litter might prove difficult. Even so, littering generally passes the grandson test. I can tell any of them not to litter, tell them why, and bawl them out if they do.

Starting a Flood

When we examine catch-and-release, antismoking, and recycling norms, we see common patterns. Time is required. These are not overnight changes that emerged from one infomercial. The catch-and-release norm took a couple of decades, and the antismoking norm took a half-century. As we know it today, the recycling norm is tied to structural fixes or recycling programs that began in the 1970s and continue to evolve and expand.

Most important, the behavior must be clear and specific. Throw the fish back, don't light up, don't litter, and put specific items in appropriate containers. It's better if the behavior is public, so the possibility of informal and, where appropriate, formal sanctions can be applied.

High-status public leadership helps. This is most evident in the catch-and-release norm, where elite trout anglers set the norm. Through fishing contests, television, and media coverage, a new form of elite bass fishermen modified catch-and-release. Smoking is a great example of how high-status leadership can influence social norms. Just as support from doctors benefited the smoking industry by reinforcing a smoking norm, once we banned doctors from cigarette advertisements, the health community spearheaded the change and helped create an antismoking norm.

Finally, norms must be consistent with values. It is not clear if norms arise from values, or if combinations of norms produce values. Most likely it's both. At the bottom of the catch-and-release norm was a shift of basic ideas about how aquatic ecosystems ought to be managed, a value change necessary for the norm to emerge. The concept of recycling had a recent history, so it was easy to reinvent during the environmental crisis when people searched for visible ways to represent newfound pro-environmental attitudes.

The antismoking norm is gradually pushing out even the physically addictive drug nicotine.

Awareness of Consequences and Norm Emergence

The antismoking norm grew from evidence that there were direct negative consequences for smokers—they are more likely to die—and for others, as society pays more for sick smokers. Of course, when freedom is a dominant value, one can deactivate the norm by saying, "It is none of your business." For the antismoking norm to produce structural fixes like smoking bans, it was necessary for science to show that smoke hurt nonsmokers, too. Data then showed that second-hand smoke hurt bartenders and waitresses, and these workers basically "had no choice" but to face these negative consequences.[52] This moved smoking to the status of a moral norm because other people were being hurt. You might wonder if the antismoking norm is really an environmental norm. Notice how all this consequence rhetoric neglects the broader environment. If anyone has claimed we can reduce global warming by reducing cigarette smoking, I have not seen it. Nor has anyone claimed we can save endangered species if we all quit smoking. Interpersonal, rather than environmental, consequences are the driving force of the spread and strengthening of the antismoking norm.

I once argued that consequences for the environment drove environmental action.[53] Dunlap and Van Liere disagreed, arguing it was really the ramifications for humans, not environmental consequences, that were moving actions that affected the environment into the realm of moral norms.[54] Their point was that "sanctions against such behaviors stem more from the widespread acceptance of the Golden Rule . . . than from acceptance of an environmental or land ethic stressing the inalienable right of nature." More recently, Dunlap wondered privately how much distinction to make between whether consequences are faced by humans directly or by the environment affecting humans.[55] Stern and Dietz conclude, "The distinction between altruism towards humans and altruism towards other species and the biosphere has not been demonstrated empirically in samples of the U.S. general public."[56] The consequences empirically seem to blend together.

The catch-and-release norm grew from an increasing number of fishermen and an interest in providing recreational benefits. The Heberlein patriarchs kept and ate fish because they wanted to "get 'em" before anyone else did. As angler numbers increased on Western trophy trout waters, it became clear that taking fish home and eating them "hurt other fishermen just like you" and you personally, for there would be fewer fish when you returned. The solution to this commons problem—natural incentives encouraging individuals to take more than their fair share, which destroys the collective resource—was to institute formal sanctions (i.e., a regulation) as a signal that one should throw back fish. This generalized to other types of fishing and was supported by formal and informal sanctions. Anglers seemed to support catch-and-release, but not because it made streams healthy, produced cleaner water, or caused other environmental consequences. Rather, it was simply self-interest: more fish to catch. Here were both kinds of human consequences—to yourself and other anglers—and catch-and-release solved a classic "commons problem."

What's most interesting about catch-and-release is that when society focuses on environmental consequences, we get a norm for the opposite behavior. Catch-and-release is *illegal* in Switzerland and strongly opposed in Germany.[57] In those societies, the broader public and anglers themselves look at consequences not to *fish populations*, but to individual fish that get caught. These fish are thought to suffer from the catching process; hence, we inflict negative consequences on a sentient being through catching and releasing it.[58] Human benefits from the recreation are not seen as justifying fish torture. Rather than ending sport fishing, the norm developed that you *must* keep and eat fish you catch, and stop at the limit. Fish are food. One should not continually hurt sentient beings for fun. You should not catch them "for no good reason." Catching them, hauling them up by their lip, and holding them in the air (tantamount to smothering them) creates pain and is not an appropriate way to treat another sentient being. This shows how important it is for norms to correspond to a society's value base, as well as the role of consequences in establishing norms. Moving from human to environmental consequences can shift the whole norm.

Conclusion

Bringing in norms gives real traction to behavior. Attitudes are internal states, but norms add the social: what other people do and where they do it. The norm concept also incorporates sanctions from others and yourself that are not part of the attitude concept. Norms are so powerful they can even get people to do the opposite of their behavioral intentions, as they did in LaPiere's study.

If we want to "improve" environmental behavior, assuming most people hold pro-environmental norms, we must focus on factors that deactivate these norms to keep them from influencing action. How do we change a setting or situation so people are less likely to deny responsibility, and how do we get people to accept the negative consequences of their actions? Sometimes it's as easy as keeping hallways and walkways clean. Often, of course, it's more difficult. My point is that by focusing on behavior—on what people do and on how they do it—along with their perceptions of other people's norms, we have a better chance of promoting pro-environmental behaviors.

Norms that influence environmental behaviors grow and change. That's the good news. The bad news, for those of us who want action now, is that it might take decades or longer for norms to emerge and strengthen. Norms focus on behavior, and they're much more specific than values. For a norm to emerge, it must apply to clear, specific, observable, public, or semipublic behavior. In addition, individuals must feel responsible for their acts and consequences of their acts. Human consequences, unfortunately, still seem to outweigh environmental consequences. In several cases, support from high-status groups helped norms emerge.

Leopold's trout-fishing trip retold in *A Sand County Almanac* provided good markers about norm change. Even more important, Leopold went on to propose, as a solution for environmental problems, something that looks a lot like a norm but isn't. He called it a "land ethic," and that's the subject of inquiry in the next chapter.

7

Aldo Leopold and the Flying Horse

SO FAR, WE have dissected Aldo Leopold's attitude toward pine trees, and we have examined his beliefs and emotions to show the structure of an attitude. From there we explored how and why Leopold changed his attitude toward wolves. Like all of us, we discovered, Leopold sometimes acted inconsistently with that attitude. The previous chapter showed how society moves on and norms change, and today even Leopold would sometimes be out of step with the crowd. By studying Leopold, the person, we've learned more about him and something about social psychology.

Leopold was trying to solve environmental problems of his day while working with the three fixes, even though he did not use those terms. He was dissatisfied with the cognitive fix, observing, "Despite more than a century of propaganda, conservation proceeds at a snail's pace."[1] He realized this change was mostly in attitudes. "Conservation," he lamented, "consists largely of letterhead pieties and convention oratory."[2] Regarding behavior, he found the familiar gap: "On the back forty we still slip two steps backward for each forward stride."[3] Nor was Leopold satisfied with a structural fix that simply changed behavior by changing the context. He noted free labor from the Civilian Conservation Corps, along with cash during the Depression, got Wisconsin farmers to adopt remedial practices to prevent soil erosion. But "the practices were widely forgotten when the five-year contract was up,"[4] just as my department returned to plastic-foam cups when the grad student left. Successful structural fixes require permanent structural change.

Leopold sought something more powerful than the cognitive fix and more sustainable than the structural fix to influence behavior. He called his fix "The Land Ethic."

"The land ethic," Leopold argues, "simply enlarges the boundaries of the community to include soils, waters, plants, and animals, or collectively: the land. . . . In short, a land ethic changes the role of *Homo sapiens* from conqueror of the land-community to plain member and citizen of it."[5] Many today, like Leopold, hold great hope for the land ethic as the solution to environmental problems. The land ethic has been analyzed by historians,[6] philosophers,[7] and wildlife ecologists,[8] but not yet by social psychologists. This social psychology perspective, using concepts I've been trying to explain in this book, more realistically assesses the land ethic's usefulness and its future possibilities. Let's take a look.

Land Ethic as a Value

On its face, the land ethic fits the definition of a value, as described in chapter 2. It is broad and general, and should be the base of many unspecified behaviors. Rather than solely using self-interest or personal economic well-being as a guide, Leopold wanted our actions toward the land or broader environment to be evaluated on collective or community interest. Leopold proposed an extension of values, from individual to collective concerns and then—here is the big leap—to include nature, our "relation to the land and to the animals and plants which grow on it," in that collectivity.[9]

Some humans, he noted, were property in Odysseus' time, and you could do what you wanted with them without moral obligation. Just as we broadened the idea of community to include all humans, we need to add nature to our community. Reflecting on the values underlying Leopold's attitude toward pine trees (chapter 2), it's clear he wanted us to strengthen our environmental values until they become primary drivers of attitudes, even behaviors. Like a value, a land ethic is not observable. It is inferred from observed behaviors, and written and oral statements. Like the values driving Leopold's attitude toward trees, the land ethic affects many evaluative beliefs. Values, of course, often conflict. The idea of a land ethic runs hard against the values of freedom and individuality, the core of American society.

We still struggle thinking of all members of society as members of a community rather than as competition in some kind of survival-of-the-fittest contest. So, this first step to a land ethic is a big change. Leopold wants us to adopt actions where individuals contribute to the community good, even though it costs them time and money. Leopold hoped this could happen, observing the "existence of obligations over and above self-interest is taken for granted in such rural community enterprises as the betterment of roads, schools, churches and baseball teams."[10] He wondered why this sense of responsibility could not broaden to include nature.

Values are powerful. This attracted Leopold. We can see this power, not so much when looking at individuals (those living in a single society mostly share the same values), but when looking across different societies. Swedes, who value collective action, have a special word, *"lagom,"* which means "appropriate or in the middle." It's used as a basic standard to judge action in almost all settings. The comparable expression in American society would be "freedom, independence, and self-reliance" all rolled into one. I discovered, while living in Sweden, that if a proposal is not *"lagom,"* it is not proposed. I further discovered in my struggles to learn Swedish that they have no word for "management." When discussing nature, they use words like stewardship and care-taking. If they want to say "management," that powerful control word, they turn to English, just as we turn to French for "coup d'état." This reflects a different value orientation toward nature.[11]

Occasionally when two societies occupy the same landscape, you can see values and their influence in starker relief. Few American Indians live in Wisconsin, but their values lie closer to Leopold's land ethic than to those of the dominant society. The Exxon mine, discussed in earlier chapters, caused much strife and conflict, but it no longer represents a threat because the Mole Lake Sokaogon Chippewa and the Potawatomi bought the land and its mineral rights.[12] Two days later, the request for the mining permit was withdrawn. Even though they are among the poorest citizens of Wisconsin's North Woods, there's no possibility the Indians will develop a mine. They have different values. Wisconsin's state government, with all the dominant society's wealth, earlier refused to purchase and preserve the site.

A Swedish commission once visited the United States to learn about wolves. After days of being bombarded with numbers, science, legal documents, and lawsuits from the dominant society, they met with Chippewa representatives. The Chippewa said, "The wolves are our brothers," and little more. Wolves are part of the Chippewa's creation story, but where Adam got Eve as his partner, the Chippewa got wolves. The Swedes pressed, asking, "How many wolves are enough?" This is the question preoccupying bureaucrats, ranchers, and conservationists elsewhere in America. The Chippewa looked puzzled. They finally answered, "How many brothers are enough?"[13]

The Land Ethic as a Norm

At the same time Leopold calls for a massive value change to the land ethic, he asks that this value function like a norm. That's a problem. Norms, as we know, differ greatly from values. Norms are observable as behavioral regularities, while values—like attitudes—are invisible. Norms direct behaviors. Norms involve feelings of personal obligations, and internal and external sanctions. Although the land ethic starts as a value, it turns into a norm when Leopold focuses on behavior and, more important, on sanctions.

An ethic, he claims, is a standard that differentiates "social from antisocial conduct"[14] and "social approbation for right actions: social disapproval for wrong actions."[15] If you violate a social norm, you should expect punishment. The problem, according to Leopold, is that sanctions don't exist for behaviors affecting the environment. The farmer who abuses his land, Leopold notes, is "still (if otherwise decent) a respected member of society."[16] No fines, shunning, strong words, or jail sentences result if you abuse nature. In short, there are no community sanctions.

Leopold complains that our orientation toward land involves "no right or wrong, no obligation."[17] With a personal norm comes obligations, and internal sanctions of pride and guilt, typical parts of what's commonly called conscience. When Leopold argues for "the extension of the social conscience from people to land,"[18] he's calling for a personal norm or obligation associated with certain behaviors. These behaviors can then be evaluated as "right" or "wrong." He also distinguishes between personal and social norms, suggesting that internal standards drive our behaviors, and they might differ from the larger society's norms.

Leopold is in step with Schwartz's activation theory, because he includes awareness of negative consequences and ascription of responsibility. He also discusses "land health." Unhealthy is clearly bad. If we do "sick making" things to land, we harm it. That's a clear environmental consequence. Just as we don't want to make a human sick, we should not, according to Leopold's land ethic, want to make nature sick. He then notes that the land ethic "reflects a conviction of *individual responsibility* [emphasis added] for the health of the land"[19] and argues that the ethical obligation "on the part of the private landowner is the only visible remedy."[20] It is the individual, not the government or markets, who should be ultimately responsible for pro-environmental behavior.

However, this is where the land ethic as a norm has serious problems: Have you ever tried defining a land-ethic behavior for someone? Why is one behavior ethical and another behavior not? Who or what is hurt—and who isn't—when the land ethic is violated? It takes lots of words, and when you finish, it still won't be clear, at least not to your grandchildren, your neighbors, or politicians, who well understand the norms of recycling, antismoking, anti-littering, and catch-and-release fishing. Norms direct specific behavior.

Leopold and the (Great) Grandson Test

This problem of identifying appropriate behaviors to sanction became clear when I met Leopold's great-grandson years ago at the shack. I could scarcely believe my ears when he apologized for the stately white pines Leopold and his children (including the great-grandson's grandmother) planted in the 1930s. In the hot sun of those Dust-Bowl years, seedlings withered and died no matter how much water the Leopolds brought them. However, with the persistence of people who knew "The Right," they replanted year after year until today we're blessed with these beauties. During those drought years, pines were about the only thing you could grow to hold sandy soil. By such standards, this behavior and persistence personified the land ethic:

1. It embodied hard work with little hope of economic gain.
2. It was performed by individuals feeling personal responsibility, knowing they were restoring the land's health.
3. It produced pride at the day's end, knowing the family would eventually have "a woodlot of distinction."[21]

Unfortunately, when applying 21st-century standards, a solid stand of white pines *is* ecologically unsound. It provides little understory for other plants and animals, and hence does not support biodiversity. So if the land ethic as a norm is an uncertain guide for the Leopold property, how can it guide actions for the rest of us? Simple behaviors directed by recycling, anti-smoking, anti-littering, and catch-and-release norms are more obvious. I also expect they're less likely to change as scientific knowledge changes. That's why they can more clearly influence behavior and why they're easier to sanction. The land ethic remains an unsettled, and perhaps unsettling, value with vague normative specifications that led to dismay for at least one Leopold progeny.

The Land Ethic as a Standard

Two things are necessary for sanctions: observability and a standard to judge right and wrong. Norms require clear behavioral standards, so there's some way to judge right from wrong. So we ask, "Okay, Professor. *What* is right and *what* is wrong?" Near the end of his essay, almost hidden, Leopold finally tells us: "A thing is right when it tends to preserve the integrity, stability, and beauty of the biotic community. It is wrong when it tends otherwise."[22]

Things are right and wrong when they "tend" to do something? Huh? This is exactly the kind of answer professors like to give, and why society sometimes keeps us locked away in ivory towers. How do we judge tendencies? This lacks the precision we prefer in natural sciences. Removing the messy tendency stuff gets us no further. Integrity is not a clear, measurable, scientific standard either. And beauty always gets dismissed as "in the eye of the beholder." Stability can be estimated, but, obviously, takes time to judge. This, too, is complex, because we expect natural systems to be dynamic and change over time, but how much change is enough? Leopold's standard for behavior—to reward good and punish evil—is not sufficiently precise to judge good and evil.

With the land ethic, Leopold welded the breadth and vagueness of a value to the specificity and sanctions of a norm. That is its central problem. A value is powerful, like a horse. By asking the value to act as a norm, Leopold requires it to do something it cannot. Sure, artists and philosophers can weld wings to a horse, but the question remains: Will Pegasus fly?

Realizing a Land Ethic Today

Compared to the environmental norms that grew and flourished since the first Earth Day celebration, what progress have we made toward realizing the land ethic? Did our behaviors and sense of obligation for the environment change as we built bigger houses, paved more roads, and gobbled more energy with air-conditioners in every house? Or do we still, as Leopold asserted, "slip two steps back for each forward stride"?[23]

Leopold certainly did not think his era established a land ethic. In *A Sand County Almanac* he writes, "There is as yet, no ethic dealing with man's relation to land and to the animals and plants which grow upon it."[24] A few pages later he asserts, "We have no land ethic yet."[25] Yet the *idea* of a land ethic has been around a long time; Leopold writes, "Individual thinkers since the days of Ezekiel and Isaiah have asserted that the despoliation of land is not only inexpedient but wrong."[26] However, this ethic has not been adopted as a major value premise of society.

In his time, Leopold saw signs that we were moving toward a land ethic. Referring to the movement he lived through during his professional life, he wrote: "I regard the present conservation movement as the embryo . . . [of an extension of ethics to the land.]"[27] He also noted progress in bird preservation: "We have at least drawn nearer the point of admitting that birds should continue as a matter of biotic right, regardless of the presence or absence of economic advantage to us."[28] Furthermore: "We hear the more honest arguments that predators are members of the community, and no special interest has the right to exterminate them for the sake of a benefit, real or fancied, to itself."[29] These are small but important steps.

Progress, according to Leopold, was still slow: "Conservation still proceeds at a snail's pace."[30] He is clear on this: "I have no illusions about the speed or accuracy with which an ecological conscience can become functional. It has required nineteen centuries to define decent man-to-man conduct and the process is only half done; it may take as long to evolve a code of decency for man-to-land conduct."[31] For Leopold, realizing a land ethic might take not just centuries, but millennia.

Will the land ethic evolve at a steady pace or ascend in uneven, unpredictable steps? Clearly, a dramatic change in attitudes and a documented change in concern about pollution occurred between 1965 and 1970 (chapter 3). Keying on moral outrage over civil rights and the Vietnam War that sent marchers to the streets during that era, a middle-of-the-road politician from a small town in northern Wisconsin proposed holding teach-ins for the environment. From the vantage of almost a half-century, it's hard to believe the sweep of that action on the first Earth Day in 1970. Some 10,000 protesters crowded Washington Mall, and marchers closed New York's Fifth Avenue for two hours as they passed. Across the country, people acted. As much as 10% of the nation's population was estimated to have taken part.[32]

I passed up the marching and stayed in my office in the UW's social science building, working on a paper with the overly optimistic title, "The Land Ethic Realized."[33] I argued we had made important progress in moving our actions toward land into the moral specter of right and wrong. Science had shown that humans were having clear impacts on the environment, that DDT was hurting wildlife, and there were strong implications humans would be hurt as well. Thus, what we did to the environment hurt people *and* the environment. Indeed, this dual impact of *both* environmental and human consequences is dominant in Rachel Carson's *Silent Spring*,[34] which is often heralded as the single book that inspired Earth Day and the environmental movement. Further, highlighting these human consequences was vital to that first Earth Day. In New York, Mayor John Lindsay said this as a simple question: "Do we want to live or die?"[35]

This shift, I argued, made environmental actions the subject of social evaluations. According to Schwartz's theory, we could deactivate norms by denying responsibility. Technology gave us the ability to reduce pollution. This made humans responsible for negative consequences because we could no longer deny we had a choice in the matter. Thus, the then villains of environmental degradation, science, and technology sowed the seeds for an emerging ethic by identifying negative consequences and making us responsible for them. To me, this seemed a start.

The Missing Road Map

Although fundamental conditions for realizing the land ethic are emerging, the process has lacked direction and a map. Leopold's land ethic is attractive because, basically, it's tautological. The ethic, complete with internal sanctions, is much the same as behavior. He judges the lack of an ethic by our collective actions toward various parts of nature. He tells us our behaviors affect "the soil, which we are sending helter-skelter downriver . . . the waters, . . . to turn turbines, float barges, and carry off sewage . . . the plants, of which we exterminate whole communities without batting an eye . . . [and] the animals, of which we have already extirpated many of the largest and most beautiful species."[36] Note these are all observable behaviors. How do we know people lack a land ethic? Because they don't engage in pro-environmental behaviors. Leopold wants them to perform pro-environmental behaviors even when they're hard or expensive. The land ethic should be strong enough to defeat the many factors that influence action. If people don't engage in pro-environmental behaviors, they don't have the ethic. To solve environmental problems, we need people to hold a land ethic because those holding the land ethic engage in pro-environmental behaviors. So the circle turns. The land ethic is the solution because behavior is the problem. Like many natural scientists and the public, Leopold thought attitudes and behavior were virtually the same thing, but they are not, which is the point of much of this book. Racing around this circle doesn't get us far.

More important, Leopold gives little hint about how to create a land ethic, the idea proposed in the final chapter of a book he never saw published. This missing road map in *A Sand County Almanac* is in stark contrast to his earlier book, *Game Management,* that began with a simple, elegant sentence: "Game management is the art of making land produce sustained annual crops of wild game for recreational use." Leopold then spent 18 chapters reviewing the science and practices necessary to realize that objective. However, *A Sand County Almanac* sorely misses those how-to chapters. Leopold leaves us on our own, and there we struggle.

Getting Pegasus off the Ground: A Small Lesson in Horse Flying

How can Leopold's ethic influence behavior if those on land who are busy farming, hunting, and building subdivisions have never heard of him or the land ethic? Environmentalists and natural-resource professionals trumpet Leopold's words. They are required reading in classrooms and necessary citations in articles. Every Earth Day speech needs at least one Leopold quote. The problem is that he is not well known by the public. Big ideas are often associated with specific people, but Leopold is all but invisible to the public we wish to educate.

In a personal effort to make progress on this front, I organized a couple dozen environmentalists and community leaders in the village of Lodi, Wisconsin, for a public reading of *A Sand County Almanac*. On one early spring Saturday in March, we read the book aloud, beginning to end. I figured this zaniness would attract the press (it did), that it would be fun (it was), and that I would learn something (I did: The recitation revealed humor I had missed when reading alone). But how many people besides the readers showed up? You could count them on your fingers and toes and you wouldn't have to remove your shoes.

The next year I invited politicians, some of whom—in Wisconsin, at least—like praising Leopold. A few more people came. Then the local newspaper editor suggested, "Get the school kids reading, and their parents and grandparents will come." The next year we did, and just as he predicted, they did come. We topped out at about 60 listeners if we counted the whole day.

Politicians who read Leopold liked the idea, and the next year the legislature passed and the governor signed a bill declaring March's first weekend as Aldo Leopold weekend in Wisconsin. Lodi spent thousands of dollars in advertising, including a giant banner hung over Main Street (a major state highway with thousands of cars passing daily). Articles in the local and Madison newspapers also touted the reading. It was further featured on Wisconsin Public Radio. However, during the event's first 10 years, we never drew more than about 60 people, including 30 readers, during a weekend.

So, where does Leopold rank with the public? One spring, The Friends of Scenic Lodi Valley, the group that continued organizing the Leopold reading, sponsored a naturalist to give an evening presentation on frogs. Seventy adults and 95 kids (more than 160 people—we know the attendance because the speaker received two dollars a head) showed up on a Thursday evening for the talk. Afterward, 6 carloads of people went to Goose Pond, and 12 carloads went to my pond to listen to spring peepers. On a Thursday evening two months before, when Leopold's biographer visited Lodi to give a talk as part of the Leopold weekend, 9 listeners attended.

Leopold says we must think like a mountain. But frogs are cool. People like nature and individual animals. Reading about land ethics? Well, I'm afraid that pleasure is reserved for a very select group. To change behavior, I fear, we must think less like mountains and more about frogs.[37]

Conclusion

Unfortunately, Leopold's proposed land ethic is not a quick fix for environmental problems. Then again, he thought it might take 19 centuries to create a land ethic, so perhaps we shouldn't expect so much in 60 years. The problem with his conception of a land ethic is that it's half value and half norm. It also requires two major shifts in American values:

1. A move from individual values to more collectivist values.
2. The inclusion of nature, plants, and animals, and the entire environment into that collectivity.

In a practical sense, the land ethic fails to specify clear norms because it's such a vague standard. People cannot be expected to develop personal norms based on the land ethic because the implied behaviors are complicated and subject to change. If we want to rely on an emerging land ethic to solve today's environmental problems, we'll wait a long time for a Pegasus to swoop down and save us. We must get on with the business of solving environmental problems by designing with attitudes rather than hoping a land ethic will rapidly take root.

After all, the water's roaring around the next bend, and we must deal with immediate challenges. So we leave Leopold and his pines at the shack, and head downriver armed with a realistic assessment of the land ethic and our scientific knowledge of how attitudes and norms work.

8

Avoiding the Cognitive Fix Keeper Hole

WE'VE BEEN WORKING on fundamentals in the previous seven chapters. What are attitudes? How do they influence behavior? Which principles are behind attitudes? What are norms and how do they work? This is like practicing kayak rolls in a pool or paddle strokes on a lake—a good place to start. But, finally, it's time to go to the river and get some lessons from experts who successfully navigated real rapids. We'll stay ashore and watch them put these principles into practice, and see how to design with attitudes rather than try changing them. These strategies halted power-plant construction in the Pacific Northwest, saved enough energy to power four university campuses, cut traffic congestion by 25% in Stockholm, Sweden, and got me to turn out the lights—every time. All were accomplished without changing attitudes.

Miracle at Hood River

About the time the cognitive fix ran aground in my time-of-use electricity experiment (our attempts to change attitudes and behavior through information barely nudged either), a team of experts implemented structural and technical fixes by navigating with attitudes in Hood River, Oregon. An environmental psychology textbook describes the Hood River Conservation Project as an "almost unqualified success" for "changing behavior that is harmful to the environment."[1] From an academic point of view, it was better than a miracle. It was a veritable textbook case, and I had to see it for myself.

Hood River today is nothing like it was in 1985, when billboards met visitors by shouting, "Welcome to the Nation's Conservation Capitol" [sic]. It's now the "Unofficial Sail Board Capital of the World." Coffee shops with high prices and no refills line the old main street. Brewpubs dot the downtown. The Hood Valley's many wineries give it a Napa Valley feel. The 700 jobs at a factory making U.S. military drones boost a flourishing tourist economy. I have done fieldwork in declining rural communities in the Great Plains, northern Wisconsin, and Sweden's forests, so I welcomed having a choice of upscale restaurants, fine local wines, and high speed Internet. This was no declining rural community.

The Hood River Conservation Project grew from a structural change: a 1980 law pushed through by environmentalists required that power in the Pacific Northwest be provided at the lowest possible cost and that *"conservation was to be assessed on equal terms with generation as a source of new power supply"*[2] (emphasis added). Power plants cost money, pollute air, warm water, devour nonrenewable resources, and inflict unavoidable environmental impacts. Not building them is a good thing, as I argued in my futile efforts to stop my hometown's power plant. So, how can we live just as well without building them? What if we invested the same amount of money in insulating and retrofitting existing houses as we did in expanding our energy-generating capacity? Could we save energy more cheaply than producing it? Because of the 1980 law, the Bonneville Power Administration went all out to "construct a 'conservation power plant' in a single community as quickly as possible."[3]

Retrofitting is a technical fix. You install insulation and replace windows, changing things that should reduce energy consumption, and then measure their effectiveness. People don't have to change their behavior. They just keep living in their homes while the houses save energy and electric bills fall. But recalling those who moved into flood plains when dams kept rivers at bay, would these people change their behaviors in unexpected ways after this technical fix? When electric bills go down with new insulation, will people buy new appliances, dial up the thermostat, or quit heating with wood? This is why technological fixes, no matter how good they look on paper, must be tested.

Hood River residents with electric heating were asked to engage in two pro-environmental behaviors. First, get their houses audited to see if they could save energy by retrofitting. Second, sign a contract for retrofitting. In the end, 91% of eligible households engaged in the first behavior, and 85% agreed to retrofitting. The 6% difference? The audit found these houses were sufficiently insulated, so a retrofit would be ineffective.

The first and most important step in designing with attitudes is to involve experts from day one. We need experts to "read the water." The second step is collecting data rather than guessing about attitudes. The third step is assessing and understanding the community, realizing that attitudes are individual constructs, but people living in groups and communities that interact with others form important contexts that influence behavior.

The "river guides" for this endeavor included four PhDs in sociology who worked for Pacific Power and Light or Bonneville Power.[4] Ken Keating was

Bonneville's conservation evaluator[5] and H. Gil Peach directed the project's evaluation and research for Pacific Power and Light. Ruth Love, also with Bonneville, advised on the project. Cynthia Brown Flynn was a consultant hired to do community assessments.

To get a reading on the water, the survey research center at Oregon State University conducted attitude surveys in Hood River.[6] Flynn built on these with 60 personal interviews in the Hood River area. This analysis identified 8 distinct community groups: "orchardists," "settled-out Mexican-Americans," "migrant Mexicans," "Japanese Americans," "counterculture," "business/professional," "blue-collar workers," and "residents of Mosier."[7] The project's ultimate success proved to come from understanding these groups, how they participated in the community, what motivated them, and what barriers to action existed. Even more important were additional interviews during the program's life that provided almost real-time assessments of attitude changes as participants gained experience with the program. This information helped project managers make midcourse corrections.

Hood River was a good pick for an energy-demonstration project because it was a light bulb that really wanted to change. The community was relatively poor. Its population dropped during the 1970s. The orchard economy was declining. Its canning company had closed, eliminating seventy full-time and 250 part-time jobs. Electricity prices had shot up 40%, and people had cut back on electric heating, substituting electricity with wood. Even before the project, electricity use was low. Residents were ripe for a fix that would save energy and reduce electric bills. No attitude change was necessary. People didn't need to be convinced that staying warm in winter or paying less for electricity were good things. It's easy to understand how insulation and storm windows keep houses warm. They simply had to learn about the program and how to get involved. The motivation that the cognitive fix expects from information was already in place.

People will likely engage in easy pro-environmental behaviors. In my time-of-use pricing experiments, we tried to get people to change many behaviors: put timers on appliances, wash clothes during off-peak hours, and reduce air-conditioning on hot afternoons. In contrast, Hood River residents only needed to call for an audit and sign a contract. Like voting, these behaviors were one-time decisions, not daily behavioral changes. To make it even easier, the project set up an office in a prime downtown location. To participate, you walked in or made a local phone call. Or, in later stages, said "yes" when someone knocked at your door.

We know people more likely act consistently with their environmental attitudes if they encounter few barriers or costs to the action (discussed in chapter 4). Retrofitting's biggest barrier is cost. Only the most committed environmentalists front money for weatherization just to "see if it would pay for itself in the future." Certainly, renters (34% of participants) and poor people would not get aboard. To lower this barrier, participants paid nothing for an audit and, if necessary, complete weatherization. "We were poor and it was free," a woman told me when I asked why she participated. "Free is good," explained an environmentalist participant who helped found the recycling program in the 1980s.

Free is also suspect. When visiting Hood River I asked, "Suppose I knocked on your door and said, 'I represent Heberlein Insulators from Wisconsin and I will insulate your house for free.'" Siding, gutters, insulation, and driveway-sealing have long been household scams. There must be more to this success than free. Free *is* good . . . but it doesn't explain 90% participation. We must account for "Why Free?" and "Why Me?" In the first newspaper article about the project, the Hood River District utility manager announced, "It is kind of exciting. . . . Hood River County could be in the limelight of the nation." The Hood River Conservation Project was built on community identity. The local power company operated it, employed local contractors, opened a local office to supervise the work, and used outside money to make houses warmer and reduce electricity bills. The program was built on community trust, not sidewalk salespeople.

Eighteen months later, a full-page advertisement announcing the project's official beginning differed greatly from most newspaper ads. Rather than shouting, "FREE, FREE weatherization," it featured a large picture of community leaders, each endorsing the project. In large type inside a bold box, Ted Perry of the Hood River Electric Cooperative, said, "Future generations, our children, will be guided by what we accomplish with this project." This was awareness of consequences writ large: Don't sign up because you save money; sign up to help people of the future. The mayor, in a similar box, spoke to community identity, "We can put ourselves on the map in a way no other city in the Northwest or the nation has done." In other words, don't do this for yourself; do it for the community. The local manager of Pacific Power and Light increased individual responsibility, saying, "The Hood River Project's success rests with citizen support and involvement." Billboards at the edge of town further enhanced community identity as a conservation capital.

Part of the project's success was the research process. The summer before the project began recruiting participants, 10% of households were randomly selected for data collection and fitted with special meters. Representatives explained the project to these homeowners, telling them their homes would be the first to be retrofitted with free insulation, new windows, and other features to make them energy efficient.

Think about this. You live in a small, economically depressed rural community, and suddenly you're picked "by the computer" to get something free. Not only that, but you'll get that something from a reliable source. You just won the lottery! What do you do? Brag to the neighbors and trumpet your good luck at church suppers, and, of course, they'll want to get involved, too. So even before the formal announcement in the *Hood River News* three months later, hundreds of customers had signed up. Two months later, more than 1,000 households (nearly one-third of eligible participants) were aboard, mainly because they first heard about it from friends and neighbors. According to Flynn's ongoing interviews, "Media sources were only secondary sources of information. . . . These sources were frequently ignored until *after* the respondent had heard about the Project by word-of mouth."[8] The struggle was to keep up with requests. Therefore, much of the planned marketing was unnecessary.[9]

Flynn's interviews furthered the word-of-mouth marketing program. People from all eight community groups mentioned earlier were asked five questions:

How did you first hear about the project?
What did you understand the project to be?
What is your experience with the project?
What do you think about it?
Do you have any questions about the project?

The last question provided a perfect opportunity to explain the project and "educate the public." Respondents were then asked if others should be interviewed. This is called "snowball sampling" and, although it does not lead to a representative sample, it does reach opinion leaders and other influential people in the community. So, we can expect the Flynn team got to "educate" face-to-face key individuals from each distinct community group through these open-ended interviews. In total, 359 community residents (more than 10% of eligible households) were interviewed. Further, about one-fourth of the households (including 15% in various metering studies) had personal contact with researchers.

However, even with two years of planning, billboards, implementation, local presence, positive attitudes ("free is good"), front-page newspaper coverage, and personal contacts with 25% of the potential participants, only about 60% had signed up. That's consistent with what we learned in the attitude-behavior chapter. Attitudes predispose us to act, but behavior is influenced more by external than internal factors. Further, many people don't act even when their attitudes are positive. So how did the research and utility staff sign up the last thousand households? They called or visited *every* nonparticipating household and personally requested that each sign up.[10] When asked why they hadn't signed up, many said they were waiting to be called or visited. Free retrofitting was good, but it was not a major deal in their lives.

Most pro-environmental marketing campaigns would have broken their arms patting themselves on the back for 60% participation rates, but the Hood River team wanted to determine maximum possible participation to see if a "conservation power plant" was really possible. It showed that in a research context, 90% participation by eligible households was possible, so utilities could not argue the public would refuse even free retrofitting.[11]

The continuous surveys showed how attitudes changed during the project. As you could imagine, attitudes were overwhelmingly positive with "free is good" at the beginning. However, just as real wolves give people direct experience, once the weatherization program gave residents direct experience, they were not so happy. Contractors could not keep up with the work, and people were disappointed with delays and quality. Others (about 10%) found they had to pay to repair dry rot, remove old insulation, and exterminate vermin discovered during the retrofit. "Free" was not completely "free." With early knowledge from the surveys, however, the team countered the emerging counterattitudes before they became well developed or widely shared. Indeed, one team member told me that information from the attitude surveys helped them "break their promise" to the community and justify bringing in outside contractors to solve delays and quality concerns.[12]

Sensitivity to attitudes and community issues weaves throughout this project. My favorite example involves radon monitoring. Radon is a naturally occurring radioactive gas that can build up in attics and basements. It's possible that insulating houses can increase radon levels. What was needed, of course, were baseline data on radon before insulating a house to determine if the retrofitting made things worse. Radon detectors, unfortunately, had not been installed with the end-use meters on test houses. The challenge became this: How do you return to install a radon meter, an innocuous-looking cardboard package that's hung on a door? Given what we know about risk perceptions, the team wanted these installations to seem as normal as possible. The idea or image of scientists in white coats measuring radioactivity in houses could scare the public and scuttle the project overnight. However, because of its many Hood River interviews, the team knew the high school band was raising money for new uniforms. The project offered to buy band uniforms if the kids distributed and retrieved the radon meters. Although we can't be sure how well band members explained the meters' purpose, we know they got them into two-thirds of participating households.[13] The meters and their role were, of course, explained in writing to participants, but the delivery system was totally nonthreatening. This sensitivity to attitudes and community issues influenced the decision to hire a consulting sociologist rather than a traditional marketing firm. According to Ruth Love:

> The contract administrator organized an interview session with the contract finalists. One was a marketing expert and the other was Cynthia [Flynn Brown, the consulting sociologist]. The marketing guy said all the right things about contacting movers and shakers, and using a network approach and some sampling. But he did not seem to capture the idea of contacting the full social spectrum. I asked him how he planned to approach the folks who live "on the wrong side of the tracks," so to speak. He paused and said very carefully that in marketing studies it doesn't pay to interview these people![14]

The surveys showed pro-environmental behaviors in the Hood River Project were *not* driven by environmental attitudes. According to Flynn, of the 97 interviews conducted at the project's start, only 3 people mentioned that the project was preferable to nuclear plants or more hydro plants. In interviews with 149 respondents near the project's end, only 6 mentioned conservation as a positive attribute. When people signed up, they were asked to take a marketing survey. When asked to give their reasons for participating in the project, 57% cited rising electricity prices and the need to control them, whereas only 15% cited beliefs in energy conservation and environmental protection.[15]

When considering the effects of the Hood River Project, I would like to report that a community norm developed, with praise from neighbors for participants and external negative sanctions for nonparticipants. I would also like to have discovered community awards or recognition for participants, but I found no editorial support for the project in the newspaper, neither in a list of names of participants nor awards for them. Any thought that the project changed the community's identity had certainly vanished when I arrived 25 years later. When I told people I was in Hood River to visit "The Nation's Conservation Capital," they looked at me as if I were lost. Was I, by chance, confusing conservation with sail-boarding? When I mentioned a "weatherization project back in the 1980s," a few older homeowners dimly remembered.

By now you're wondering if the program worked. From our point of view, it worked like a charm, with 91% participation. Did it save energy? Yes. Energy consumption fell 15%. That's considerably less than the projected 43% savings.

It would have fallen more if some people hadn't quit heating with wood and others hadn't dialed up their thermostats.

What about the costs of achieving 90% participation? For those wanting to try the Hood River Conservation Project at home, don't overlook the money spent. In today's dollars, the project cost $40 million, about half of which funded the research. To enroll 3,000 households, the marketing budget today would exceed $250,000. Much of the marketing costs ended up as part of the research and local administration budgets. It's possible to get high participation rates with simple behaviors in communities eager to save energy, but even that costs lots of time and money.

For homeowners, the payback from investing in retrofits based on energy savings was *not* justified. It did not pay to retrofit because savings in the electric bill were too small. *However*—and this is the key factor for energy conservation—*it was cheaper for Bonneville to retrofit houses than to build new generating capacity*. A dollar spent retrofitting an existing home produced more kwh than a dollar spent building a power plant. The Hood River Conservation Project showed that a conservation power plant *was* cost-effective.

In the face of clear benefits, did Bonneville Power stop building power plants and start retrofitting all homes in the Pacific Northwest? The simple answer is yes. According to Ken Keating, the Bonneville Power Administration (BPA) and other utilities in the Pacific Northwest eventually weatherized more than 800,000 electrically heated homes, almost all of which were single-family houses. By the end of 2005, Pacific Northwest utilities had saved energy equivalent to three times the Bonneville Dam's annual output. Bonneville Power Administration did not build, or cause to be built, any power plants since constructing the Richland nuclear plant in 1984. No other nuclear plants have been built in the region, and one was closed.[16] Structural and technological fixes designed with attitudes changed electricity generation in the Pacific Northwest.

Avoiding the Cognitive Fix Keeper Hole

The best advice I can give anyone trying to negotiate big water is to avoid "keeper holes," places where water swirls and turns on itself, trapping your craft. You go round and around, sometimes upside down, and sometimes never come up. The cognitive fix is like a big keeper hole. It's easy to get sucked in and go nowhere. Even smart people need guides to help them avoid these vortexes.

I wasn't thinking about river-running on a cold November morning as ice formed along the shore of Madison's Lake Mendota. Along with a couple-dozen faculty, I trudged up the steps of the Memorial Union for Bill Cronon's biweekly environmental seminar. Cronon, an environmental historian, founded the seminar to help faculty from across campus learn from each other and promote interdisciplinary discussion of environmental issues. We met at dawn, the only time free from demands of teaching, research, and departmental responsibilities. The topic that day was how to make the UW-Madison campus "greener" while saving energy, and reducing our impact on the planet.

Predictably, the conversation headed straight for the cognitive fix.[17] Before I could wet my paddle, several colleagues asserted that, to save energy, we just had to "educate" our 40,000 students to turn off their computers. Perhaps we could educate ourselves to bicycle to work when it's minus 20 degrees. Even better, form a committee. In spite of the wisdom and experience of this august group, many of whom were natural scientists of international repute, they were no better informed than average citizens in running rivers or changing human behavior.

Although dressed in a suit rather than river gear, a tall stranger in the back of the room saved us. First, he introduced himself: Al Fish. Fish was a legendary campus administrator in charge of all buildings and infrastructure of our city-sized campus. I had never met him, but he had a reputation as a no-nonsense type. I was curious how he would respond to this "educate the public" business.

He did not disappoint. Rather than commenting on educating students, putting professors on bicycles, or (thankfully) forming faculty committees, Fish started discussing ventilation. Every campus building has big fans. Because ventilation fans sit on roofs where you can't see them, they don't jump to mind when discussing energy conservation. Heating, ventilation, and air-conditioning use about 72% of the campus's energy, whereas 4% is spent on computing, of which student-run computers are a small part. During Wisconsin winters, ventilation fans pull out millions of cubic feet of warm air and replace it with ice-cold air. Fans devour lots of energy moving those tons of air, while furnaces below burn fuel heating it. The question is, how often must a building's air be circulated? Fish said state codes for building ventilation had problems.

The state required all new buildings to exceed energy-code performance requirements by 30%. That's good for our future energy use. However, ventilation safety standards for existing buildings often required more air changes per hour and 100% fresh air where it might not be needed. Fish also said some UW rooms have 20 or 30 hourly air changes when 8 would be plenty. The UW could save lots of energy by changing conservative air-change requirements in some cases, and by calibrating rooms and repairing air-circulation equipment in others.[18] All that without one sign or brochure. Fish combined a structural fix, change the building codes, with a technological fix, new fans to move air. The UW would save energy, and let students and faculty go about their usual business while avoiding the cognitive fix keeper hole.

Just how much energy did UW-Madison save? Faramarz Vakili, director of the WE CONSERVE program, was at the seminar. He later amazed us when reporting that since April 2006, the program cut energy consumption by a trillion BTUs, saving $9 million. The goal was to reduce energy consumption by 20% by 2010, which was achieved.[19] In addition, water usage dropped 46% in 6 years, saving 178 million gallons (enough to fill two Olympic-size swimming pools daily). Vakili later told me the program saved enough energy to power four other UW campuses (Green Bay, Parkside, Stout, and Superior).

Technological fixes delivered savings through things like replacing cold-water air-conditioning systems, controlling lawn-watering practices, and installing low-flow plumbing fixtures. No one posted signs asking students to take shorter showers. Technological fixes worked similar magic with electricity. Energy audits and retrofits of seven campus buildings decreased energy use by 40%, for a total annual savings of $3.5 million. Upgrading to more efficient lighting decreased lighting costs 57% for a $400,000 annual savings.

During a later visit with Vakili I asked, "If you get these big savings on buildings, why bother asking people to turn off individual computers?" The 27,000 computers across the campus use only 4% of the university's energy. Vakili said putting these computers into the sleep mode after they're idle 20 minutes would cut their energy usage 85% and save $1.5 million annually, about as much as the combined retrofits of Chamberlain Hall and the Engineering Building. How do you do that? Vakili, the master of avoiding cognitive fix keeper holes, said: "I don't have to deal with each computer user. I just have to work with the IT managers who control the network. I can get them to set this up, and then we don't have to worry about individual behavior."[20]

Of course WE CONSERVE tried the cognitive fix, with predictable results. Vakili barely mentioned that fix when relating the program's spectacular achievements. On that cold gray morning, I was grateful he and Al Fish told the faculty what *did* work, and for sparing me from telling them their proposals would feel good but surely fail.

The Stockholm Crowding Tax

River guides come in all varieties: sociologists at Hood River, engineers and administrators at UW-Madison, and—as we're about to see—transportation planners and economists in Stockholm, Sweden. One April, the leader of those transportation experts—Jonas Eliasson—hurried back to his office at the Royal Institute of Technology after a life-changing meeting at Stockholm City Hall. During his 20-minute walk, a cliché scene from an American World War II movie ran through his head. The off-screen voice boomed: "This is not an exercise. This is what you have been trained for. Make us proud!"[21] Eliasson and his team had 26 days to design a toll system to reduce traffic in Stockholm's center. His discipline had been hoping for this opportunity since the first paper on congestion charges was presented 150 years earlier.[22] Such charges had only recently been tried in Singapore, London, and Trondheim, Norway. Now it was Stockholm's turn, and time was short.

What came to be called the Stockholm Congestion Tax (in Swedish, *Trängselskatt*)[23] is a classic example of a structural fix, where one changes the situation, and attitudes and behavior follow. The fix itself, built on a strong attitude base, perfectly illustrates how experience changes attitudes and even trumps the media. It also shows when and why general environmental attitudes are important. Finally, as I will explain in chapter 10, the Stockholm case further demonstrates how pro-environmental norms can emerge and persist in influencing behavior.

Eliasson's team designed an electronic barrier around the city's center that charged each vehicle between one and two Euros, depending on time of day.[24] This fee for driving into the city resembled the time-of-use fee for electricity that we tested in Wisconsin. Of course the public was reminded to use public transportation in place of driving. The focus was to change the situation with economic incentives: the costs and rewards of driving into Stockholm's center. If the program was effective, drivers would get something in return: less crowding and shorter lines. However, outcomes couldn't be certain without a full-scale trial.

To succeed, structural fixes must be designed with attitudes. The idea of congestion charges was not new in Stockholm. "Such charges were discussed in 1972, and by the end of the decade all parties basically understood they couldn't build more roads in city center."[25] However, most wanted to build ring roads west and east of the city. Financing was the main obstacle, along with winning enough support from smaller parties to get a majority in Sweden's parliamentary system. In the 1980s, specific plans surfaced for reducing congestion. Later, various commissions made recommendations, and the topic was again on the political agenda in the 2002 elections. Thus, Stockholmers were familiar with the idea of congestion charges.

The specific proposal was, however, a new attitude object. Most of us don't consider solving transportation problems with a tax. For that matter, we think little about transportation beyond deciding how to get to work or to the ball game. Except for guys like Eliasson, congestion charges are neither tied to identities nor central to belief systems. When we hear about such things, we ignore or try linking them to things we have attitudes about. Eliasson believed Stockholmers had developed negative attitudes about cars in the city. "There are a lot of people who consider cars to be evil," he said, as we chatted in his Royal Institute of Technology office, but like any attitude, this one was inconsistent. He also noted, "At the same time, people see cars as necessary." The trial period would reveal just how necessary.

The Stockholm crowding tax further built on existing positive attitudes toward the city, taxes, and the environment. Can you imagine trying to implement something called a tax in the United States? U.S. politicians who support tax increases soon become former politicians. Yet in Stockholm, "tax" was part of the word used in naming the congestion charge. Obviously, Swedes have more positive attitudes about taxes than do Americans.[26] They see benefits returning to them in free healthcare, paid parental leave, nearly free day care, and excellent public transportation. Political parties often run on platforms with specific types of tax increases, explaining how they would use the money for your benefit. Sweden uses direct incentives to support things society desires, so you get money (rather than tax credits) from the government each month for each child. In Sweden, it's common to use money to influence behavior.

Swedes also have strong positive attitudes toward the environment. Thus, Stockholm pitched the tax as "miljöavgifter\trängselskatt" or "Environmental Fees\Crowding Tax." In promoting the program, the city noted environmental benefits like less air and noise pollution from fewer cars in the central city. Stockholmers take special pride in their city, so things that reduce its noise, traffic, and air pollution are all seen as positives.

Stockholm has excellent mass transit, so people have alternatives to paying to drive downtown. The program was designed to give drivers alternatives, be it noncharged times, modes, routes, or destinations. Because the charged area is relatively small, driving around the central city rather than through it was an option. Six months before beginning the trial, Stockholm masterfully established 16 new nonstop bus routes from its suburbs to the city. Drivers could no longer deny responsibility by saying, "I have no choice." Widely noted and expensive improvements to mass-transit before the trial period, *whether the public used them or not*, likely made drivers feel more responsible for negative behaviors (driving evil cars into the city). Eliasson sums up Stockholm's situation: "Compared to many other cities, car use is low, transit satisfaction is high, and environmental concerns are high."[27]

Some argue that environmental or congestion charges are difficult to implement in many countries because of "strong resistance from citizens."[28]

However, Stockholm's first attitude survey found 52% of the public supported the program, whereas less than one-third thought it a very bad idea. This support surprised Eliasson and his colleagues, but politicians, it appears, had a good intuitive reading of the public. With strong pro-environmental attitudes, excellent public transit, and a history of relevant discussion, Stockholm seemed ready for congestion charges.

Launching the trial was neither simple nor cheap.[29] Cars required transponders, and a reader system was set up to photograph all license plates of cars going in and out of the city's center. If you didn't have a transponder, you had five days to pay your fee at a convenience store or online. Otherwise you faced a large fine.[30] Officials faced other worries, too. If the trial didn't work or the public hated it, who would pay the system's costs?

The press, indeed, worried. Remember, though, that the press sets agendas and frames discussions. It does not change strong, well-established attitudes, and it certainly framed the crowding tax in negative fashion. Only 3% of media coverage before the test period was positive, compared to about 40% negative. The rest were neutral, just providing facts like the time of day the tax applied, and so forth.[31]

If media coverage had been taken as a measure of public support, one would have thought the public hated the idea. Even scientific surveys showed support dropped to 43% just before the program started. This 9 percentage-point decline was nothing, however, like the 30 percentage-point shift in upstate New York when the press reframed wolf restoration (chapter 3) by linking weak attitudes toward wolves with stronger value-laden attitudes. In Stockholm, despite almost overwhelming negative news coverage, attitudes toward the crowding tax remained relatively stable, most likely because support was tied to stronger attitudes about the environment and using taxes for collective projects.[32]

Speculation about the crowding tax ended January 3, 2006, the day the 6-month trial began. That day, Stockholmers began getting direct experience, including a miracle: "Every fourth car disappeared!" shouted a headline in *Metro*, along with before-and-after pictures at a main entry point to central Stockholm. This was no overstatement. During January, traffic volume decreased 28%. Even Eliasson was shocked: "Practically all the experts were convinced traffic would decrease, but few—and certainly not me—expected it could be *seen with the naked eye*"[33] (emphasis in the original). Eliasson recalled that when he saw the *Metro* picture published a week later (see Figure 8.1), "I gaped in astonishment."[34]

Within days, newspapers declared the program a success,[35] and drivers discovered that, even though they had to pay, they got something in return: less time sitting in traffic jams.[36] Drivers found they could shift their behavior

FIGURE 8.1 Newspaper Front Page Showing Decrease in Traffic. "Stockhomers, where have you gone?"

and the effects weren't so bad. The press quickly reframed the story. Positive articles went from almost none to more than 40%.[37] In two months, public support hit 54%. By the time the trial ended, media coverage was even more favorable. The number of positive articles increased to 50%, and negative articles dropped to 20%. Post-trial surveys showed 35% of the public was more positive after several months of direct experience.[38] Even opinion leaders in the press announced they changed their minds.[39] Support increased to 65% in 2007 and 74% in 2009.[40] In the 2010 elections, no political party opposed Stockholm's congestion tax.

These increases in positive attitudes through direct experience in Stockholm are not uncommon. Surveys in London showed support increased from minority to majority after implementing a congestion charge. The acceptability of toll rings in Bergen, Oslo, and Trondheim, Norway, all increased during implementation.[41]

Stockholm's experience also gives special insight into the important role of general pro-environmental attitudes. In previous chapters I've repeatedly shown general attitudes have little to do with pro-environmental actions like recycling, littering, saving energy, purchasing environmental goods, and so forth. Therefore, it's reasonable to ask, what good are general pro-environmental attitudes if they don't influence what people do?

The answer was clear in Stockholm. You can't implement a structural fix unless it's consistent with general attitudes. Stockholm had majority support for reducing crowding long before the trial. Direct experience with the trial further increased positive attitudes. In 2007, the team finally had enough information to study the role of individual factors (age, income, etc.) and attitudes that influenced the crowding tax's support. *General pro-environmental attitudes* were front and center in every model predicting support.

Among those saying they strongly cared about the environment, 79% supported the congestion tax. Further, 76% of those saying they often worry about environmental issues supported the tax. These general pro-environmental attitudes were more important than where people lived or whether they drove their car to the city center. In Stockholm, more than two-thirds of the population held strong *general pro-environmental attitudes.*[42] Eliasson's models showed that, if support for the environment were cut to half the baseline level, support for the congestion tax would have dropped 13%. If awareness of consequences were reduced along with pro-environmental attitudes, support would drop 23%. Both effects were bigger than the effect of increasing the number of people owning or using cars who were dissatisfied with public transit.

Without strong pro-environmental attitudes, there's little doubt the Stockholm congestion tax would never have reached the test stage, and it would have certainly lost in a public referendum after the trial. I asked Eliasson if Stockholm would have backed down from the trial's huge fixed costs if the tax had failed to shift attitudes or if support had fallen to 30%. He didn't hesitate: "No party would have supported the continuation under these circumstances." General environmental attitudes don't influence specific actions, but the Stockholm experience shows they play a big role in influencing support for structural fixes that *can* dramatically influence pro-environmental behaviors.

Smaller Fixes: Key Cards

Fixes designed with attitudes don't all have to be major million-dollar projects implemented by teams of engineers, PhD sociologists, and transportation economists. Much simpler fixes can avoid keeper holes. For decades, I've stayed at hotels imploring me to save energy, reminding me (especially in the 1970s) there was an energy crisis. About half the time, I'm cynical, thinking corporate owners care not one whit about the environment, just their profits and electricity bill. My socialist self hits my environmental self, and I don't walk back across the room to switch off the lights.

While working on this book at a Budapest hotel, I turned out all the lights when leaving the room every time, without fail! No one had posted signs with dire warnings about global warming, and no one pledged the money saved to combating greenhouse gases. How did I engage in such miraculous behavior? It was a small-scale structural fix. Although it uses technology, it's a structural fix because it changes human behavior (mine, in this case) and then the environment, rather than directly changing the environment.

When I first entered the room and flipped the light switch, nothing happened. Next to the switch was a plastic slot that read "Main Switch" and ⌊CARD⌋. I shoved my key card into ⌊CARD⌋ and left it there. The lights came on. No sign educated me. The room did that. This fix works because we can be pretty sure about the wants and needs of most hotel customers. Whether they are an environmentalist or Donald Trump, they want a hot shower, lights in their room, and power for their computer. The role (hotel guest) and the setting (hotel room) pretty much bound these choices and preferences.

When you leave the room, this fix assumes you want to get back in, so you take your key with you (a common behavioral regularity among hotel guests). The room quits using electricity once you pull out the card. Simple. This structural fix solved another problem for me, and I suspect many others: I often lose my key inside the room. When I'm about to leave, usually late for something, I must tear the room apart to find the key. In Budapest, the key was always handy, next to the door. Whoever invented this structural win-win fix should get an environmental award.

Microsoft in Paris devised a similar innovation.[43] It noticed about 40% of documents sent to printers were never retrieved. Think of the wasted paper and energy, and the great opportunity for a cognitive fix. Microsoft might have launched all sorts of electronic signs on your computer to warn you of the problem and remind you how many trees would be spared by not printing. Microsoft's crew was smarter than that: A keystroke sends your print job to a printer, but it will not print until you walk to the printer and use your key card to start the job. No signs and no exhortations, just problem-solving. Notice how this fix capitalized on behavioral data. Rather than having a heavy-handed manager dictate paper savings, Microsoft studied what people were doing—or in this case, not doing—and saw an opportunity. People wanted a paper copy enough to hit the print button, but did not want it enough to retrieve it. By requiring key cards, the company saved resources without requesting major sacrifices in productivity and worker satisfaction. No education necessary.

Conclusion

The cognitive fix keeper hole is everywhere. It's *so* easy to badger hotel guests to turn off lights, shame employees into reducing their printing, urge students and professors to turn off computers and ride bicycles, encourage Hood River residents to dial down thermostats, and beg Stockholm drivers to take the subway rather than driving into the city center. These "solutions" make us feel good but drag us into that keeper hole. We spin around and around, thinking we're going somewhere, but in reality, accomplish little for the environment.

Bypassing the attitude-change process does not mean you can ignore attitudes. The technical fix of New Deal dams was derailed because the so-called fix changed attitudes and behavior. We try big dams because they're consistent with our attitudes, rather than creating flood-plain zoning and spending tax dollars to remove structures from the flood plain. The keys to the Stockholm crowding tax were the knowledge base, positive attitudes, and collective values revealed by repeated surveys, along with efficient public transportation that encouraged alternative behaviors. However, just as every rapids is different, a fix that works in one place cannot be torn up and laid in another. Implementing a technical or structural fix, as we saw in Hood River, requires careful community assessments and designing with attitudes. Our knowledge of these attitudes must be based on good science and repeated surveys in the context of experimental design, not just guesses.

As key cards show, fixes need not be complicated. The secret is thinking carefully about behaviors you want to change and then creatively trying to change them without trying to change attitudes. Follow the moving water, paddle hard, and beware that keeper hole.

9

Going with the Flow

THE BEST WAY to avoid keeper holes and smashing up on rocks is to read the river correctly and, most important, go with the flow. Find the river's main chutes and keep your boat within them. Don't fight the river. Work with its current to stay well-positioned. Don't stare at the rocks. They aren't going anywhere.

Similarly, we can't let ourselves think, "If I could just change somebody's attitude . . . ." That's like hoping a rock looming ahead will somehow vanish. If we're wishing instead of watching, we won't notice the water flowing smoothly around it. By going with the flow, we can avoid catastrophe. When attitudes are positive or changing in positive directions, they create eddies going upstream and into new channels. Look for them and go with the flow. As the following stories illustrate, this happens more than you might expect.

Navigating the River Wolf

Going with the flow might seem obvious, but I've found it's not always easy to convince managers they're trapped in the cognitive fix keeper hole. They want to change attitudes—whether the attitudes need changing or not. Stephen Kellert and I discovered this in Michigan during 1990. Our surveys (chapter 2) showed the public had positive attitudes toward wolves. The river was flowing our way. "Educating the public" would not improve attitudes because those with the *least* knowledge were just as positive about wolves as those with the most. Only a few hardscrabble Upper Peninsula farmers had well-developed, identity-based negative attitudes. That is, they hated wolves. Nothing short of brainwashing would have changed them. The good news for wolf restoration was that the Upper Peninsula's farmer population was small and declining, and perhaps as endangered as wolves. Leave them alone, we counseled managers.

Members of the major group whose attitudes needed changing were our clients. These scientists and managers were convinced *before* our study that Michigan residents hated wolves. It was all Kellert and I could do—armed with data, years of experience, and academic credentials—to change one simple belief among the managers. PEOPLE IN MICHIGAN LIKE WOLVES. It was a tough sell, requiring lots of numbers and many hours answering questions. Even then, I doubt we convinced them. The four short-lived wolves introduced 15 years before proved to the managers, no matter what our data said (remember the direct-experience principle), that Michigan residents *hated* wolves. That's the common mistake of thinking that behavior and attitudes are virtually the same. Fortunately, low budgets and inexperience, not our ability to persuade, scuttled the proposed information campaign.

Shortly after the fateful meeting at which Kellert and I failed to convince the wildlife managers, a Michigan forester called to say that a truck driver killed a wolf. He saw a wolf on a forest road, sped up, and ran it over. My heart sank as even I began doubting our data. Perhaps our clients were right. Perhaps people in Michigan did hate wolves. Then the forester added, "Someone saw it and reported him. The driver is being charged." My heart soared. Here was clear evidence that protecting wolves had reached normative status. The attitude had become part of the community, and informal as well as formal sanctions were being invoked. No longer could you walk into a cafe and brag you killed a wolf. I knew then that wolves would continue howling in Michigan.

In the ensuing years, wolves returned to Michigan's Upper Peninsula without further educating the public. The Upper Peninsula held fewer than 20 wolves when we did our study, and in 2012 it had nearly 600. We don't have attitude data from the early 1970s to compare with our 1990 survey, but the likely hypothesis is that public attitudes toward wolves had been changing, just as Leopold's had changed. By the 2000s, more people found pleasure in the wolf's presence in the forest (and even glimpsing them occasionally) than took pleasure in killing them. Prowolf attitudes were part of the community norms. Our surveys found no rocks in River Wolf's main channel. Although managers were scared by roaring waters and standing waves, the rocks were well below the surface. We were riding high on currents of social change.

Catching the Eddy: Designing with Deer Hunter Attitudes

Bo Shelby and I once scouted Blossom Bar, the biggest rapids on Oregon's Rogue River. The main chute, a big tongue of water, ended at a set of killer rocks. It looked impossible until Bo spotted a small eddy to the right where water ran back upstream. The goal was to slip off the main tongue sweeping toward those rocks and "catch that eddy." From there, one could go through a secondary channel and slip through the rapids.

"What if we miss the eddy?" I asked.

"No problem," he said. "We'll catch the eddy."

"But what happens *if* we miss the eddy."

Bo said, "Look, Tom, if you're going to run this rapids, you catch that eddy."

Deer hunter attitudes are as solid as rocks in Blossom Bar, and the current of conventional thinking is as powerful as the Rogue. However, against all odds, a Georgia deer manager in the mid-1990s read the water right and spotted an eddy. I was skeptical when the Sand County Foundation invited Terry Kile to visit Wisconsin and "describe how he had changed attitudes" and modified deer hunting in Georgia's Dooly County. Kile's program succeeded, I discovered, because he designed *with,* not against, attitudes. He worked one part of an attitude structure against another, using a powerful evaluative belief to leverage a couple of other beliefs. Kile is no social psychologist, but his program followed our theories to a T. It might have seemed magical to him, but based on the logic of attitudes, his success was predictable.

White-tailed deer were all but extinct in Georgia by the Great Depression. In those years, when low cotton prices put growers out of business, Georgia bought up empty fields, planted trees, and created deer habitat. The state trucked in deer from Wisconsin and banned hunting until 1952, when the herd numbered 30,000. By 1992 Georgia held 1.2 million deer, and during the years that followed, hunters shot about 400,000 deer annually to try controlling the population.

Why would Kile try to improve such success? In his view, there was a problem: Even with fields full of deer, big trophy bucks—the kind hunters dream of hanging over their fireplaces—were not there. They were so rare that it would take 50 hunting seasons on average for one hunter to shoot a trophy buck. Plus, even with heavy hunting pressure, deer remained so plentiful they were devouring the habitat supporting them. Hunting regulations that created Georgia's big deer herds worked against producing trophy bucks and controlling the herd. Hunters were prohibited from shooting does or young bucks without antlers. As soon as a male deer grew antlers it died, long before it reached bragging size.

Kile knew things could be fixed. The biology was simple. Pass up small bucks and shoot more female deer to reduce the population so there would be more feed and healthier deer. Although this solution sounds simple, hunters for decades had chanted, "Dead does bear no fawns," and refused to shoot female deer and risk shooting young antlerless bucks. Hunters like to see and shoot deer, so they often pass up does. Getting hunters to believe it was good to shoot does—and then actually do it—was Kile's first challenge. The second was changing another behavior: passing up small-antlered bucks. Few had heard of passing up a buck, no matter how small. If you didn't shoot it, your neighbor would.

What gave Kile hope was that one part of the attitude was solid: Hunters had strong positive attitudes toward shooting trophy deer. To achieve his goal, Kile didn't need to convince hunters that deer hunting was bad and that they should stop hunting deer. That would have been a *major* attitude change, like making rivers run upstream. He simply had to change two beliefs and behaviors that would help hunters do what they most desired: shoot trophy bucks. They could still harvest antlerless deer, and if they did that, Kile could all but guarantee they would see more big bucks and have better chances of bagging a trophy. Kile's strategy was to show hunters how changing their behavior could increase their odds of shooting big bucks.

His real insight was realizing social attitudes are just that, *social* attitudes— beliefs held by people living in a community and looking to others to determine what's appropriate. Hunters' attitudes are more influenced by other hunters and community leaders than by state wildlife managers. So when Kile visited Dooly County, where he thought this program might have a chance, he went straight to the sheriff's office and told him of the opportunity. Then he visited one community leader after another and told the same story. He avoided reactance[1] by giving the community a choice. He said, "You don't have to support this, but if you want to shoot big bucks, here's how." He told stories about Texas ranches that fenced 30,000 and 40,000 acres to protect deer from poachers and the neighbors, and then passed up small bucks. Over the years this strategy produced big bucks for the ranch owners and their hunting buddies. Nobody owns that much property in Dooly County, so fences were not an option. Instead, Kile argued that regulations would act like fences. As a state wildlife manager, he could build a regulatory fence if hunters supported it. This wasn't a "government regulation." It was a fence, a direct experience for people, and something they understood.

Now if you asked Kile, he would say he changed attitudes, but that isn't clear. Across the nation, grassroots groups of hunters were implementing what's called quality deer management (QDM), which promotes passing up young bucks and shooting more does. The idea was regularly discussed in most hunting magazines. Texas ranchers and Wisconsin locals who were tired of shooting small deer were implementing QDM without help from the state. Georgia hunters aren't immune from cultural trends. The same broad attitude change that sent Kile to Dooly County was making local hunters receptive to the idea. A survey the year before the program began showed that 66% of hunters supported the concept.[2]

However, when success seemed at hand, Kile got blindsided. He forgot to consider the attitudes of some others with a big stake in deer management: his superiors at the Georgia Department of Natural Resources (DNR). Once the program won community support, he went to his bosses and proposed changing Dooly County's deer season. They refused. They agreed the program would create more big bucks for hunters and that hunters would like it, but they said the current program had restored deer and they didn't want to risk change. Because the attitudes of DNR professionals wouldn't budge, Dooly County would not have trophy-buck regulations.

However, Dooly County's community leaders didn't care about the attitudes of DNR bosses. They were fired up and ready to go, so they went to the governor. The governor cared more about his constituents' attitudes than those of his wildlife managers. The new rules were implemented, and hunters began shooting more does and bragging about little bucks they passed up. A new norm was emerging. After a few years, Dooly County hunters began seeing and shooting more big deer. A survey after the third year showed 87% of hunters supported this management.[3] That's attitude change based on direct experience. For his *trouble*, Kile was officially reprimanded twice by his department.

A Light Bulb That Really Wants to Change

When people with positive attitudes are motivated, it can be easy to implement fixes, as Faramarz Vakili discovered. As discussed in the previous chapter, Vakili made great progress saving energy at the University of Wisconsin-Madison through technological and structural fixes. The positive energy of the WE CONSERVE program attracted attention from others who, like light bulbs, "really wanted to change." With the program in place, Vakili started to get irritating calls from folks in the 16-story Atmospheric, Oceanic and Space Sciences (AOSS) building. They wanted to help with the program and save energy in *their* building. Of the 300 or so buildings on the UW campus, this one wasn't high on Vakili's list because it had relatively little potential compared to the laboratory buildings, but he couldn't keep rejecting them.

He finally met with two of the building's three departments. A simple technological fix to save energy is to turn off the air conditioning at night, which the UW's physical plant usually does at 9 P.M. The AOSS departments asked, "Well, no one is here after 5 P.M., so can't you turn it off earlier?" After further checking, however, they discovered some people stayed late, but those people who stayed late all agreed if the air conditioning shut off at 5 P.M., they would bring a sweater.

Yes, you read that right. Turning *off* the air conditioning in summer made the air *colder*, not warmer. To prevent condensation and other problems, water used to cool UW buildings is chilled to 55 degrees. The offices drop to 55 overnight and are *reheated* to 68 degrees before people return to their offices the next morning. Paradoxically, folks who turned up their thermostats during the day to save on air conditioning actually used more energy heating the cold water. This was big news and shows how "common sense" can be deceiving in complex systems.

The air conditioning was turned off at 5 P.M., and at least some of the 400 people in the building were advised to quit raising their thermostats to "save energy" during the day. This saved more than 868,000 BTUs of chilled water annually. They also changed the building's ventilation (remember Al Fish from the previous chapter), reducing air circulation by 30% during workdays and by 70% on nights and Sundays. This saved 403,000 kwh or, at 11 cents a KWH, $44,330 in a single year. A lighting study identified an additional annual savings of 416,000 kwh through upgrades that consist primarily of swapping older fixtures and fluorescents with new T-8 5000K energy-efficient lighting. These are all technological fixes that require no attitude and little behavior change by building residents.

Educating self-selected, highly motivated people works, which is how we can build on positive environmental attitudes. The changes here were based on a few people, and group process played a role. They were no doubt motivated by internal sanctions of pride for bringing their sweaters, and the entire group (who delivers informal sanctions) was in on the deal. They might have created a local norm, but this norm required neither major value changes nor particularly high personal costs. This norm did not diffuse far outside the AOSS building, however. In spite of the WE CONSEVE program, only one other UW building followed this model.

Back to the River Wolf

A few chapters back, we noted that in spite of overwhelmingly positive attitudes toward wolves in Wisconsin, 99.6% of car owners did not pay $25 to put a wolf on their license plates. Even of those who did pay—less than 2%—gave additional money to the Timber Wolf Alliance. So even if we could change positive attitudes and make them even more positive, prowolf behavior would not likely follow.

This is why we sometimes get pessimistic about attitudes, but that doesn't mean they're useless or should be ignored. How do you think wolves got on license plates in the first place—because Wisconsinites hated wolves? How many plates feature pictures of the plumb curculio? Because millions of Wisconsinites like wolves and want them in the ecosystem, politicians felt safe proposing to put them on license plates to raise money for endangered resources. Remember, a structural fix must be consistent with attitudes. This fix allowed people to act on their prowolf attitudes. Even though only a small percentage of people gave money, they brought in more than $500,000 annually over 12 years to fund endangered resources work by the Wisconsin DNR.[4] So even if many did not act on their positive attitudes, they did much good for the environment without anyone trying to change their attitudes. Clever administrators simply read the water and went with the flow.

To give you an idea of the current's strength on the River Wolf, realize Wisconsin offers 28 specialized plates. In 2009, the wolf plate was the second-best seller with 15,203 sold. That's far more than the Ducks Unlimited plate, 1,678; Wisconsin Salutes Veterans plate, 934; or the Women's Health Foundation plate, 226. Only the Green Bay Packers exceeded the wolf plate, with 15,882 sold.

Avoiding Rocks: Adjusting to Attitudes in Washington D.C.

We don't always have to change attitudes. Nor can we. However, it's important to know where attitudes lie so we can adjust to them. With pollsters as their guides, politicians adjust to attitudes all the time. After the 1994 elections, with a congressional majority for the first time in 40 years, Republicans busily cut environmental programs from national parks to EPA water-quality standards. With an eye to the 1996 elections, they conducted a survey and found boulders ahead. "Our party is out of sync with mainstream American opinion,"[5] reported pollster Linda DiVall. Fifty-five percent of Republicans said they did not trust their party to protect the environment, whereas 72% of Democrats *trusted* theirs. The survey also showed Democrats and Republicans alike rejected the GOP's environmental policies. This opposition included most women, independents, and young people.

Faced with this view of the river, did Republicans call for a nationwide campaign to convince the public theirs was the environmental party? Did they try to "educate the public"—the equivalent of blasting rocks or rerouting the river? They were smarter than Exxon Minerals in Wisconsin and the American Nuclear Energy Council in Nevada. They knew the American public was unlikely to change its environmental attitudes, so the GOP's only choice was steering clear of these rapids. Thirty Republican congressional representatives pleaded with House Speaker Newt Gingrich to "correct the course during the continuing budget talks."

DiVall's report was especially powerful because she surveyed not just positive and negative feelings, but also voting intentions. The survey asked, "Would you vote to re-elect" those who supported the Republican-backed bill that cut EPA financing by one-third? Forty-six percent said they would vote against those supporting the bill, whereas only 35% said they would vote to re-elect.

Democrats scouted the river and read it the same way. It was no accident, said the *New York Times*, that Bill Clinton—seeking re-election himself—"spoke at length about environmental issues" in his 1996 State of the Union address. These issues, the *Times* article noted, "usually take the back seat to others."[6] The course through environmental attitudes was safe for President Clinton, amid a boulder-field of mishaps in other areas, and his State of the Union address was designed accordingly. The president's canoe went down the main chute, whereas Republicans missed that channel.

This doesn't mean we can always "get around public attitudes" the same way we can slide around rocks in a rapids. We must realize attitudes are sometimes so strong and pervasive they're like a waterfall. In this case, the Republicans backed down on their anti-environmental agenda. Reading the river with attitude surveys doesn't always mean you'll find safe passage, but it can make you less susceptible to nasty surprises.

Conclusion

Attitudes are forever changing naturally. Attitudes toward wolves have grown more positive since Leopold's time, and as the public becomes more urban and better-educated, that will likely continue. Michigan's wildlife managers were locked into outdated views of public attitudes based on their inferences from observing behavior. They all but ignored data that Kellert and I presented documenting a change in society—even in Michigan's Upper Peninsula—that yielded better social habitat for wolf survival. Even though we cannot change attitudes at will, repeated surveys to understand how attitudes are naturally changing are as important in resource management as they are in politics. You need experts to read the water, and you need some faith in the experts.

In the natural process of social change, attitudes can create upstream eddies that go against the flow. Even deer-management attitudes are not homogeneous and one-dimensional. Terry Kile and others took advantage of that dynamic. Resource managers should note that Kile did not go forth with a heavy-handed "I have to educate the public" mission. Rather, he modestly proposed, "I have something to offer." Rather than trying to change the attitudes of all hunters, he first worked with community leaders. It's important to recognize the social context of attitudes.

Positive attitudes that people hold about the environment form an important foundation for building. Even if a low percentage of people participate, the sheer number of Wisconsinites with positive attitudes toward wolves and endangered resources placed wolves on license plates; it was a structural fix that poured money into a nongame WDNR program. People with positive attitudes toward saving energy in one UW building attracted the attention of administrators and got energy-saving fixes implemented. Lots of good attitudes are out there. We need to chart them and build on them to deliver environmental change.

10

Increasing the Flow

ACTIVATING AND CREATING NORMS

READING THE RIVER and going with the flow help us negotiate attitudes rather than trying to change them. However, what if river runners could make rocks disappear? Before the days of railroads, lumberjacks did just that. Logs floated out of the North Woods often hung up on rocks, creating tremendous jams. Rather than dynamiting the rocks (like trying to change attitudes), loggers turned to a more powerful force: water.

They opened dams built near the headwaters and flooded the rapids. The flood didn't change or move the rocks. It just took them out of action. Norms, like water surges, can swamp attitudes, create new channels, and even trigger the occasional upstream eddy. So, to change environmental behavior, let's raise the water through norms. This chapter shows how we can get almost magical results by focusing and activating norms, providing normative information, and even creating norms through structural fixes.

Reduce Litter? Get Rid of the Barrels!

During a visit to the manicured picnic area at Devil's Lake State Park in Wisconsin, I noticed that litter barrels were missing. They were all gone. The results were predictable. Not a scrap of litter was in sight. I looked table to table for litter and drew a blank. No pop cans, dirty paper plates, or used diapers were in sight. No barrels, no litter. My science side hoped someone had read the research that described how litter barrels create litter, but I knew better. Resource managers seldom read scientific journals, but when budgets get cut, they'll try *anything*, including getting rid of litter barrels, to save money. And it worked!

Removing litter barrels is a classic case of working with existing norms rather than trying to change attitudes or educate the public. Just about everyone shares the anti-littering norm, especially middle-class families who picnic and swim at Devil's Lake. So removing the barrels was the right fix. People bring food and picnic supplies, lounge on the beach, and when they're done . . . say what? No litter barrels? They're confronted with two choices: leave garbage as litter or take it elsewhere, such as home to their own trash can. And that's what people did.[1]

When I talked with the park superintendent in his office on a midwinter day, he confessed they had doubts whether removing the barrels would work.[2] To make it easier for visitors, the park distributed free garbage bags. Bad idea! The bags created a counter-norm. Although many folks used the bags to take their trash home, others took this as a sign that the government would take care of their trash but had "forgotten" to put out litter barrels. So they took their garbage and stuffed it into the bags, transforming it from litter to nonlitter. Then they placed the full bag next to a charcoal grate so it was easily found by park staff, and left with a clear conscience as nonlitterers. In technical terms, they suffered no negative internal sanctions. Once one person did this, a new norm took root. People said to themselves, "Aha, that's where they want the trash," and the bags soon became a haystack. Even one bag was sure to attract a local raccoon . . . and hence nonlittering (bagging your trash) begets what researchers call "unintentional litter." After a couple of years, the DNR got smarter and got rid of the bag dispenser, saving $1,500 a year and removing raccoon food. Predictably, litter didn't increase.

Litter creates a "descriptive norm," as Cialdini would call it, and implies it's all right to litter.[3] Litter likely reduces awareness of consequences (one more piece won't hurt) and reduces personal responsibility (others have caused the litter, . . . someone else will pick it up, . . . it is not my job), as my research showed. However, that's easy to fix. The park crew cleans the area every morning. On weekdays this takes about 30 minutes; on weekends, about 90 minutes. This might seem like a lot, but 1.5 million visitors use this park annually. Norms need maintenance, just like cars, houses, and fences. The cleanup crew erases signs that others have violated the norm, thus preventing the norm from being deactivated.

Because people expect some shared responsibility from the park, dumpsters were available some distance from the picnic area so one could haul trash there. This avoided reactance, "an aversive affective reaction in response to regulations or impositions that impinge on freedom and autonomy . . . especially common when individuals feel obliged to adopt a particular opinion or engage in a specific behavior."[4] Reactance could lead to symbolic littering when people, so angry that they have no alternatives, violate the norm just to prove something. Dumpsters gave people a choice and made them feel responsible if they littered, just as more buses—whether used or not—gave Stockholmers choices.

Of course, formal norms are backed by formal sanctions. Devil's Lake employs five armed rangers. They break up beer parties, settle family disputes, and write speeding tickets. They issued 565 citations during a recent year, none for littering.[5] Littering behavior is controlled by personal norms and occasional informal sanctions, not by guns and uniforms.

Based on this single case at Devil's Lake, I don't recommend immediately removing litter barrels from parks and cities worldwide. In Stockholm, where I live, it's clear much litter comes from tiny overflowing trash bins dotting city parks and playgrounds. The Swedes use these spaces differently than Wisconsinites use Devil's Lake. Families, picnickers, young people, and street drunks all contribute to Stockholm's litter load. They usually have no handy car to haul trash home. Furthermore, Swedes pay high taxes and expect governmental services in return. Who knows what they might do if barrels were removed?

The point is, norms are local, and tied to settings and social groups. Using normative solutions requires serious research and field experiments to test possible solutions. Just as the crowding tax that worked well in Stockholm would not easily export to Madison, the vanishing litter barrels of Devil's Lake might be disastrous in downtown Stockholm, but for well-manicured U.S. parks, removing litter barrels can force people to take trash home *and* reduce litter.

Reduce Litter? Advertise!

Can we change attitudes and reduce littering with advertising? The Keep America Beautiful (KAB) campaign thinks so. Although that first part is not true, the second is. By capitalizing on the media's agenda-setting function— remember, the press tells us what to think *about*, not *what* to think—we can reduce litter by focus and activation. Have you ever heard anyone say litter is good? When we get people thinking about litter, they think about not littering. Advertising activated and increased the salience of the *existing* anti-littering norm.[6] To spread KAB's message in Oklahoma, the state bought commercial advertising, and gave away litterbags and bumper stickers. They even had a song and slogan.

In addition to norm-awareness advertising, KAB introduced a structural fix, an "adopt a highway" program. Oklahoma signed contracts with more than 1,300 groups to pick up highway litter. Guessing that groups average 10 people, the state now had 13,000 people invested in litter. These folks feel proud (internal sanctions) when picking it up, and when seeing their organization's name on roadside signs, litter becomes their problem, not someone else's.

We would expect roadside signs along these sections to raise awareness of negative interpersonal consequences and activate antilittering norms. When passing a roadside sign that says that litter you toss will have to be picked up by the 4-H club, workers at Hill's Restaurant, or the Friends of Scenic Lodi Valley, you're hurting your neighbors.[7] So, based on Schwartz's theory, the program should keep people from deactivating antilittering norms.

The unique thing about Oklahoma's program is that we got to see how focusing the norm changed internal sanctions. We can thank the quick-thinking Harold Grasmick for that. Grasmick, a well-known criminologist at the University of Oklahoma, wasn't so interested in littering or the environment but more serious crimes like theft. To compare violations of the weak antilittering norm, he used two questions on a survey to measure guilt and shame (internal negative sanctions) associated with littering.

Q1. "Generally, in most situations I would feel guilty if I were to litter the highways, streets, or a public recreation area." (Strongly agree to strongly disagree)

Q2. "Would most of the people whose opinions you value lose respect for you if you were to litter the highways, streets, or a public recreation area?" (Definitely would to definitely would not)[8]

Most important, this survey was done *before* the KAB program began. After the campaign, Grasmick repeated the survey and found Oklahoma City's guilt levels for littering skyrocketed 80%. Litter-associated shame more than doubled. Intentions to litter dropped 18%. Getting people to think about the existing norm clearly raised internal-sanction levels and increased behavioral intentions to comply. However, we know from chapter 4 that positive attitudes, even behavioral intentions, don't always lead to behavior. However, these data show that when you make people think about norms, and they feel guilt and shame, negative internal sanctions and behavior follow. Measuring the litter along roadsides before and after the program showed a 23% reduction in litter. That's a clear case of how activating norms can influence public behavior by increasing internal-sanction levels, but to be effective, the norm must already be in place.

Save Energy? Check on the Neighbors!

Norms are powerful because we follow the actions of others, such as I did in the Stockholm bank after being clueless about the queue system. I watched everyone else to see what they were doing. But, what happens when we can't see what others are doing? What happens without direct experience? It turns out you can get people to reduce energy consumption by telling them what neighbors are doing.

This worked for a random sample of households in San Marcos, California, a city of 85,000 north of San Diego.[9] First, psychology graduate students read the homes' outside electric meters to establish a baseline. Then they hung a packet on the door with information about how much electricity the household used daily and the neighbors' average daily consumption. A week later, the students hung another feedback packet on their doors. The final measure showed those who were above average decreased consumption 5%, moving toward their neighbors' use level.

However, norms are like magnets. They pull behavior toward the average or the "normal." Those below average *increased* their electricity consumption by 8%. Maybe they told themselves, "Well, I'm using less electricity than my neighbors, so it won't hurt to use a little more." Information about others' behavior exerts influence, good or bad.

The question was how to deactivate the norm's upward pull on low consumers to keep them from moving toward the average. After the baseline and initial-feedback session, the research team applied informal sanctions. They put hand-drawn smiley faces on information material left with those using less than the norm. This communicated someone was watching, it provided a small positive sanction for their behavior. The smiley face kept this group from increasing consumption toward the norm compared to the control group.

However, this was just a pilot test and it had some baggage. All messages carried the logo of California State University at San Marcos, not the utility company's logo. Did this provide special motivation for San Marcos residents? The information packet was hung on the door, not mailed or sent electronically. Did this make it more noticeable and more likely to be read? Would it be cost-effective for the electric company to make such deliveries? The information was handwritten, implying a "real" person knew and—with hand-drawn smiley faces—presumably cared about the household's energy use. Finally, the experiment ended after a few weeks. Would the savings be sustained for months or years? Although promising and consistent with theory, it needed larger-scale testing.

A company called Opower took this from the pilot stage to broader application, first with the Sacramento Municipal Utility District east of San Francisco. The company provided normative feedback to a random sample of 35,000 customers and compared them to 50,000 who got nothing more than their regular bill. A second client, Puget Sound Energy in northwestern Washington state, also began a full-scale experiment. These field experiments showed miraculous results. In the California trial, if all customers received normative feedback, electricity consumption would fall 110 million kwh per year, the equivalent of saving 9 million gallons of gasoline and reducing carbon emissions by 80,000 metric tons. The Washington state study showed similar savings.[10]

One sheet of paper mailed monthly changed behavior and saved tons of energy. It did this not only by providing information about what others were doing, but by attending to many things I've tried to show in this book. Information first must reach the actor's sense organs to be effective. That's no small thing in a busy world where everyone fights for your attention. The graduate students in San Marcos with handwritten notes and smiley faces had a good chance of engaging people, but that wasn't practical for big electricity companies. The next best solution was sending a personally addressed envelope. People were likely to open it because it looked official but wasn't a bill.

Once the curious customers opened their envelopes, they found only one sheet of paper. Its graphics were in color and easy to read, although the figure here does not show color (see Figure 10.1). It was also personalized and provided short answers (20 words or fewer) to some basic questions: What is this? Why am I receiving this? How do the comparisons work? Once you reach people's eyes and ears, you must work fast, so make it easy.

The letter's next section provided the all-important *normative information* in words and pictures. You were told you used X% more (or possibly less) electricity than your "efficient neighbors." Note the positive label on the comparison to neighbors. Next was a simple three-bar graph: one bar for you; one for all neighbors (100 occupied homes nearby of similar size to yours and with the same type of heat); and one for your most efficient neighbors (the 20% using the least electricity). You easily saw if you were above or below average that month. Below that was a line graph providing the exact same information for a year (not just one month). So you could check to see if the previous month was unusual.

The informal sanction came in a little box labeled, "Your efficiency standing." An arrow pointed to one of three labels. The one fitting you was in bold. The standings were as follows:

"GREAT ☺☺"
"GOOD ☺"
"BELOW AVERAGE"

At the bottom were three personalized action steps based on consumption levels and appliance-ownership patterns. Each step was six or fewer words.

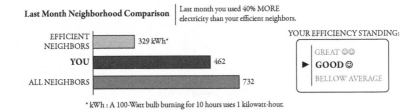

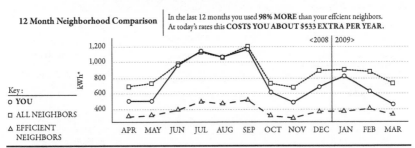

FIGURE 10.1 **Normative Information on Side One of Sacramento Metropolitan Utility Test (original in color)**

Thus, customers knew what they could try to reduce consumption and thereby reduce their ability to deny responsibility, as in, "There's nothing I can do to lower my consumption, so who cares if I use more than other customers?"

People who looked only at the letter's first side got, within seconds, normative information about their behavior, an informal sanction, a notice of an economic incentive, and three suggestions for reducing energy. End of story. Remember the specificity principle: behavior is always specific. To provoke a behavior, give people specific information and tell them exactly what to do. This single page followed the formula to a T. The normative information acted as a surrogate for direct experience. It told you what you did and what your neighbors were doing.

On the letter's reverse side (see Figure 10.2), a two-bar graph compared household consumption for the current month with consumption for the same month the previous year. A statement noted whether the household

Personal Comparison | How your electricity use compares to last year

Feb 1-Feb 28 Usage (kWh/day)

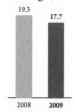

2008 2009

You used 8% LESS electricity in February than you did last year.

STARS ARE AWARDED WHEN YOU USE LESS THAN IN 2008

★	★	?	?	?	?	?	?	?	?	?	?
-16%	-8%										

JAN FEB MAR APR MAY JUN JUL AUG SEP OCT NOV DEC

So far this year, you're using 13% LESS electricity than you did last year.

Action Steps | Personalized tips chosen for you based on your energy use and housing profile

Quick Fixes
Things you can do right now

☐ **Turn off lights when not needed**
Itls a common misconception that turning a light off and on consumes energy so that you might as well leave it on. This is not the case.

While some lights do require an initial burst of energy to start, the amount is very small when compared to the energy needed to keep the light operating

Turning off lights (and other devices too) when not needed will save you energy and money.

Save up to 20% on lighting energy cost

Smart Purchases
Save a lot by spending a little

☐ **Save by covering your pool**
The best way to reduce the cost of heating your pool is to keep it covered when it's not in use.

A cover will keep the water temperature about 10° warmer, greatly reducing the energy and cost to heat the pool.

A cover will also help keep your pool clean, saving additional cost by reducing the need to run the filter pump.

Finally, a cover will greatly reduce evaporation, saving hundreds of gallons of water.

Save up to 50% or more on pool heating cost

Great Investments
Big ideas for big savings

☐ **Install a variable speed pool pump**
A pool pump uses more energy than most of the other devices and appliances in your home.

If you don't currently have a variable speed pump, you could be wasting hundreds of dollars by pumping at a higher speed for more hours than needed.

Get ready for summer by installing a properly sized variable speed pump, and you can save between 30-75% on your energy costs. Pool pump savings often pay back their cost in less than two years.

SAVE UP TO

$**200**PER YEAR

SMUD
SACRAMENTO MUNICIPAL UTILITY DISTRICT
The Power To Do More

Powered by
Positive Energy

1-888-742-SMUD (7683)
electricityreports@smud.org

For information about this home electricity report please visit www.smud.org/reports.

FIGURE 10.2 Normative Information on Side Two of Sacramento Metropolitan Utility Test

used more or less energy this year, and awarded a green STAR if it used less. Below this information was a grid with 24 boxes. The household's reduction (or increase) appeared in the lower box, and a star "check-marked" the upper box if energy consumption decreased. If the household used less energy each month compared to the previous year, it received 12 green stars.

The message at the page's bottom was again specific to the household. The text was a bit longer, assuming those who actually turned the letter over were more interested.

Although aggregate savings across hundreds of thousands of utility customers loom large, remember individual behavioral shifts were small, no more than a 2% reduction in energy use. What we're doing is shifting the flow, causing small behavioral changes. We're working the eddies, not making the river run backward. People wouldn't look at this one page and take their home off the grid.

Astute readers might ask if this is a cognitive fix. Yes, but it's a particular kind of cognitive fix. The unusual thing is that it works, and here's why:

1. The simple information it gives provides motivation, not simply knowledge (like how much energy a refrigerator uses).
2. It builds on what most people feel they "should" do (the injunctive character of norms). Saving energy is good.
3. It's specific. It gives information about the individual reading the message, not the public in general.
4. It does not clutter the message with distracting information about global warming or energy conservation to provide motivation.

In retrospect, our failure to change the time-of-day electricity use three decades before (chapter 5) could have resulted from bombarding customers with too much general, rather than specific, information. Nor were our meters sophisticated enough to give customers monthly feedback. Most important, our sample sizes were too small to detect small behavioral changes. When you have 35,000 people rather than 250 in your treatment group, you can identify tiny effects. Our intervention might have had effects, but our methods and measures might not have been sensitive enough to detect them. The cognitive fix as a broad brush *usually doesn't work*, but these field experiments show that when you focus on normative information, and informal sanctions and incentives, and deliver this message in ways people can't miss, small but important changes in pro-environmental behavior *can* follow.

Even so, these apparently successful programs had problems. First, as in the San Marcos pilot study, Sacramento customers in the lower 20% consumption level *increased* energy use after receiving normative information.[11] Second, normative information is effective only if people hold injunctive norms. What if a lot of people think using *more* energy is good? Third, will the effect last over time? The first of these problems can be handled by not sending normative information to customers who use little energy. Simply avoid risking the increase, and save on metering, postage, and printing costs. If regulators require all customers receive feedback, just send the low-consumption group information on their energy use with a couple of green stars, but no comparative information. Research on the second problem shows it's possible to identify subpopulations who don't appear to care about using less energy, but they are probably no more than 10% of the population.[12] Finally, studies of second-year effects of these normative programs show no backsliding. Indeed, some evidence shows people might strengthen their personal norms for energy conservation and start replacing appliances with more energy-efficient models.

Carefully delivered normative information can affect small amounts of electricity consumption. Across millions of customers, this can save significant energy. Let's move to Chicago to show the money value of normative information.

Norms and Light Bulbs in Chicago

According to Chicago economists who did the study, if every American house replaced one incandescent light bulb with a compact fluorescent light (CFL), energy savings would exceed $800 million and reduce greenhouse gases as much as removing 420,000 cars from the road. So, for an entire year, students tried selling energy-conserving light bulbs. The resulting study showed again that normative information can change consumer behavior *and* was worth real money.[13] However, because few people bought the bulbs, we might say that instead of starting a flood, they barely raised the water in a small creek.

How do we increase CFL use? A structural fix includes lower prices, and the cognitive fix gives people information. How do the two compare? The first thing economists discovered was that selling light bulbs door-to-door is tough. Students had to knock on nearly 9,000 doors to sell bulbs to 300 families. One reason sales were dismal was that two-thirds of the people weren't home or they didn't answer the door. When students talked to somebody, about 10% bought bulbs. Because this was an experiment, half the households were offered bulbs at $5 for a box of four, about retail price. The other half got a deal: $1 for the same box. Price, one kind of structural fix, made a difference; 15% bought low-priced bulbs and 6% bought high-priced bulbs.

However, here's the interesting part: In the sales pitch (the cognitive fix), one-third of prospective customers received no reference to norms. In this group, 8% bought light bulbs. Adding one sentence of normative information to the pitch—"For instance, did you know that 70% of U.S. households own at least one CFL?"—increased sales to 11%. When that normative information was focused locally to "70% of households that we surveyed *in this area*," sales rose to 12%.

The normative sales pitch worked better with the higher price. Adding the national normative information for $5 bulbs had the same effect as reducing the price to $3.50, and adding the local normative information had the same effect as reducing the price to $1.50. Norms are worth real money and make real differences in sales.

Even *with* normative information, however, 87% *did not buy* light bulbs even when personally asked. Think how many would purchase energy-saving bulbs if they were the only ones on the shelves. This structural fix would dramatically change the targeted behavior more than price or information about other people's behaviors.

Creating a New Norm? Check out Stockholm!

A real step forward would be *creating* norms that direct behavior toward the environment, not just activate existing norms. Can that happen? Evidence is sparse, but Stockholm's crowding-tax trial provided hopeful data.

When fees were removed after six months, inner-city traffic did not rebound completely, suggesting the tax had created a norm for some. According to basic economics and behavioral psychology, people should have resumed their old behaviors, because they would no longer be sanctioned for it. This concerned Leopold when seeing farmers revert to their old ways when the government ended incentives for adopting conservation practices.[14]

Granted, trips by car into the city increased when the tax was removed, but only about half as much as they had decreased. The first month's traffic to and from the inner city after the tax was removed was *still* 11% lower than the baseline and remained 5 to 10% lower for the *entire* year when no fees were charged.[15] Every month, there were 10–20 *thousand* fewer trips into Stockholm's center. That's a huge behavior change.

So we have a new behavioral norm: fewer people driving into the city. Why? Is this represented in the individual's social psychology? Did Stockholm create a personal norm during the trial? Before implementing the crowding tax, motorists had no norm about where to drive their cars. When the trial began, if you drove into the city during peak hours, you suffered a formal sanction: a tax, or a small "fine." What you did was labeled a bad thing: You created crowding and inconvenience for other drivers, and increased noise and air pollution in the inner city.

Surveys showed the public was aware of these negative consequences for others and the environment, which is a condition for activating norms.[16] Could it also be a precursor for creating norms? Stockholm's public-transit system gave drivers alternatives, which should make them feel responsible for negative consequences. Conditions were right for a new personal norm against driving into the city to emerge.[17]

We can't be certain what happened to beliefs, attitudes, or norms about driving in Stockholm, because no one surveyed people who changed their behavior. When the crowding tax added incentives for people to change, many might have discovered they didn't really need to make so many trips into Stockholm's center. Others tried mass-transit and maybe learned to use it effectively. Hence, maybe they gained positive attitudes toward continuing its use (remember the direct-experience principle). Internal sanctions of pride might have come with forgoing automobile trips. Likewise, internal sanctions of guilt might have arisen when people thought about making a trip. When we change behavior in a nonreactive way, and when people feel they have choice, it appears pro-environmental norms might follow or at least strengthen.

Good examples of creating norms are rare. The Stockholm crowding tax shows the power of the structural fix. It further suggests that with such fixes, new ethics might emerge to guide environmental actions.

Conclusion

Understanding and working with norms can lead to effective and counterintuitive results, like reducing litter by removing litter barrels. Normative feedback on the behavior of others can inspire small but important behavioral changes. The 2% reductions in West Coast utility projects are significant, but they are still modest compared to weatherization efforts in the Pacific Northwest that grew from the Hood River Conservation Project. Norms help sell a few more light bulbs, but the effect is tiny compared to a structural fix like banning incandescent bulbs. Activating existing norms can be effective, as the KAB programs showed, but structural reductions in litterable material don't require continual hoopla and advertising to do the same job. We can activate only existing norms. Creating norms that direct pro-environmental behaviors could be the key, and results from Stockholm's crowding tax suggest this might be possible under the right circumstances. This norm creation, in my opinion, should be the direction of our future research in environmental social psychology.

11

Thinking Beyond the Rim

AS THE SUN sank below the Grand Canyon's rim and the blazing heat retreated, Bo Shelby leaned back on his oars, the big rapids behind us. He looked around and said, "It's a nice time of day to be on the river." A beach campsite, a good dinner, and a Dutch-oven cobbler lay ahead. We broke out our beer and reflected on the day. What did we learn? What mistakes did we make? How could we do better?

This book's principal point—that one cannot solve environmental problems by simply changing attitudes—is not big news. Those who have dealt with environmental problems for years know that changing attitudes and behavior is nearly impossible. What's new in this book is that it shows *why* that's the case and—more important—how to navigate when finally conceding you can't change attitudes.

Attitudes Redux

Attitudes are invisible and overused in common language. They're everywhere and nowhere, and that's why they're so difficult to handle. They're composed of beliefs, they're built on broad values, and they have objects. We don't have an attitude. We have an attitude toward something.

We often forget that attitudes have two parts, the cognitive and the emotional, and too often research focuses on the cognitive. The real power of attitudes is the emotional dimension. My student Howard's attitude toward Exxon, you'll recall, was overpowered by emotion. Emotion can often make attitudes impervious to change, as when the American Nuclear Energy Council (ANEC) in Nevada tried changing the public's attitudes toward a nuclear repository. Emotion can work the other way, too. Fear associated with chronic wasting disease in Wisconsin was sufficient to sway even strong attitudes about deer hunting. You'll soon find yourself in trouble if you ignore emotion in attitudes.

Attitudes are generally stable, which makes them important. Some change, but only slowly. They're more likely to change at certain stages in life. The social context, rather than information alone, has much to do with that change. Leopold changed roles and learned from past mistakes. The Bennington women changed at college. Attitudes of the young replace the old. Attitudes sometimes change rapidly when a new attitude object is hooked to stronger attitudes and values, as we saw when wolf restoration was proposed in the Adirondacks. Society changes and attitudes change with it, but they change in ways we cannot predict or control. The point to remember is that although attitudes change, we cannot change them at will.

The media play a role in changing attitudes, mostly by setting and framing agendas. When wolf restoration became news in the Adirondacks, framing turned wolves into a local control issue. In Wisconsin, with so few facts about chronic wasting disease (CWD), the story became one of fear and uncertainty. In both cases attitudes changed in the "wrong" direction, as viewed by conservation biologists and wildlife managers. People had little information about, and no direct experience with, wolves or CWD. The media took these attitude objects and linked them to much stronger attitudes. Even paid advertising can backfire, as when Exxon Minerals tried to get Wisconsinites to like the mine or when ANEC tried to get Nevadans to favor a nuclear repository.

We have faith in attitudes as solutions to environmental problems because we think behaviors are perfect reflections of attitudes. They aren't. Context, setting, and norms—all outside the individual—have much more influence on what we do. Attitudes are important, of course, but we often overrate their importance by ignoring context, much as Leopold did when trying to figure out why he cut birch on his own land. Multiple attitudes surround any act, so Professor Temple and millions of others can have positive attitudes toward wolves but still not buy a wolf license plate. We showed that attitudes are a necessary condition for behaviors: People with negative attitudes toward wolves don't buy plates, just as people with negative attitudes toward hunting don't hunt. The correlations are low because many people who never hunt have positive attitudes toward hunting. Positive attitudes, *even though they don't influence actions of individuals,* are important, because they're necessary for winning public support for structural fixes, like offering wolf license plates in the first place. Although only a small percentage of Wisconsinites buy them, they provide $500,000 to support endangered resources. From the hunters' view, broad, positive attitudes toward hunting among nonhunters are important to maintain hunting.

Norms are the heavy hitters for changing environmental behavior. Unlike attitudes, norms can be seen, and unlike attitudes, they have much to do with behavior. Norms grow from social environments and actions of others. Formal and informal sanctions outside the individual are part of the action context. Norms must be focused (again, usually by the context) before they work. They can be deactivated by context, and by responsibility and consequence denial. They sometimes fail, but not often. Norms exist at the individual level in what's called a "personal norm," but unlike more general attitudes, norms imply specific behaviors and come with internal sanctions if you comply or disobey. The problem with norms is that, like attitudes, we cannot change them at will. They do change, as we saw with Leopold's smoking and fish-killing, but such changes are slow.

Then we reach the land ethic, Leopold's solution to environmental problems. To a social psychologist, the land ethic resembles a value: It's big, powerful and the base of many attitudes. Because of its size and strength I compare it to a horse. However, Leopold wants it to function like a norm, guiding specific actions. That's where he asks the horse to fly, but horses, though useful and powerful, do not fly. Change is the bigger problem. If changing attitudes and norms is a slow, uncertain process, asking for value change is dreaming.

Although attitudes are complex, and much is written about them, I believe four principles are "true forward, true backward, true even before breakfast," as Leopold would say.[1]

The Direct-Experience Principle: Attitudes based on direct experience are stronger, more central, harder to change, and more tied to our behavior. Conversely, attitudes not based on direct experience are easier to change but likely have little impact on what we do. If we can give people direct experience, their attitudes will likely change and the changes will likely persist.

The Identity Principle: Attitudes tied to our identities are hard to change because changing them would require major restructuring of our belief system. Such attitudes also tend to have strong emotional components that make them further resistant to change. We should not waste time trying to change identity based attitudes.

The Consistency Principle: Attitudes *tend* to be consistent. The key word is *tend*. All attitudes have inconsistency, some more than others. That's why the theory of cognitive dissonance is so attractive. You can always point to some kind of attitude inconsistency to explain why people do or don't do something. That's why I don't find this theory helpful. Because inconsistent information can be uncomfortable—by creating dissonance—people often invent ways to avoid it. The lesson of the consistency principle is that attitudes are not like gears. You cannot try to change one belief and, under normal conditions, hope other parts of the attitude follow in lock-step.

The Specificity Principle: We have general attitudes about broad objects like the environment, specific attitudes toward taking public transit, and even more specific attitudes about driving in central Stockholm. More specific attitudes are better predictors of behaviors, because behaviors are specific. There is some, but more limited, evidence that general attitudes affect broad spectrums of behaviors. We cannot count on those with strong environmental attitudes to engage in specific pro-environmental behaviors, but they're more likely to engage in at least some.

The Three Fixes Redux

We try to fix environmental problems by changing the environment directly (the technological fix), relying on people to change themselves in response to information (the cognitive fix), or changing human behavior by changing the context (the structural fix). Although this notion of technological, cognitive, and structural fixes helps us understand how we approach environmental problems, real solutions are more complex and often require all three fixes simultaneously. Attitudes do not go away just because we choose a technological or structural fix. Effective structural and technological fixes designed with attitudes take advantage of social contexts rather than relying on attitude change to produce new behaviors.

Hood River was a successful technological and structural fix because it was designed with attitudes. It saved energy by retrofitting houses with insulation. The technological fix saved energy and required no changes in attitudes or behavior. In fact, people reduced technology's effect by using less wood and turning up their thermostats after installing insulation. The structural fix was making the retrofit free rather than trying to persuade people to buy and install insulation on their own (the cognitive fix). However, this program worked by imbedding it in the community (signs, local office, and community leader support), conducting a preproject community assessment, and administering attitude surveys throughout the project. The team's responsiveness to new attitudes that arose from direct experience also aided its success. Rather than trying to change attitudes, they adjusted the project to fit these attitudes.

How can you replicate this in your neighborhood? It's not easy. It took an outside interest group (Natural Resources Defense Council) pushing, the legal demand (from Congress) to estimate the effect of a "Conservation Power Plant," and huge amounts of outside money. But most important, I believe, was the density of social science expertise. Four PhDs in sociology—three working for the utility and one as a consultant—were on location doing attitude studies. Never have I seen such depth of social science talent focused in one project to balance the engineering and natural-science expertise. The Stockholm Crowding Tax also designed with attitudes, thanks to social science depth: transportation economists, social psychologists, and others. For fixes to succeed, we need more social science involvement in projects, start to finish.

How do we weave fixes together to solve environmental problems? How do we craft effective structural fixes? It's not easy, and we must learn from our mistakes. For example, as Bo and I relaxed on our raft late that day after surviving the big Grand Canyon rapids mentioned at the beginning of this chapter, he reminded me why we hit the big hole in House Rock rapids: I pulled on the oar when I should have pushed. Let's look at three other cases and see what we can learn.

Use Enough (Social) Science: The Lake Mendota Project

A giant technological fix to clean Madison's Lake Mendota was threatened because we knew lots more scientifically about planktivores than people. Lake Mendota, a 10,000-acre lake in Wisconsin's capital, has suffered severe algae problems for decades. As the city grew and paved more land, and farming practices in the watershed intensified, the lake's fertility increased and turned its water green each summer. Efforts to curb Madison's growth and to control farmers' spreading of manure and fertilizer didn't work, so the Wisconsin Department of Natural Resources (DNR) and university scientists turned to nature.

It turns out Lake Mendota has water fleas (a zooplankton called *Daphnia*) that eat algae. The idea was to increase the number of water fleas by decreasing the number of small fish that eat them. How? By dumping in lots of big fish to eat lots of little fish. The strange thing about the proposal, at least in retrospect, is that, in considering predation, scientists forgot the top predator: Wisconsin anglers.

Anglers threatened the experiment in two ways. First, they and some DNR fish managers opposed taking walleyes and northern pike from far off hatcheries and putting them into Lake Mendota rather than northern lakes.[2] The initial stocking, therefore, was lower than it would have been if the scientists had complete control. Second, and even worse, the human predators changed their behavior, increasing their own numbers more than 600%. They caught lots of the fish that were supposed to reduce zooplankton predators.[3]

Putting a couple of million walleye and northern pike into Lake Mendota got lots of media attention, way more than that single *Outdoor Life* article that doubled angling pressure at the Escanaba lakes (see chapter 5). Plus, Madison is home to many anglers. They, and others from Milwaukee to Chicago, came by the thousands. Scientists in UW-Madison's Limnology Laboratory watched daily as these top predators reduced the key independent variable in this grand experiment. Ice fishermen even walked into the lab to use the phone (these were the days before cellular phones) to order pizzas, which, I suppose, was fitting in a food-web management study. Top predators must eat too, and kind-hearted scientists helped feed them, even to their research's peril.[4]

Maybe the anglers, their attitudes, social networks, and behaviors should have been studied before designing the experiment. Maybe anglers should have been monitored throughout the project, just as fish, algae, zooplankton, and water quality were monitored for decades. Unfortunately, although UW-Madison and the Wisconsin DNR had enormous scientific expertise about the lake's many variables, they had no cadre of social scientists studying anglers and their habits to the degree necessary to understand, predict, and learn from human behavior as part of the experiment.[5]

It would be incorrect to say ignoring the anglers destroyed the experiment, but it seriously crimped an already complex analysis.[6] It would have been far better to unleash higher densities of walleyes and northerns. Steve Carpenter observed later that, despite the surprising increase in anglers, "the magnitude of the water flea effect . . . has been large and consistent since 1987. Our recent report on the past thirty-three years of water quality . . . shows that there are no real trends in phosphorus. . . . The failure to decrease phosphorus is largely due to failure to change farmer behavior."[7] The reason Lake Mendota still turns green each summer is that, although the biomanipulation worked, the big problem lies in less well-studied human behavior beyond the lakeshore.[8]

Missed Structural Fix at Delavan Lake

Steve Carpenter also wondered about structural fixes. "The successful structural fixes seem to emerge from a deep understanding of how the social-ecological system works. Does it follow that a deep interdisciplinary social-ecological systems analysis will always reveal a good structural fix? I am not sure that a fix is guaranteed. There seems to be an intuitive leap, or flash of genius, or luck involved in the success stories. And the failures are not (always) the result of blundering by dummies: well-thought-out plans can fail."[9]

Carpenter might be right. I missed a structural fix, but not because of the missing "flash of genius." No, much like the Lake Mendota case, I missed for lack of social science. As faculty adviser for the Water Resource Management masters program, I directed 16 environmental students writing a plan to restore another algae-choked lake in southern Wisconsin, Delavan Lake.[10] As you can assume, I insisted on a balance of social science, but balance was difficult because only a couple of students had undergrad degrees outside the natural sciences. To provide some relevant expertise, we added an economics professor to our staff and had the students survey lakeshore owners and anglers. These data showed cleaner water was more valuable, and people would willingly pay as much as $180 annually for clean water and fish.

The good news is that our plan, implemented by the community and Wisconsin DNR, worked. They sealed off phosphorus in the sediments by dumping many truckloads of alum. Then, they diverted the stream bringing in dirty water at the north end of the lake. Next, they poisoned carp and rough fish, and replaced them by stocking walleyes and northern pike. These are all technological fixes consistent with public attitudes. The lake cleared up in a few years, the fish grew, and fishermen came. Because lakeshore owners could once again swim, boat, and fish in a clean lake, property values soared. Everybody won. Or at least they seemed to.

Though our team was clever, we did not consider sustainability. Would Delavan Lake stay clean forever? No. Fast forward 20 years. Its water quality declined and it needed further rehabilitation. However, that costs money, and no one was paying. People who sold their much more valuable houses during the clean-water years walked away with the profits of the initial lake rehabilitation. They put no money in a kitty to keep the lake clean. The hundreds of lakeshore property owners, who would have paid $80 to $160 annually for improved water quality, never had to pay. Neither did the thousands of anglers attracted to the lake pay their share. We missed obvious structural fixes: user fees on anglers and a tax on property appreciation devoted to a water-quality fund. Maybe it could have been paid when selling a house or through annual taxes on lakeshore property. Such taxes could have built an endowment to keep the lake clean.

I offer two excuses. First, I'm an attitude mechanic, not a policy analyst. If you want to know about attitudes, I'm your man, but building structural fixes requires broader expertise than I (and I think most other social psycholgists) possess. Attitudes are *not* everything. Successful structural fixes involve expertise from those who study governance in natural resource systems. Social psychology, even resource economics, is not enough. Second, our team lacked such expertise. The students worked long and hard on details of rerouting the stream, poisoning the lake, and determining the number and kinds of fish to stock. This fit their backgrounds, interests, and career aspirations, but our crew had no aspiring social engineers to explore how to develop sustainable structural fixes to sustain our success.

Thinking Beyond the Rim: Motors in the Grand Canyon

To end this chapter and book, let's return to the Grand Canyon. The big issue after the Glen Canyon Dam evened out flows and made that segment of the Colorado River "runable" was whether to allow motor- and oar-powered float trips. Park managers saw no clear negative biological or safety differences in these recreational options, so they turned to social psychologists. Attitude data further suggested the trip type made no difference because visitors on motorized trips and oar-powered trips were equally satisfied.[11]

On the other hand, anyone who has run the river in a boat with oars versus a boat with a motor sees huge differences. But here's the rub: The people surveyed had made only one trip. Without direct experience with both types of trips, how could they tell? Bo Shelby was doing research on river visitors at the time, and set up an experiment to give them direct experience with both trips. Visitors were randomly assigned to oar-powered and motor-powered trips.[12] Several days later, they switched from oars to motors or vice versa. This gave a group of people direct experience with both types of propulsion.

As they left the river, he asked which trip they preferred. The data couldn't have been clearer: Eighty-seven percent picked oars and four percent chose motors. Seventy-nine percent said they would recommend oars to a friend and six percent said they would recommend motors. Nine of ten said oars gave a better experience of the canyon. They described the motor-powered segment as "loud," "noisy," "big," and "crowded." In contrast, the oar-powered segment was described as "quiet," "relaxing," "natural," and "friendly."[13]

Thirty-five years later, when sitting on our raft in the Grand Canyon and reminiscing on the day's run and past research, we heard a distant motor. Before long, a 32-foot raft driven by a 30-horsepower motor roared past, water flying and 15 passengers waving greetings. In a few minutes they were gone. Peace returned to the canyon. We heard birds singing, and the gasoline fumes soon faded. How could the National Park Service (NPS) still allow motors in the Grand Canyon's wilderness? How could they ignore Shelby's compelling attitude data? Oar-powered trips are quiet and close to nature, just what management objectives for the Inner Canyon are supposed to be.

One explanation for science failing to influence policy is that few managers read studies and even fewer believe them (especially social science).

However, rather than simply handing out Shelby's tables, the planning team's leader persuaded the brass to take a "best of both" trip. Among the participants was NPS Director Bill Whalen, who came from Washington with his assistant and a staff member from the Secretary of the Interior's office. Also present were Merle Stitt, superintendent of the Grand Canyon National Park, and Howard Chapman, the NPS's legendary regional director. Steve Martin, who later became the Grand Canyon National Park's superintendent, was a ranger on this trip.

Once this group experienced both trips, they were further committed to removing motors from the Grand Canyon. Marv Jensen, then Inner Canyon manager, said the reasons for their "very decided preference and greater enjoyment on the oar-powered segment of the trip were fully analogous with the reasons given in the 1975 Shelby study."[14]

Armed with the results of Shelby's research, the enthusiastic endorsement of the planning team, and concurrence at the highest levels of NPS management, the Inner Canyon Management Plan proposed phasing out motorized trips. A year later, however, a Congressional rider was attached to a Department of Interior appropriations bill. It stated, "If the River Management Plan with the motorized rafting phase-out (was) implemented, funding for river management at GRCA would be stripped from the budget."[15] A powerful senator and the perceived interests of small Utah communities trumped science and the best judgment of National Park managers.

Rather than blaming politics for this setback, we must consider the science. I was the primary designer of NPS visitor studies to establish social carrying capacities. But like the scientists at Lake Mendota, where all the science was in the lake, all the science I recommended was in the canyon. There's more to managing a river than studying the attitudes, behaviors, and norms of its visitors. We should have worked beyond the canyon's rim to better understand the small raft-rental industry. How would the rules affect them? What alternatives did they have? Were there ways they might have accommodated the phase-out that would have made their jobs easier and made them more money, while also helping the communities and giving visitors better experiences? No such research was recommended. I pulled the oar when I should have pushed, thus missing a chance for a structural fix.

Conclusion

In each of these cases we missed crafting technological and structural fixes that worked, not only because we didn't understand the attitudes of those involved, but also because we lacked the social science resources to fully illuminate the human dimensions of fishing, farming, the tourism industry, and lake-front-property ownership. The balance of science is out of whack. As Bill Freuden-burg, the scholar to whom this book is dedicated, observed:

> Forty years ago, when a new trend called 'environmentalism' swept the country and much of the planet, respected professors were pretty sure they knew what needed to be done. In a nutshell, their ideas involved careful research on every single species on the planet except one—the one that was actually at the root of almost everything they called an 'environmental' problem. For that one species, they said that, instead, what we needed to do was "educate the public."[16]

That's the shame of it. Because we relegate the human dimension to "an education problem" rather than an interesting scientific question, we know far more scientifically about zooplankton in Lake Mendota than about human's use of that lake. Leopold (quoted in the frontispiece of this book) foresaw what he called "the inevitable fusion" of those who study the human community with those who study the plant and animal community as something that will "constitute the outstanding advance of this century."

Leopold penned those words late one night in a Berlin hotel room. The year was 1935. I hope—and I expect his spirit hopes—that we might achieve this goal before the end of the 21st century. We need more water, better boats, and more social scientists pulling on the oars. And we must, above all, avoid the keeper hole.

Acknowledgments

I'M ALWAYS SURPRISED when books begin with acknowledgments. Why distract your poor readers before they even read the book? Colleagues and others who think they deserve thanks will find this section, even at the back of the book. Readers ought to get on with it.

Now that you have finished, here are the people to whom I am (and you should be) grateful. If you didn't like the book, it's all my fault. Read no further.

This book is indebted to Bill Freudenburg, Rich Bishop, and Elizabeth Thomson.

It's dedicated to the memory of William R. Freudenburg, my friend and colleague. While at the University of Wisconsin-Madison, where we taught together for 15 years, and later as Dehlsen Professor of Environmental Studies at the University of California-Santa Barbara, Bill pushed me to first start and then complete this project. In his final letter of support, written from his hospital bed, he argued that the assumption that "all we need to do to solve environmental problems" is "the most dangerous of all assumptions in environmental management." Bill thought this diverted students and scientists from the broader social causes of, and solutions to, environmental problems.

Economist Rich Bishop, co-conspirator on some of this research, critiqued my arguments over the years during trips between Madison and northern Wisconsin's lakes and forests. Most important—after watching me flailing on this manuscript more than a decade—he put me on a writing schedule that worked. At his suggestion, I wrote every weekday morning for over two years, treating Rich as my "boss" and sending him each completed chapter.

Elizabeth Thomson, Chaired Professor of Demography at Stockholm University, took me on as a project some 25 years ago and stuck with it. In this part of our relationship, I must thank her for reading and marking up the "in progress" drafts of each chapter again, and again, and again. When the book's review draft was finally done, she read it on and off for a couple of weeks and then blasted out a 5,000-word review in one afternoon. During the years this book languished as a partially written manuscript, she warned that if I died, she and Rich Stedman would NOT finish it. Okay, you guys are finally off the hook.

My second debt is to the University of Chicago and University of Wisconsin-Madison. I consider this book my take-home final for Conservation of Natural Resources, taught at Chicago by geographer Gilbert White. As a high school student, I was recruited to Chicago by the Small School Talent Search Program. There, in addition to White, I was privileged to study with social psychologists Fred Strodtbeck, Milton Rosenberg, and Richard Flacks. They sowed the seeds.

At the University of Wisconsin-Madison I earned my degrees in sociology as Shalom Schwartz's first PhD student. After a brief stay at the University of Colorado-Boulder, I returned to Madison and spent the rest of my career in the Department of Rural Sociology (now the Department of Community and Environmental Sociology). The Agricultural Experiment Station supported some of the research discussed here, and my research appointment allowed me to take risks unavailable to other scholars. I was blessed with incredible students and supportive colleagues, many of whom I acknowledge in these pages.

At UW-Madison, anything environmental is touched by Bill Cronon. Bill read an early précis in 1994 and urged me to continue and expand Leopold as a leitmotif. His faculty environmental seminar was a source of ideas and inspiration and the link with Oxford University Press was made with Bill's assistance.

The writing began during my 1995–1996 sabbatical to Sweden and, therefore, owes much to *Svenska Jägarförbundet*, Mid-Sweden University, Tomas Willebrand, and Lars Emmelin. It was later supported by colleagues Kjell Danell and Göran Ericsson in the Department of Wildlife, Fish and Environmental Studies, Faculty of Forestry, at the Swedish University of Agricultural Sciences.

I also thank Bill Freudenburg, Richard Stedman, and Walt Kuentzel for beta-testing some early chapters with their students in "Critical Thinking About Human-Environment Problems and Solutions" (University of California-Santa Barbara), "Society and Natural Resources" (Cornell University), and "Human Behavior and Environmental Management" (University of Vermont). Thanks also to my students at the Swedish University of Agricultural Sciences in Umeå, Sweden, who helped sharpen these ideas over the years.

Besides those noted earlier or in the text, I thank the following who read all or part of the many drafts: Rich Stedman, Walt Kuentzel, Jim Tantillo, Curt Meine, Steve Carpenter, Sharon Dunwoody, Paul Stern, Ken Keating, and those stalwarts of science, Anonymous Reviewer 1 and Anonymous Reviewer 2, who turned this manuscript around in barely a month.

I further thank many others for providing information, answering questions, and otherwise guiding my thinking, particularly Riley Dunlap, an environmental sociologist and my sometime intellectual sparring partner. Riley provided articles, reading lists, comments, reflections, and encouragement. Most impressive was the day he searched files in his garage to find an unpublished paper I gave at the AAAS in 1975. He preserved this paper more than 35 years, hauling it from Pullman, Washington to Turku, Finland; Orlando, Florida; and finally, Stillwater, Oklahoma. He scanned it and sent a PDF to me in Stockholm. That manuscript, complete with Riley's notes, is on my Web site.

Others who have given generously of their time include Øystein Aas, Jim Addis, Duane Alwin, Robert Arlinghaus, Frank Bernheisel, Steve Born, Connie Burton, Ralph Cavanagh, Betty Chewning, Robert Cialdini, Jay Coggins, John DeLamater, Mark Duda, Jonas Eliasson, Alan Fish, Cynthia B. Flynn, Buddy Huffaker, Marv Jensen, Karyl Kinsey, Bob Krumenaker, Ruth Love, Loren Lutzenhiser, John Magnuson, John Miroslaw, Margaret Mooney, Kirby Neumann-Rea, Steve Newman, Fiona O'Brien, Pallavi Patwardhan, H. Gil Peach, Harry Peterson, Rolf Peterson, Bill Pielsticker, David Policansky, Bill Provencher, Ann Saxby, Steve Schmelzer, Daniel Schuller, Shalom Schwartz, Bo Shelby, Linda Steg, Dan Syrek, the University of Wisconsin-Madison Applied Population Laboratory, Faramarz Vakili, Kent Van Liere, Jerry Vaske, Theresa Wantz, Keith Warnke, Richelle Winkler, Doug Whittaker, and Adrian Wydeven.

Finally, there are those who make books happen: my assistant Chelsea Schelly, who saved me months of work by fixing every footnote and finding every reference; Jean Dailey, writing specialist at West Virginia University; Betsy Thorp, my literary consultant; and Patrick Durkin, who did the final editing. Any remaining errors are, of course, Pat's fault.

Niko Pfund at Oxford was an early supporter of this project and Becky Clark helped at the end stages. Finally, special thanks to my editor, James Cook. This manuscript was much improved by his gentle touch and good advice.

Tom Heberlein
Stockholm
April 20, 2012

Notes

CHAPTER 1

1. Graeme Wood, "Re-Engineering the Earth," *The Atlantic* July/August 2009, http://www.theatlantic.com/magazine/archive/2009/07/re-engineering-the-earth/7552/, accessed May 24, 2011.

2. David Wilma, "U.S.S. *Lexington* Provides Electricity to Tacoma Beginning about December 17, 1929," HistoryLink.org. The Free Online Encyclopedia of Washington State History. January 24, 2003C:\Users\Tom\AppData\Local\Temp\ZGTemp\<a href=http://www.historylink.org/index.cfm?DisplayPage=output.cfm&;File_Id=5113, accessed May 24, 2011.

3. Nine billion dollars was spent between 1935 and 1960, which would inflate to $44 billion spent between 1985 and 2010. According to the Army Corps of Engineers, 19,562 dams were completed in the United States between 1930 and 1959. http://geo.usace.army.mil/pgis/f?p=397:5:684470416924157:NO, accessed May 30, 2011.

4. Task Force on Federal Flood Control Policy, *A Unified National Program for Managing Flood Losses*, Report No. 67–663 (Washington, D.C.: U.S. Government Printing Office, 1966); Howard L. Cook and Gilbert F. White, "Making Wise Use of Flood Plains," *United States Papers for United Nations Conference in Science and Technology. Vol. 2* (Washington, D.C.: U.S. Government Printing Office, 1963); Gilbert F. White, "Optimal Flood Damage Management: Retrospect and Prospect," in *Water Research*, Ed. Allen V. Kneese and Stephen C. Smith (Baltimore: The Johns Hopkins Press, 1966), 251–69.

5. Gilbert F. White et al., *Changes in Urban Occupance of Flood Plains in the United States* (Chicago: University of Chicago Department of Geography Research Papers No. 57, 1958).

6. Thomas A. Heberlein, "The Three Fixes: Technological, Cognitive and Structural," in *Water and Community Development: Social and Economic Perspectives*, eds. Donald Field, James C. Barren, and Burl F. Long (Ann Arbor, MI: Ann Arbor Science Publishers, 1974), 279–96. Social psychologists have recently been calling this the Knowledge Deficit Model. See P. Wesley Schultz, "Knowledge, Information and Household Recycling Examining the Knowledge-Deficit Model of Behavior Change," in *New Tools for Environmental Protection: Education, Information, and Voluntary Measures*, eds. Thomas Dietz and Paul C. Stern (Washington, D.C.: National Academy Press, 2002), 67–82.

7. Wolf Roder, "Attitudes and Knowledge in the Topeka Flood Planner," in *Papers on Flood Problems*, ed. Gilbert F. White (Chicago: Department of Geography Research Paper No. 70, 1961), 62–83.

8. Ibid, 78–79.

9. White, G. F., "Optimal Flood Damage Management," 261.

10. Aldo Leopold, *A Sand County Almanac* (New York: Oxford University Press, 1949), available in Japanese, Czech, German, Italian, Spanish, French, Russian, Portuguese, Korean, Polish, and Chinese (at least 2 different dialects).

11. See, for example, Susan L. Flader, *Thinking Like A Mountain: Aldo Leopold and the Evolution of an Ecological Attitude Toward Deer, Wolves and Forests* (Columbia, MO: University of Missouri Press, 1974); J. Baird Callicott, ed., *Companion to A Sand County Almanac* (Madison, WI: University of Wisconsin Press, 1987); Curt Meine, *Aldo Leopold: His Life and Work* (Madison, WI: University of Wisconsin Press, 1988); Richard L. Knight and Suzanne Riedel, *Aldo Leopold and the Ecological Conscience* (New York: Oxford University Press, 2002).

CHAPTER 2

1. This discussion is based on Thomas A. Heberlein, "Environmental Attitudes," *Zeitschrift fur Umweltpolitik (Journal of Environmental Policy)* 2 (1981): 241–70.

2. Aldo Leopold, *A Sand County Almanac* (New York, Oxford University Press, 1949), 68–69.

3. Milton Rokeach, *The Nature of Human Values* (New York: John Wiley, 1973). More recent and complex statistical work on values has been done by Shalom H. Schwartz. See Shalom H. Schwartz, "Are There Universal Aspects in the Structure and Contents of Human Values?" *Journal of Social Issues* 50/4 (1994): 19–45. But "Most of Rokeach's (1973) tenets are accepted by Schwartz's (1994) model of values," according to John DeLamater. See John DeLamater, Ed., *Handbook of Social Psychology* (New York: Kluwer-Plenum, 2004), 287. Accordingly, I will stick with Rokeach's labels because they match Leopold's words precisely. For those interested in reading more about environmental values, see Thomas

Dietz, Amy Fitzgerald, and Rachael Shwom, "Environmental Values," *Annual Review of Environment and Resources* 30 (2005): 335–72.

4. Robert P. Abelson and Milton J. Rosenberg, "Symbolic Psycho-Logic: A Model of Attitudinal Cognition," *Behavioral Science* 3/1 (1958): 1–13.

5. Daryl J. Bem, *Beliefs, Attitudes, and Human Affairs* (Belmont, CA: Brooks/Cole, 1970).

6. Leopold, *A Sand County Almanac*, 70.

7. Ibid., 69.

8. Ibid., 69.

9. This discussion is based on Stephen R. Kellert, *Public Attitudes and Beliefs about the Wolf and Its Restoration in Michigan* (Madison, WI: HBRS, 1990). For a more accessible version, see Stephen Kellert, "Public Views on Wolf Restoration in Michigan," *Transactions of the 56th North American Wildlife and Natural Resources Conference* (1991): 152–61.

10. Thomas A. Lewis, "Cloaked in a Wise Disguise," *National Wildlife* October/November (1992): 4–9; see also Alistair J. Bath, "The Public and Wolf Reintroduction in Yellowstone National Park," *Society & Natural Resources* 2/1 (1989): 297–306; Matthew A. Wilson and Thomas A. Heberlein, "The Wolf, the Tourist, and the Recreational Context: New Opportunity or Uncommon Circumstance?" *Human Dimensions of Wildlife* 1/4 (1996): 38–53; Matthew A. Wilson, "The Wolf in Yellowstone: Science, Symbol, or Politics? Deconstructing the Conflict Between Environmentalism and Wise Use," *Society & Natural Resources* 10/5 (1997): 453–68. Wolves elicit strong emotional responses not only in America, but also around the globe. For example, the center-right government in Sweden received more letters about the country's 2010 wolf hunt than any other issue during its first four years in power.

11. See L. David Mech, *The Wolf: The Ecology and Behavior of an Endangered Species* (Minneapolis, MN: University of Minnesota Press, 1981); Bruce Hampton, *The Great American Wolf* (New York: Henry Holt, 1997), 184.

12. Alan D. Bright and Michael J. Manfredo, "A Conceptual Model of Attitudes Toward Natural Resource Issues: A Case Study of Wolf Reintroduction," *Human Dimensions of Wildlife* 1/1 (1996): 1–21.

13. John Andrew Zuccotti, "A Native Returns: The Endangered Species Act and Wolf Reintroduction to the Northern Rocky Mountains," *Columbia Journal of Environmental Law* 20 (1995): 329–60; cited in Bright and Manfredo, 1996.

14. Stephen Kellert, "The Public and the Timber Wolf in Minnesota," *Transactions of the 51st North American Wildlife and Natural Resources Conference* (1986): 152–61; Christopher K. Williams, Göran Ericsson, and Thomas A. Heberlein, "A Quantitative Summary of Attitudes Toward Wolves and their Reintroduction (1972–2000)," *Wildlife Society Bulletin* 30/2 (2002): 575–84; Wisconsin Department of Natural Resources unpublished data; See also Lisa Naughton-Treves, Rebecca Grossberg, and Adrian Treves, "Paying for Tolerance: Rural Citizens' Attitudes Toward Wolf Depredation and Compensation," *Conservation Biology* 17/6 (2003): 1500–511.

15. Williams, Ericsson, and Heberlein, "A Quantitative Summary," 2002.

16. For those interested in more on dissonance theory, see E. Harmon-Jones and J. Mills, eds., *Cognitive Dissonance: Progress on a Pivotal Theory in Social Psychology* (Washington, D.C.: American Psychological Association, 1999), and the very readable Joel M. Cooper, *Cognitive Dissonance: 50 Years of a Classic Theory* (London: Sage Publications, 2007).

17. Thomas A. Heberlein et al., "Rethinking the Scope Test as a Criterion for Validity in Contingent Valuation," *Journal of Environmental Economics and Management* 50/1 (2005): 1–22.

18. Our review of all published attitude studies on wolves between 1972 and 2000 showed that in the nine studies that included hunters, five showed that being a hunter was positively associated with support for wolves, three showed the opposite, and one had no significant relationship. See Williams, Ericsson, and Heberlein, "A Quantitative Summary," 2002.

19. Hunters and rural people who lived in wolf areas were, now that wolves are back, less positive than other groups. However, these people knew more about wolves because they lived close to them. On the positive side for education, within any group (hunters, rural people, and city people), those with more knowledge were more positive toward wolves. See Göran Ericsson and Thomas A Heberlein, "Attitudes of Hunters, Locals and the General Public in Sweden Now That the Wolves Are Back," *Biological Conservation* 111/2 (2003): 149–59. I am not arguing against environmental education or education in general. Indeed, our meta-analysis showed that 20 studies found a positive relationship between years of education and attitudes toward wolves.

20. Russel H. Fazio, "On the Power and Functionality of Attitudes: The Role of Attitude Accessibility," in *Attitude Structure and Function*, eds. A. R. Pratkanis, S. J. Breckler, and S. G. Greenwald (Hillsdale, NJ: Earlbaum, 1988), 153–79.

21. This is true not only of Michigan farmers, but also of farmers in Minnesota and ranchers in Wyoming and Idaho. See Stephen Kellert, *The Value of Life: Biological Diversity and Society* (Washington, D.C.: Island Press, 1997).

22. Jon A. Krosnick and Robert P. Abelson, "The Case for Measuring Attitude Strength in Surveys," in *Questions about Questions: Inquiries into the Cognitive Bases of Surveys*, ed. J. Tanur (New York: Russell Sage, 1992), 177–203; Richard E. Petty and Jon A. Krosnick, *Attitude Strength: Antecedents and Consequences* (Mahwah, NJ: Erlbaum, 1995).

23. Leopold, *A Sand County Almanac*, 69.

24. J. C. Farman, B. G. Gardiner, and J. D. Shanklin, "Large Losses of Total Ozone in Antarctica Reveal Seasonal Clox/Nox Interaction," *Nature* 315/6016 (1985): 207–10.

25. John J. Magnuson et al., "Historical Trends in Lake and River Ice Cover in the Northern Hemisphere," *Science* 289/5485 (2000): 1743–46.

26. Martin Fishbein and Icek Ajzen, "Attitudes and Opinions," *Annual Review of Psychology* 23 (1972): 487–544. Fishbein and Ajzen "found 500 different operational definitions of attitudes and that in 70 percent of the 200 studies in which

attitudes was defined in more than one way, different results were obtained depending on which definition was used." From William J. McGuire, "Attitudes and Attitude Change," in *Handbook of Social Psychology* 3rd ed., eds. Gardner Lindzey and Elliot Aronson (New York: Random House, 1985), 238–39. The reader must remember that the research on attitudes is vast. "Between 1995 and 2010 alone, more than 13,000 articles on the topic of attitudes have appeared." From Mahzarin Banaji and Larisa Heiphetz, "Attitudes," in *Handbook of Social Psychology* 5th ed., eds. Susan Fiske, Daniel Gilbert, and Gardner Lindzey (Hoboken, NJ: Wiley, 2011), 353–427.

CHAPTER 3

1. Aldo Leopold, *A Sand County Almanac* (New York, Oxford University Press, 1949), 130. For a long time, no evidence could be found that this event actually occurred. Even though Leopold kept a journal and wrote many letters, no mention of the incident was found in any letter, leading some to suggest the event was apocryphal. Finally, the key letter describing the event was found and reported in the introduction to the 2010 edition of Leopold's biography. See Curt D. Meine, *Aldo Leopold: His Life and Work* (Madison, WI: University of Wisconsin Press, 2010), xxxi. Meine also cites a 1919 article in which Leopold reports shooting "three big lobo wolves" (Ibid., footnote 10, 543). So, Leopold clearly and repeatedly attempted to kill wolves during at least a 10-year period.

2. The first quote is from a resolution passed by the New Mexico Game Protection Association in 1916 (Meine, 1988, 154). Leopold was the one of the founders, secretary, and self-described "committee of one in charge of educational and publicity work" (153). He no doubt helped write and support the resolution. It was reprinted in *The Pine Cone*, which he edited. As Meine notes, at this time Leopold "was fired up enough . . . to call for total eradication of predators" (155). The second quote is from a report that Leopold presented at a national scientific meeting in New York in 1919 (181).

3. Aldo Leopold, *A Sand County Almanac*, 130.

4. Göran Ericsson and Thomas A. Heberlein, "Attitudes of Hunters, Locals and the General Public in Sweden Now That the Wolves are Back," *Biological Conservation* 111/2 (2003): 149–59.

5. Daryl J. Bem, *Beliefs, Attitudes, and Human Affairs* (Belmont, CA: Brooks/Cole, 1970).

6. For a more detailed discussion of the original Bennington study, see Theodore Mead Newcomb, *Personality and Social Change* (New York: Dryden, 1943).

7. Carl Bernstein, *A Woman in Charge: The Life of Hillary Rodham Clinton* (New York: Alfred A. Knopf, 2007).

8. Theodore Mead Newcomb et al., *Persistence and Change: Bennington College and Its Students after 25 Years* (New York: Wiley, 1967), 48. This measure compares

behavioral reports in the national sample with attitude (preference) in the survey data, which could account for some of the difference. Nevertheless, a 30-point spread remains impressive.

9. Ibid., 49.

10. Newcomb et al. write, "[T]he women who had not changed their political attitudes since college had, to a greater extent, moved into a social environment which supported their existing political view points" (Ibid., 65). See also Duane F. Alwin, Ronald L. Cohen, and Theodore M. Newcomb, *Political Attitudes Over the Life Span: The Bennington Women after Fifty Years* (Madison, WI: University of Wisconsin Press, 1991), Chapter 9.

11. Maxwell E. McCombs and Donald L. Shaw, "The Agenda-Setting Function of Mass Media," *Public Opinion Quarterly* 36/2 (1972): 176–87.

12. Bernard Cecil Cohen, *The Press and Foreign Policy* (Princeton, NJ: Princeton University Press, 1963), 13.

13. Christopher K. Williams, Göran Ericsson, and Thomas A. Heberlein. "A Quantitative Summary of Attitudes toward Wolves and Their Reintroduction (1972–2000)," *Wildlife Society Bulletin* 30/2 (2002): 575–84.

14. Mark Damian Duda, Steven J. Bissell, and Kira C. Young, *Wildlife and the American Mind: Public Opinion on and Attitudes toward Fish and Wildlife Management* (Harrisonburg, VA: Responsive Management, 1998).

15. Virginia A. Sharpe, Bryan G. Norton, and Strachan Donnelley, *Wolves and Human Communities: Biology, Politics, and Ethics* (Washington, D.C.: Island Press, 2001).

16. Jody W. Enck and Tommy L. Brown, "New Yorkers' Attitudes toward Restoring Wolves to the Adirondack Park," *Wildlife Society Bulletin* 30/3 (2002): 16–28.

17. Thomas A. Heberlein and Bruce Laybourne, "The Wisconsin Deer Hunter: Social Characteristics, Attitudes, and Preferences for Proposed Hunting Season Changes," Working Paper 10 (Madison, WI: University of Wisconsin Center for Resources Policy Studies and Programs, 1978).

18. Thomas A. Heberlein, "Foreword" in *Legendary Deer Camps*, by Rob Wegner (Iola, WI: Krause Publications, 2001), 6–7. For a broader discussion of hunting camps and their culture, see Marc Boglioli, *A Matter of Life and Death: Hunting in Contemporary Vermont* (Amherst, MA: University of Massachusetts Press, 2009).

19. Citations for these quotes and an extended analysis of the response to CWD in Wisconsin can be found in Thomas A. Heberlein, "Fire in the Sistine Chapel: How Wisconsin Residents Responded to Chronic Wasting Disease," *Human Dimensions of Wildlife* 9/3 (2004): 165–79.

20. Ron Seely, "Scientists are Alarmed by Chronic Wasting Disease," *Wisconsin State Journal*, March 21, 2002, A7.

21. Paul Slovic, Baruch Fischhoff, and Sarah Lichtenstein, "Facts and Fears: Understanding Perceived Risk," in *The Perception of Risk*, ed. Paul Slovic (London: Earthscan, 2000), 137–53.

22. See Thomas A. Heberlein and Richard C. Stedman, "Socially Amplified Risk: Attitude and Behavior Change in Response to CWD in Wisconsin Deer," *Human Dimensions of Wildlife* 14/5 (2009): 326–40.

23. Ibid. Heberlein and Stedman provide a report on the results of the seven 2002 surveys and an analysis of CWD in Wisconsin in the social amplification of risk framework.

24. Joshua A. Compton and Michael Pfau, "Inoculation Theory of Resistance to Influence at Maturity: Recent Progress in Theory Development and Application and Suggestions for Future Research," *Communication Yearbook* 29 (2005): 97–145; William J. McGuire, "Inducing Resistance to Persuasion: Some Contemporary Approaches," in *Advances in Experimental Social Psychology*, ed. Leonard Berkowitz (New York: Academic Press, 1964), 191–229.

25. Leon A. Festinger, *A Theory of Cognitive Dissonance* (Evanston, IL: Row Peterson, 1957).

26. Williams, Ericsson, and Heberlein, "A Quantitative Summary," 575–84.

27. Conrad Kanagy, Craig Humphrey, and Glenn Firebaugh, "Surging Environmentalism: Changing Public Opinion or Changing Publics?" *Social Science Quarterly* 75/4 (1994): 804–19.

28. Environment as a term came into use in the 19th century, referring to the space around the individual. In social sciences it has had two previous incarnations. In the early part of the century, environmentalists referred to a school of thought that felt the natural environment had strong influences on culture and society. In its second incarnation, the social environment outside the individual took precedence over the natural environment. This contrasted "environment" with heredity as causes of behavior. Today, environmental psychology generally looks at how people affect the environment, not how social factors influence human behavior. According to the *Oxford English Dictionary*, the term *environmentalist*, meaning those who actively worked to preserve and protect the environment, came into use only in the 1970s.

29. The very notion of environmental attitudes came not from some fundamental theory of attitudes but rather from the appearance of questions on national surveys. These questions aren't asked accidentally. Enough people must be discussing the issue so that those who sell survey data to newspapers and politicians think something is important. The presence of the question itself is a significant social fact.

30. Riley E. Dunlap, "Trends in Public Opinion Toward Environmental Issues, 1965–1990," *Society and Natural Resources* 4 (1991): 285–312.

31. Robert C. Mitchell, "Public Opinion and Environmental Issues," in *Council on Environmental Quality: The Eleventh Annual Report of the Council on Environmental Quality* (Washington, D.C.: Government Printing Office, 1980), 401–25.

32. Hazel Erskine, "The Polls: Pollution and Its Costs," *Public Opinion Quarterly* 36/1 (1972): 120–35.

33. See Riley E. Dunlap, "Public Opinion and Environmental Policy," in *Environmental Politics and Policy: Theories and Evidence*, ed. James P. Lester (Durham, NC: Duke University Press, 1995), 63–114.

34. Anthony Downs, "Up and Down with Ecology: The 'Issue-Attention Cycle,'" *Public Interest* 28 (1972): 38–30; Even sociologists Riley Dunlap and Don Dillman reported declines in support between 1970 and 1974 as evidence of Downs's claim. See Riley E. Dunlap and Don A. Dillman. "Decline in Public Support for Environmental Protection: Evidence from a 1970–1974 Panel Study," *Rural Sociology* 41 (Fall 1976): 382–90.

35. Riley E. Dunlap, "An Enduring Concern: Light Stays Green for Environmental Protection," *Public Perspective* (2002): 10–14.

CHAPTER 4

1. Aldo Leopold, "Thinking Like a Mountain," in *A Sand County Almanac* (New York: Oxford University Press, 1949), 137–40.

2. Curt Meine, *Aldo Leopold: His Life and Work* (Madison, WI: University of Wisconsin Press, 1988), 507.

3. Richard T. LaPiere, "Attitudes vs. Actions," *Social Forces* 13/2 (1934): 230–37; Irwin Deutscher, "Words and Deeds: Social Science and Social Policy," *Social Problems* 13/3 (1966): 235–54.

4. Philip Banyard and Andrew Grayson, *Introducing Psychological Research: Sixty Studies That Shape Psychology* (New York: New York University Press, 1996); Roger R. Hock, *Forty Studies that Changed Psychology: Explorations into the History of Psychological Research*, 2nd ed. (Englewood Cliffs, NJ: Prentice Hall, 1995).

5. Robert Baumgartner, transcript of an interview with Richard LaPiere, June 8, 1983; Baumgartner and I later returned to interview LaPiere a second time. Unfortunately, this second session was not recorded. Several quotes are from my recollection of the interview.

6. Always the methodologist, LaPiere asked the question two ways on the questionnaire: "In one this question was inserted among similar queries concerning Germans, French, Japanese, Russian, Armenians, Jews, Negros, Italians and Indians. In the other the pertinent question was unencumbered." LaPiere also secured responses from a control sample of 32 nearby hotels and 96 restaurants they did not visit. Neither the type of questionnaire nor the previous experience with the actual visit affected the responses. LaPiere, "Attitudes vs. Actions," 230–37; Deutscher, "Words and Deeds," 235–54.

7. See Howard Schuman and Michael P. Johnson, "Attitudes and Behavior," *Annual Review of Sociology* 2 (1976): 161–207.

8. Martin Fishbein and Icek Ajzen, *Belief, Attitude, Intention and Behavior: An Introduction to Theory and Research* (Boston: Addison-Wesley, 1975); Icek Ajzen and Martin Fishbein, *Understanding Attitudes and Predicting Social Behavior* (Englewood Cliffs, NJ: Prentice-Hall, 1980).

9. Icek Ajzen and Martin Fishbein, "The Influence of Attitudes on Behavior," in *The Handbook on Attitudes*, ed. Delores Albarracín, Blair T. Johnson, and Mark P. Zanna (Mahwah, NJ: Erlbaum, 2005), 173–222.

10. Donald T. Campbell, "Social Attitudes and Other Acquired Behavioral Dispositions," in *Psychology: A Study of a Science*, ed. S. Koch (New York: McGraw-Hill, 1963), 94–172.

11. Of course, we don't know that is the case. LaPiere could have been wrong, just as when he started out he thought the Chinese were going to be treated badly and even turned away. As Michal Firmin notes, one thing that makes LaPiere's study classic and problematic, like some other experiments (e.g., Milgram's and Zimbardo's classic studies), is that they can't be replicated. Michal Firmin, "Commentary: The Seminal Contribution of Richard LaPiere's Attitudes vs. Actions (1934) Research Study," *International Journal of Epidemiology* 39/1 (2010): 18–20. See Stanley Milgram, "Behavioral Study of Obedience," *Journal of Abnormal Social Psychology* 67 (1963): 371–78; Stanley Milgram, "Some Conditions of Obedience and Disobedience to Authority," *Human Relations* 18 (1965): 57–76; Phillip Zimbardo, "The Pathology of Imprisonment," *Society* 9 (1972): 4–8.

12. Meine, *Aldo Leopold*, 456–57.

13. Ibid, 458. Leopold's response to Waldo Rinehard, a hunter from Shawano.

14. Ibid, 468.

15. Susan L. Flader, *Thinking Like A Mountain: Aldo Leopold and the Evolution of an Ecological Attitude toward Deer, Wolves and Forests* (Columbia, MO: University of Missouri Press), 215, footnote 11.

16. Aline Kühl et al., "The Role of Saiga Poaching in Rural Communities: Linkages between Attitudes, Socio-Economic Circumstances and Behaviours," *Biological Conservation* 142/7 (2009): 1442–49.

17. Ibid, 1447.

18. Ibid.

19. Ibid.

20. Ibid, 1442.

21. Matthew A. Wilson, *Appendix H: Public Attitudes towards Wolves in Wisconsin*, Wisconsin Department of Natural Resources, http://dnr.wi.gov/org/land/er/publications/wolfplan/appendix/appendix_h.htm, accessed May 18, 2011.

22. The site is http://www.dnr.state.wi.us/org/land/er/donate/, accessed May 18, 2011. I expect all readers with prowolf attitudes to stop right now and send a check, which I believe further illustrates the point of this argument.

23. Aldo Leopold Foundation, *Green Fire: Aldo Leopold and a Land Ethic for Our Time*. See http://www.greenfiremovie.com/, accessed May 18, 2011.

24. Stanley Temple, e-mail to the author, April 18, 2011.

25. Thanks to Per E. Ljung for this analysis. For information about the sample and the measurement of attitudes see Per E. Ljung et al., "Eat Prey and Love: Game Meat Consumption and Attitudes toward Hunting." Paper submitted to the *Wildlife Society Bulletin*.

26. The binary correlation based on the two-by-two table was $r = 0.13$ (p <.01) while the Pearson correlation (r) using the full 26-item attitude scale was $r = 0.31$ (p<.001).

27. Steven Jay Gross and C. Michael Niman, "Attitude-Behavior Consistency: A Review," *The Public Opinion Quarterly* 39/3 (1975): 358–68; Icek Ajzen, "The Directive Influence of Attitudes on Behavior," in *The Psychology of Action: Linking Cognition and Motivation to Behavior*, eds. Peter M. Gollwitzer and John A. Bargh (New York: Guilford, 1996), 385–403; Laura R. Glasman and Delores Albarracín, "Attitudes that Predict Future Behavior: A Meta-Analysis of the Attitude-Behavior Relation," *Psychological Bulletin* 132 (2006): 778–822.

28. Thomas A. Heberlein and Matthew A. Wilson. "What Do Attitudes Toward Wolves Have to Do with Behavior? Not Much. But That's OK," Presented at the International Symposium on Society and Resource Management, Madison, Wisconsin (2011). We also sent out 500 requests to join the TWA to a sample of those *without* the plates. Of this group, no one sent in $25, showing that attitudes and prior behavior count for something, but not much.

29. For more information on this study, see Thomas A. Heberlein and J. Stanley Black. "Attitudinal Specificity and the Prediction of Behavior in a Field Setting," *Journal of Personality and Social Psychology*, 33/4 (1976): 474–79; Thomas A. Heberlein and J. Stanley Black, "Cognitive Consistency and Environmental Action," *Environment and Behavior* 13/6 (1976): 717–34.

30. Martin Fishbein and Icek Ajzen, "Attitudes toward Objects as Predictors of Single and Multiple Behavioral Criteria," *Psychological Review* 8 (1974): 59–74; Martin Fishbein and Icek Ajzen, *Belief, Attitude, Intention and Behavior*; Icek Ajzen and Martin Fishbein, "Predicting and Understanding Consumer Behavior: Attitude-Behavior Correspondence," in *Understanding Attitudes and Predicting Social Behavior*, Icek Ajzen and Martin Fishbein (Englewood Cliffs, NJ: Prentice-Hall, 1980), 148–72; Doug Whittaker, Jerry J. Vaske, and Michael J. Manfredo, "Specificity and the Cognitive Hierarchy: Value Orientations and the Acceptability of Urban Wildlife Management Actions," *Society & Natural Resources* 19 (2006): 515–30.

31. Ajzen and Fishbein describe this as the correspondence principle. See Icek Ajzen and Martin Fishbein, "Attitude-Behavior Relations: A Theoretical Analysis and Review of Empirical Research," *Psychological Bulletin* 84/5 (1977), 888–918.

32. Russell H. Weigel and Lee S. Newman, "Increasing the Attitude-Behavior Correspondence by Broadening the Scope of the Behavior Measure," *Journal of Personality and Social Psychology* 33/6 (1976): 793–802.

33. Riley E. Dunlap and Kent D. Van Liere, "The New Environmental Paradigm: A Proposed Measuring Instrument and Preliminary Results," *Journal of Environmental Education* 9/4 (1978):10–19; Riley E Dunlap, "The New Environmental Paradigm Scale: From Marginality to Worldwide Use," *Journal of Environmental Education* 40/1 (2008): 3–18.

34. Conrad Kanagy, Craig Humphrey, and Glenn Firebaugh, "Surging Environmentalism: Changing Public Opinion or Changing Publics?" *Social Science Quarterly* 75/4 (1994): 804–19.

35. For more details on this study, see Richard C. Bishop and Thomas A. Heberlein, "Measuring Values of Extra Market Goods: Are Indirect Measures Biased?" *American Journal of Agricultural Economics* 61 (1979): 926–30.

36. Aldo Leopold, *Round River: From the Journals of Aldo Leopold* (New York: Oxford University Press, 1952).

37. Ibid, 168.

38. Ibid, 169. Leopold was writing in the 1940s. A symphony ticket today in Madison, WI, might cost $35 or a total value of $350 using Leopold's calculus.

39. Actually, Leopold was using one measure of the value of a goose, his willingness to pay for the opportunity to hunt it. We were looking for a different—but equally valid—measure: willingness to accept compensation to give up a goose-hunting opportunity.

40. Because of this, we actually returned their permits after the week-long goose season. University and DNR lawyers agreed we were not technically purchasing them, only "holding them." Hunters could not legally hunt without the permit on their person. So, in effect, we were paying them to give up their hunting right for that season, without buying the permit.

41. Aldo Leopold, *A Sand County Almanac* (New York: Oxford University Press, 1949), 69.

42. Richard C. Bishop, Thomas A. Heberlein, and Mary Jo Kealy, "Contingent Valuation of Environmental Assets Comparisons with a Simulated Market," *Natural Resources Journal* 23/3 (July, 1983): 619–33.

43. Lee Ross, "The Intuitive Psychologist and His Shortcomings: Distortions in the Attribution Process," in *Advances in Experimental Social Psychology*, ed. L. Berkowitz (New York: Academic Press, 1977), 173–220; Edward E. Jones and Victor A. Harris, "The Attribution of Attitudes," *Journal of Experimental Social Psychology* 3/1 (1967): 1–24.

44. Malcom Gladwell, *The Tipping Point: How Little Things Can Make a Big Difference* (New York: Little Brown and Company, 2000).

CHAPTER 5

1. William R. Freudenburg, e-mail to the author, January 14, 2010. Freudenburg was, at the time of his death on December 28, 2010, the Dehlsen Professor of Environmental Studies at UC-Santa Barbara. Bill was particularly frustrated with students' preoccupation with the cognitive fix because it kept them from seeing the structural causes as well as solutions to environmental problems. Bill's work focused on these socially structured sources of environmental impacts. See William R. Freudenburg et al., *Catastrophe in the Making: The*

Engineering of Katrina and the Disasters of Tomorrow (Washington, D.C.: Island Press, 2009).

2. Irwin Deutscher, "Words and Deeds: Social Science and Social Policy," *Social Problems* 13/3 (1966): 235–54.

3. Leon Festinger, "Behavioral Support for Opinion Change," *Public Opinion Quarterly* 28/3 (1964): 404–17.

4. When a young scholar gave a presentation on attitudes toward wolves, she was met by the comment: "You keep studying attitudes, but they don't get any better," reflecting this common view that we must be able to change attitudes for them to be important.

5. Environmental sociologist Riley Dunlap observed that waiting four hours to get gas on the way home after a 1973 Christmas visit to California had a notable effect on his own thinking about environmental issues and helped influence his distinguished career. See Riley Dunlap, "The New Environmental Paradigm Scale: From Marginality to Worldwide Use," *The Journal of Environmental Education* 40/1 (2008): 3–18.

6. James R. Murray et al., "Evolution of Public Response to the Energy Crisis," *Science* 184/4134 (1974): 257–63.

7. Thomas A. Heberlein, "Conservation Information: The Energy Crisis and Electricity Consumption in an Apartment Complex," *Energy Systems and Policy* 1 (1975), 105–17.

8. Ibid. 113.

9. Thomas A. Heberlein, "Time-of-Day Electricity Pricing," in *Consumers and Energy Conservation*, ed. John D. Claxton, C. Dennis Anderson, J. R. Brent Ritchie, and Gordon H.D. McDougall (New York: Praeger, 1981), 194–204; Thomas A. Heberlein, Bonnie Ortiz, and Daniel Linz, "Satisfaction, Commitment and Knowledge of Customers on a Mandatory Participation Time-of-Day Electricity Pricing Experiment," *Journal of Consumer Research* 9/1 (1982): 106–14; Thomas A. Heberlein and W. Keith Warriner, "The Influence of Price and Attitude on Shifting Residential Electricity Consumption from On to Off Peak Periods," *Journal of Economic Psychology* 4/1–2 (1983): 107–30; Daniel Linz and Thomas A. Heberlein, "The Development of a Personal Obligation to Shift Electricity Use: Initial Determinants and Maintenance Over Time," *Energy* 9/3 (1984): 254–63; J. Stanley Black, "Attitudinal, Normative and Economic Factors in Early Response to an Energy Use Field Experiment" (PhD Dissertation, Department of Sociology and Rural Sociology, University of Wisconsin-Madison, 1978).

10. Clive Seligman and J. M Darley, "Feedback as a Means of Decreasing Residential Energy Consumption," *Journal of Applied Psychology* 62/4 (1977): 363–68; Clive Seligman, L. Becker, and J. Darley, "Encouraging Residential Energy Conservation Through Feedback," in *Advances in Environmental Psychology: Vol. 3: Energy: Psychological Perspectives*, eds. A. Baum and J. Singer (Hillsdale, NJ: Erlbaum, 1981).

11. W. Burleigh Seaver and Arthur H. Patterson, "Decreasing Fuel-Oil Consumption Through Feedback and Social Commendation," *Journal of Applied Behavior Analysis* 9/2, (1976): 147–52.

12. These results and the whole experiment are described in Robert Mathew Baumgartner, "Attitude Change and Behavior Change: A Field Experiment Investigating Responses to an Alternative Electric Rate" (PhD Dissertation, Departments of Sociology and Rural Sociology, University of Wisconsin-Madison, 1987).

13. Ibid, 157.

14. Loren Lutzenhiser, "Marketing Household Energy Conservation: The Message and Reality," in *New Tools for Environmental Protection: Education, Information and Voluntary Measures*, eds. Thomas Dietz and Paul C. Stern (Washington, D.C.: National Academy Press, 2002), 49–65.

15. Susan Lutzenhiser et al., "Beyond the Price Effect in Time-of-Use Programs: Results from a Municipal Utility Pilot 2007–2008," Ernest Orlando Lawrence Berkeley National Laboratory (LBNL–2750E). Paper presented at the International Energy Program Evaluation Conference, Portland, OR, August 12–14 and published in the proceedings, 2009. Unlike the Wisconsin research, this program was voluntary, with severe selection bias (330 participants out of 30,000 households contacted). Further, even within the experiment, the information treatments were not completely random.

16. Christensen Associates (with R. Baumgartner, D. W. Caves, L. R. Christensen, and R. Sweeney), *Analysis of the Wisconsin Electric Residential Rate Experiment, Volume 1: Summary of Findings from the Wisconsin Residential Rate Experiment*, Prepared for Wisconsin Electric, March 1987.

17. At the time, the mining company was officially called Nicolet Minerals, co-owned by Exxon and Rio Algom, a Canadian mining company. Environmentalists persisted in calling it the Exxon mine. I use that language in this section because this is how the discussion was framed and "The Exxon mine" persisted as the attitude object. This was one of the problems for the mine, since the term *Exxon* in those days instantly hooked to the Valdez disaster and all that came with it, as illustrated by my student Howard's strong negative emotional attitude in chapter 2.

18. The Wolf River is 219 miles long and flows through seven counties with about 6.5 percent of the state's population.

19. George Piper, "Only Crandon Wins in Gamble with River," *Mauston Star-Times*, March 15, 1997.

20. Ron Seely, "Local Governments Say No Thanks to Mine Plan," *Wisconsin State Journal*, November 3, 1996. Cited in Al Gedics, http://www.wsn.org/crandon/SOCIMAGN2.html, Accessed May 13, 2011.

21. Quoted in Jeff Mayers, "Moratorium on Mines Gains Momentum," *Wisconsin State Journal*, January 18, 1998, 1C.

22. Al Gedics, http://www.wsn.org/crandon/SOCIMAGN2.html. See also "The Wisconsin Public Radio-St. Norbert College: The Wisconsin Survey," March 1996, Topic: Environment/Crandon Mine, Tuesday, April 8, 1996.

23. James Flynn, Paul Slovic, and C. K. Mertz, "The Nevada Initiative: A Risk Communication Fiasco," *Risk Analysis* 13/5 (1993): 497–502. We don't know how much they spent, but leaked documents from the ANEC recommended spending $9 million for the "Nevada Initiative." See Flynn, Slovic, and Mertz, 500.

24. Ibid, 501.

25. Ibid, 498.

26. Gerard Tellis, "Advertising Exposure, Loyalty and Brand Purchase: Two Stage Model of Choice," *Journal of Marketing Research* 25/2 (1988): 134–44. Tellis presents scanner records on 12 brands of toilet tissue.

27. Charmin/Procter & Gamble spent $16.6 million in 2006 and $48.9 million in 2007; Charmin Ultra /Procter & Gamble spent $54.1 million in 2006 and $24.4 million in 2007; Kleenex Cottonelle /Kimberly-Clark spent $18.8 million in 2006 and $28.0 million in 2007; Scott /Kimberly-Clark spent $16.5 million in 2006 and $16.4 million in 2007; and Quilted Northern /Georgia Pacific spent $0.4 million in 2006 and $23.4 million in 2007. Information provided by UW-Madison's Business Library via e-mail correspondence, May 25, 2010.

28. Gerard Tellis, "Advertising Exposure, Loyalty and Brand Purchase," 134.

29. William J. McGuire, "The Myth of Massive Media Impact: Savagings and Salvagings," *Public Communication and Behavior* 1 (1986): 173–257. See particularly 174–75.

30. "How Much Is BP Spending on Google Ads?" http://blog.searchenginewatch.com/100609-140554, Accessed July 11, 2010.

31. See http://www.yourdictionary.com/edsel, accessed May 13, 2011.

32. Forbes's personal spending of $17 million was a big deal in the mid-1990s and the subject of much media attention. Today, it would be considered small. Still, personal money alone seldom gets candidates elected if they are not otherwise politically involved.

33. A. H. Rohlfing, "Hunter Conduct and Public Attitudes," *Transactions of the 43rd North American Wildlife and Natural Resources Conference* (1978): 404–11.

34. Jack Kulpa, "Secret Lakes of the North Woods," *Outdoor Life* 79/5 (1984): 108–9.

35. Steven P. Newman and Michael H. Hoff, "Evaluation of a 16-inch Minimum Length Limit for Smallmouth Bass in Pallette Lake, WI," *North American Journal of Fisheries Management* 20/1 (2000): 90–99.

36. Ibid.

37. See Thomas A. Heberlein and Richard C. Stedman, "Socially Amplified Risk: Attitude and Behavior Change in Response to CWD in Wisconsin Deer," *Human Dimensions of Wildlife* 14/5 (2009): 326–40.

38. This is not to diminish the effect of the 103,000 licenses not being sold. That's the equivalent of a social tidal wave. If antihunters had given me an unlimited

budget, there is no way I could have reduced hunting participation in Wisconsin by 12 percent in eight months. See Thomas A. Heberlein, "Fire in the Sistine Chapel: How Wisconsin Responded to Chronic Wasting Disease," *Human Dimensions of Wildlife* 9/3 (2004): 169–75. Advertising, as we have seen in this chapter, backfires when it seems excessive. A PETA (People for the Ethical Treatment of Animals) program to reduce hunting participation in Wisconsin would no doubt increase the number of hunters, because individuals would be spurred to defend a sacred state tradition. If you look at sheer numbers, in spite of the enormous amount of fear relayed by the media and the resulting attitude change, Wisconsin sold more than 700,000 licenses the year before AND the year after. The resilience of attitudes and their constant effect on behavior should impress objective observers. At least I was impressed.

39. Richelle Winkler and Rozalynn Klaas, "Declining Deer Hunters: Wisconsin's Gun Deer Hunter Numbers Are Continuing to Decline." Applied Population Laboratory, Department of Community and Environmental Sociology, University of Wisconsin-Madison. February, 2011. http://www.apl.wisc.edu/publications/APL_hunters2011_web.pdf, Accessed May 13, 2011.

40. For a particularly compelling argument supporting this point, see McGuire, "The Myth of Massive Media Impact," 174–75.

41. John T. Jost and Mahzarin R. Banaji, "William James McGuire (1925–2007)," *American Psychologist* 63/4 (2008): 270–71.

42. McGuire, "The Myth of Massive Media Impact," 173–257.

43. Sharon Dunwoody, "The Challenge of Trying to Make a Difference Using Media Messages," in *Creating a Climate for Change*, ed. Susanne C. Moser and Lisa Dilling (New York: Cambridge University Press, 2007), 89–104.

CHAPTER 6

1. These queuing systems are becoming more common in the United States. By 2011 there was one at the motor vehicle department in Madison. They are all over in Sweden, particularly in liquor stores, but also at the train station and even in the bakery and lamp shops near my apartment. According to blogs of other Americans in Stockholm, my experience and reactions were not unusual.

2. Of course, the negative attitude might be expressed in how well they perform the role. If servers dislike certain customers, the service might be overly slow, or they might work extremely fast to get rid of them. However, the general role behaviors are the same. Remember, too, the dependent variable in LaPiere's study was not how good the service was but whether they were served at all, and they were, in spite of the behavioral intention not to serve Chinese.

3. Robert B. Cialdini, Raymond R. Reno, and Cari A. Kallgren, "A Focus Theory to Normative Conduct: Recycling the Concept of Norms to Reducing Littering in Public Places," *Journal of Personality and Social Psychology* 58/6 (1990): 1015–26.

4. John L. Heywood, "The Cognitive and Emotional Components of Behavioral Norms in Outdoor Recreation," *Leisure Sciences* 24 (2002): 271–81. Heywood corroborates experiences with a survey of visitors to parks in Columbus, Ohio. Of those surveyed, 87 percent said they should never litter, and would feel guilty (88 percent), ashamed (87 percent) and embarrassed (85 percent) if they did.

5. Thomas A. Heberlein, "Moral Norms, Threatened Sanctions, and Littering Behavior," PhD Dissertation, University of Wisconsin-Madison, 1971, *Dissertation Abstracts International* 32, 5906.

6. See also Thomas A. Heberlein and Shalom H. Schwartz, "Deactivating the Anti-littering Norm: A Field Test of Schwartz's Norm Activation Theory," Paper Presented at the 9th Biennial Conference on Environmental Psychology, September 26–28, 2011, Eindhoven, The Netherlands.

7. Daniel B. Syrek, *Summary of Litter Research Findings Report S-1.1* Institute for Applied Research, Sacramento, CA, No Date, 3. Cited with permission from Daniel B. Syrek, interview with the author, March 23, 2011.

8. For a popular discussion, see Malcolm Gladwell, *The Tipping Point: How Little Things Can Make a Big Difference* (London: Little, Brown and Company, 2000), 160–63. See also Lee Ross, "The Intuitive Psychologist and His Shortcomings: Distortions in the Attribution Process," in *Advances in Experimental Social Psychology Vol. 10*, ed. Leonard Berkowitz (New York: Academic Press, 1977), 173–220.

9. Harold G. Grasmick, Robert J. Bursik Jr., and Karyl A. Kinsey, "Shame and Embarrassment as Deterrents to Noncompliance with the Law: The Case of an Antilitter Campaign," *Environment and Behavior* 23/2 (1991): 233–51, footnote 3.

10. Arlo Guthrie, Alice's Restaurant.http://www.youtube.com/watch?v=5_7CoQGkiVo, accessed May 21, 2011.

11. Robert B. Cialdini, "Crafting Normative Messages to Protect the Environment," *Current Directions in Psychological Science* 12/4 (2003); 105–9.

12. You might think the confederate in the experiment tossing the litter would be a role model for the potential litterer, but at the time of the littering event, the subject did not have a chance to litter. No interviews were done, so we don't have an exact idea of what they were thinking at either the time of observing the littering or when they later had the opportunity to litter themselves. However, given my experience with my students, I trust my explanation.

13. Cialdini, Reno, and Kallgren, "A Focus Theory to Normative Conduct."

14. Yvonne A. W. de Kort, L. Teddy McCalley, and Cees J. H. Midden, "Persuasive Trash Cans: Activation of Littering Norms by Design," *Environment and Behavior* 40/6 (2008): 870–91; E. S. Geller, W. Brasted, and M. Mann, "Waste Receptacle Designs as Interventions for Litter Control," *Journal of Environmental Systems* 9 (1980): 145–60.

15. Shalom H. Schwartz, "Words, Deeds and the Perception of Consequences and Responsibility in Action Situations," *Journal of Personality and Social Psychology* 10/3 (1968): 232–42. Later in his career, Schwartz refined and extended his

theory. See Shalom H. Schwartz, "Normative Influences on Altruism," *Advances in Experimental Social Psychology* 10 (1977): 221–79; Shalom H. Schwartz and J. A. Howard, "A Normative Decision Making Model of Altruism," in *Altruism and Helping Behavior: Social, Personality, and Developmental Perspectives*, eds. J. P. Rushton and R. M. Sorrentine (Hillsdale, NJ: Erlbaum, 1981), 189–211; Shalom H. Schwartz and J. A. Howard, "Helping and Cooperation: A Self-Based Motivational Model," in *Cooperation and Helping Behavior: Theories and Research*, eds. V. J. Derlega and J. Grzelak (New York: Academic Press, 1982), 328–56.

16. Thomas A. Heberlein, "Moral Norms, Threatened Sanctions, and Littering Behavior."

17. William C. Finnie, "Field Experiments in Litter Control," *Environment and Behavior* 5/2 (1973): 123–44.

18. E. Scott Geller, Jill F. Witmer, and Margaret A. Tuso, "Environmental Interventions for Litter Control," *Journal of Applied Psychology* 62/3 (1977): 344–51.

19. E. Scott Geller, Jill F. Witmer, and Andra L. Orebaugh, "Instructions as a Determinant of Paper-Disposal Behaviors," *Environment and Behavior* 8/3 (1976): 417–39. This study did not mention if the store was prelittered when shoppers were asked to litter their handbill.

20. Cialdini, Reno, and Kallgren, "A Focus Theory to Normative Conduct." See Study 1, Confederate not littering treatment.

21. Kees Keiser, Siegwart Lindenberg, and Linda Steg, "The Spreading of Disorder," *Science* 322 (2008): 1681–84.

22. For a more extended description of the methodology, see Thomas A. Heberlein and J. Stanley Black, "Attitudinal Specificity and the Prediction of Behavior in a Field Setting," *Journal of Personality and Social Psychology* 33 (1976): 474–79.

23. J. Stanley Black, "The Relationship of Personal Norm, Perceived Social Norms and Beliefs in Lead-Free Gasoline Purchasing Behavior." Masters Thesis, Department of Sociology, University of Wisconsin-Madison. 1974.

24. Thomas A. Heberlein, "Social Norms and Environmental Quality." Paper presented at the American Association for Advancement of Science Annual meetings, New York, 1975.

25. Kent D. Van Liere and Riley E. Dunlap, "Moral Norms and Environmental Behavior: An Application of Schwartz's Norm-Activation Model to Yard Burning," *Journal of Applied Social Psychology* 8/2 (1978): 174–88.

26. J. Stanley Black, Paul C. Stern, and Julie T. Elworth, "Personal and Contextual Influences on Household Energy Adaptations," *Journal of Applied Psychology* 70/1 (1985): 3–21.

27. Paul C. Stern, "Toward a Coherent Theory of Environmentally Significant Behavior," *Journal of Social Issues* 56/3 (2000): 407–24. Paul C. Stern et al., "A Value-Belief-Norm Theory of Support for Social Movements: The Case of Environmentalism," *Human Ecology Review* 6/2 (1999): 81–97.

28. Nina L. Bradley et al., "Phenological Changes Reflect Climate Change in Wisconsin," *Proceedings of the National Academy of Sciences USA* 96 (1999): 9701–704.

29. Aldo Leopold, *A Sand County Almanac* (New York: Oxford University Press, 1949), 38.

30. Curt Meine, e-mail to the author, June 2, 2009.

31. David Policansky, "Catch-and-Release Recreational Fishing: A Historical Perspective," in *Recreational Fisheries: Ecological, Economic and Social Evaluation*, eds. Tony J. Pitcher and Chuck E. Hollingworth (Oxford: Blackwell Science, 2002), 74–93.

32. Craig Paukert, Michael McInerny, and Randall Schultz, "Historical Trends in Creel Limits, Length-Based Limits, and Season Restrictions for Black Basses in the United States and Canada," *Fisheries Management* 32/2 (2007): 62–72.

33. Wisconsin built the nation's first hatchery in 1887. The builders used a special rail car that could keep fish alive while hauling them to northern lakes long before the North Woods had a road network for automobiles. In fact, this was before the automobile was invented.

34. For more information, visit http://www.tu.org/, accessed June 10, 2010.

35. Seventy-eight percent of TU members had college degrees. Bryan K. Moore (VP for Volunteer Operations/Watershed Programs, Trout Unlimited), e-mail to the author, May 23, 2011.

36. That fish won the week's and the month's contest. It weighed 4 pounds, 6½ (don't forget the half) ounces, and measured 21 inches.

37. Martha N. Gardner and Alan N. Brandt, "'The Doctor's Choice Is America's Choice': The Physician in US Cigarette Advertisements, 1930–1953," *American Journal of Public Health* 96/2 (2006): 222–32. See, for example, The Camel Cigarettes advertisement "I'm Gonna Grow a Hundred Years Old!" from the "More Doctors Smoke Camels" series, *Ladies Home Journal*, July 1946.

38. Lawrence Garfinkel, "Trends in Cigarette Smoking in the United States," *Preventive Medicine* 26 (1997): 447–50.

39. David E. Nelson et al., "Trends in Cigarette Smoking among U.S. Physicians and Nurses," *Journal of the American Medical Association* 271/16 (1994): 1273–75.

40. Hao Tang et al., "Changes of Knowledge, Attitudes, Beliefs, and Preference of Bar Owner and Staff in Response to a Smoke-Free Bar Law," *Tobacco Control* 13 (2004): 87–89.

41. American Non-Smokers' Rights Foundation, "Summary of 100 percent Smoke Free State Laws and Population Protected by 100 percent U.S. Smoke Free Laws. January 2, 2012" Available online at http://www.no-smoke.org/pdf/SummaryUS PopList.pdf, accessed December 30, 2011.

42. Richard Craver, "Adult Smoking Is at a Record Low," *Winston-Salem Journal*, November 15, 2008. Available online at http://www2.journalnow.com/business/2008/nov/15/adult-smoking-is-at-record-low-ar-135139/, accessed May 21, 2011.

43. Robin R. Jenkins et al., "The Determinants of Household Recycling: A Material-Specific Analysis of Recycling Program Features and Unit Pricing," *Journal of Environmental Economics and Management* 45/2 (2003): 295–318; see also Nora Goldstein and Celeste Madtes, "12th Annual Biocycle National Survey: The State of Garbage in America, Part II," *Biocycle* 41 (2000): 40–48.

44. See Martin V. Melosi, *Garbage in the Cities: Refuse, Reform, and the Environment, 1880–1980.* (Pittsburgh, PA: University of Pittsburgh Press, 1981); David N. Pellow, Allan Schnaiberg, and Adam S. Weinberg, "Putting the Ecological Modernisation Thesis to the Test: The Promises and Performances of Urban Recycling," in *Ecological Modernisation Around the World: Perspectives & Critical Debates*, eds. Arthur P. J. Mol and David A. Sonnenfeld (Portland, OR: Frank Cass Publishers, 2000), 109–37.

45. E.g., James McGuinness, Allan P. Jones, and Steven G. Cole, "Attitudinal Correlates of Recycling Behavior," *Journal of Applied Psychology* 62/4 (1977): 376–84.

46. U.S. Environmental Protection Agency, *Municipal Solid Waste Factbook* (Washington, D.C.: U.S. Environmental Protection Agency, 1998).

47. Paul C. Stern and Stuart Oskamp, "Managing Scarce Environmental Resources," in *Handbook of Environmental Psychology*, eds. D. Stokols and I. Altman (New York: Wiley, 1987), 1043–88.

48. P. Wesley Schultz, "Knowledge, Information, and Recycling: Examining the Knowledge-Deficit Model of Behavior Change," in *New Tools For Environmental Protection: Education, Information, and Voluntary Measures*, eds. Thomas Dietz and Paul Stern (Washington, D.C.: National Academy Press, 2002), 67–82.

49. Joyce McCarl Nielsen and Barbara L. Ellington, "Social Processes and Resource Conservation," in *Environmental Psychology*, eds. N. R. Feimer and E. Scott Geller (New York: Praeger, 1983), 288–312; Joseph R. Hopper and Joyce McCarl Nielsen, "Recycling as Altruistic Behavior: Normative and Behavioral Strategies to Expand Participation in a Community Recycling Program," *Environment and Behavior* 23/2 (1991): 195–220; see also Shawn M. Burn, "Social Psychology and the Stimulation of Recycling Behaviors: The Block Leader Approach," *Journal of Applied Social Psychology* 21/8 (1991): 611–29.

50. Patrícia Oom Do Valle et al., "Combining Behavioral Theories to Predict Recycling Involvement," *Environment and Behavior* 37/3 (2005): 364–96. As you might imagine, the developers of this program had high hopes for the cognitive fix component. Two TV ads were used along with billboards, newspapers, radio, and eco-spots. It surprised three statisticians and a professor of supply chains who authored the article, but it will not surprise readers of this book, that people surveyed who reported seeing the advertising were no more convinced that recycling was easy. The ads failed to "educate the public." But the structural fix part of the program worked, most likely because of activation of an existing norm.

51. Gregory A. Guagnano, Paul C. Stern, and Thomas Dietz, "Influences on Attitude-Behavior Relationships: A Natural Experiment with Curbside Recycling," *Environment and Behavior* 27/5 (1995): 699–718.

52. Michael Siegel, "Involuntary Smoking in the Restaurant Workplace: A Review of Employee Exposure and Health Effects," *Journal of the American Medical Association* 270 (1993): 490–93.

53. Thomas A. Heberlein, "The Land Ethic Realized: Some Social Psychological Explanations of Changing Environmental Attitudes," *Journal of Social Issues* 28/4 (1972): 79–87.

54. Riley E. Dunlap and Kent D. Van Liere, "Land Ethic or Golden Rule: Comment on 'Land Ethic Realized' by Thomas A. Heberlein," *Journal of Social Issues* 33/3 (1977): 200–207.

55. "At this point, I'm not sure it's all that important to distinguish between human and environmental consequences, as they are inextricably interrelated as you well know. And maybe it's not even that important to try to ferret out purely environmental values/motives." Riley Dunlap, e-mail to the author, May 10, 2010.

56. Paul C. Stern et al., "The Case of Environmentalism."

57. Robert Arlinghaus, "Voluntary Catch-and-Release Can Generate Conflict within the Recreational Angling Community: A Qualitative Case Study of Specialised Carp (*Cyprinus carpio* L.) Angling in Germany," *Fisheries Management and Ecology* 14 (2007): 191–71.

58. Victoria Braithwaite, *Do Fish Feel Pain?* (New York: Oxford University Press, 2010).

CHAPTER 7

1. Aldo Leopold, *A Sand County Almanac* (New York: Oxford University Press, 1949), 207.

2. Ibid., 207.

3. Ibid., 207.

4. Ibid., 208.

5. Ibid., 204.

6. E.g., Susan L. Flader, *Thinking Like A Mountain: Aldo Leopold and the Evolution of an Ecological Attitude Toward Deer, Wolves and Forests* (Columbia, MO: University of Missouri Press, 1974).

7. E.g., J. Baird Callicott, ed., *Companion to A Sand County Almanac* (Madison, WI: University of Wisconsin Press, 1987).

8. E.g., Richard L. Knight and Suzanne Riedel, *Aldo Leopold and the Ecological Conscience* (New York: Oxford University Press, 2002).

9. Leopold, *A Sand County Almanac*, 203.

10. Ibid., 209.

11. Thomas A. Heberlein, "Wildlife Caretaking vs. Wildlife Management: A Short Lesson in Swedish," *The Wildlife Society Bulletin* 33/1 (2005): 378–80.

12. Michael O'Brien, *Exxon and the Crandon Mine Controversy: The People vs. Giant Companies, A True Story of People Winning* (Middleton, WI: Badger Books, 2008), 169–70.

13. These different values lead, as we would expect, to different attitudes toward wolves between the Chippewa and the non-Indian residents of northern Wisconsin. See Victoria Shelley, Adrian Treves, and Lisa Naughton, "Attitudes to Wolves and Wolf Policy Among Ojibwe Tribal Members and Nontribal Residents of Wisconsin's Wolf Range," *Human Dimensions of Wildlife* 16/6 (2011): 397–413.

14. Leopold, *A Sand County Almanac*, 202.

15. Ibid., 225.

16. Ibid., 209.

17. Ibid., 207.

18. Ibid., 209.

19. Ibid., 221.

20. Ibid., 214.

21. Ibid., 69.

22. Ibid., 224–225.

23. Ibid., 207.

24. Ibid., 203.

25. Ibid., 210–11.

26. Ibid., 203.

27. Ibid., 203.

28. Ibid., 211.

29. Ibid., 211–12.

30. Ibid., 207.

31. Aldo Leopold, "The Ecological Conscience," *Bulletin of the Garden Club of America* (1947): 45–53. Reprinted in Susan Flader and J. Baird Callicott, eds., *The River of the Mother of God and Other Essays by Aldo Leopold* (Madison, WI: University of Wisconsin Press, 1991), 338–48. This is a speech delivered by Leopold in Minneapolis on June 26, 1947. This was one of the essays that he blended, along with two earlier essays, to develop his Land Ethic essay for *A Sand County Almanac*, which he composed less than a year before his death in July 1947. Although this direct quote did not make it into *A Sand County Almanac*, it accurately represents his view of time in the realization of a land ethic.

32. Bill Christofferson, *The Man from Clear Lake: Earth Day Founder Senator Gaylord Nelson* (Madison, WI: University of Wisconsin Press, 2004), 3. The prologue of this book (3–7) gives an excellent overview of that dramatic day.

33. Thomas A. Heberlein, "The Land Ethic Realized: Some Social Psychological Explanations for Changing Environmental Attitudes," *The Journal of Social Issues*

28/4 (1972): 79–87. Originally presented at the Rural Sociological Society Annual Meetings in Washington, D.C., August 1970.

34. The original *Silent Spring* was published in 1962 after being serialized in *The New Yorker*. Linda Leer, in an introduction to the 2002 edition, summarizes Carson's main thesis: we were "subjecting ourselves to slow poisoning by the misuse of chemical pesticides that polluted the environment." Rachel Carson, *Silent Spring* (New York: Houghton-Mifflin, 2002), x. Throughout the text, Carson keeps focusing on human consequences to farm workers, duck hunters, bird watchers, and normal citizens as the ultimate recipients of human-caused environmental change.

35. Quoted in Christofferson, *The Man from Clear Lake,* 3.

36. Leopold, *A Sand County Almanac,* 204.

37. One piece of good news in getting Leopold's name and the idea of the Land Ethic out is that in 2011 a film on Leopold's life was made, *Green Fire: Aldo Leopold and a Land Ethic for Today*. In the first nine months it was viewed by more than 50,000 people in 48 states and 16 foreign countries. http://www.aldoleopold.org/, accessed December 28, 2011.

CHAPTER 8

1. Gerald T. Gardner and Paul C. Stern, *Environmental Problems and Human Behavior*, 2nd ed. (Boston, MA: Pearson Custom Publishing, 2002), 155.

2. Eric Hirst, *Cooperation and Community Conservation: The Hood River Conservation Project*. ORNL/CON-235, DOE/BP-11287-18, 1987, 2.

3. Ibid.

4. Kenneth M. Keating et al., "Hood River Project: Take a Walk on the Applied Side," *The Rural Sociologist* 5/2 (1985): 112–18.

5. Keating was a student of Bill Freudenburg, the environmental sociologist to whom this book is dedicated. As Freudenburg said in an e-mail three decades later (e-mail to author, August 6, 2010), "Ken Keating was one of the smartest grad students I ever worked with, anywhere. He decided he wanted to make a difference in the real world, so he went to the Bonneville Power Administration." In the same e-mail, Freudenburg lauded Ruth Love as "one of the environmental sociologists who went to work for an agency before it was fashionable."

6. Helen M. Berg and P. K. Bodenroeder, *Hood River Community Conservation Project Evaluation Plan, Report on the Pre-Test Survey*. Oregon State University, Corvallis, OR, DOE/BP-11287-14, 1983; Helen M. Berg and P. K. Bodenroeder, *Report on the Pre-test and Follow-After Survey*, Survey Research Center, Oregon State University, Corvallis, OR, 1986.

7. Hood River is still a diverse community. The first language I heard on the street during my visit was Spanish, and when I tried my ATM card I had a choice of five languages, only two of which had Latin characters.

8. Cynthia Flynn-Brown, *Process Evaluation: Final Report, Hood River Conservation Project*, DOE/BP-11287-6. 1986, 20.

9. "As it turned out, participation was overwhelming, so many of these planned activities were not adopted." Hirst, *Cooperation and Community Conservation*, 24.

10. David Goldstein with the Natural Resources Defense Council, who sat on the HRCP Regional Advisory Council, argued 20 years later that a key to effectiveness and success was that "the motivation was, from the program implementer's side, a commitment to show what really could be done." David B. Goldstein, *Extreme Efficiency: How Far Can We Go If We Really Need To?* Proceedings from the ACEEE Summer Study on Energy Efficiency in Buildings (Washington, D.C.: American Council for an Energy-Efficient Economy, 2008).

11. A survey of 200 nonparticipants representing those who refused an audit showed 44 percent thought they had adequate insulation and did not need a retrofit. Only 13 percent said they were never contacted. Flynn-Brown, *Process Evaluation*, 81.

12. Kenneth M. Keating, e-mail to the author, August 10, 2010.

13. Ibid; see also Hirst, *Cooperation and Community Conservation*, 17.

14. Ruth Love, e-mail to the author, August 11, 2010. This is also described in Keating et al., "Hood River Project."

15. Flynn-Brown, *Process Evaluation*, 25.

16. Kenneth M. Keating, e-mail to the author, September 6, 2010.

17. This is no surprise. Professors are in the "educate the public" business, so the cognitive fix is appealing. Our students are often those "light bulbs ready to change." But outside the classroom, they are just normal people.

18. Alan Fish, e-mail to author, July 30, 2010.

19. See http://conserve.wisc.edu/, accessed May 14, 2011. However, there is some weaseling here. The goal is energy *per square foot*. In the meantime, the university built like crazy, increasing the square feet of new buildings. For example, a new student union covers 276,664 total square feet, nearly twice the size of the former student union. The point is they achieved energy reductions per square foot. The fact these new buildings might have squandered those reductions is another issue.

20. Unfortunately, this structural fix has a structural problem. Vakili noted there is no incentive for the IT guys, because having a bunch of "sleeping" computers makes it difficult to run updates overnight. "If I could give each of them $1,000 for doing this, they would do it in a minute," Vakili observed.

21. Jonas Eliasson, "Expected and Unexpected in the Stockholm Trial," in *Congestion Taxes in City Traffic: Lessons Learnt from the Stockholm Trial*, eds. Anders Gullberg and Karolina Isaksson (Lund, Sweden: Nordic Academic Press, 2009), 205–34.

22. Actually, Eliasson reports that Frank Knight at the University of Chicago demonstrated long ago that congestion charges could be socially profitable. Transportation economists went on to work out the details and practicalities over the next

half century. "But to the increasing dismay of transport economists, not a single trial run of congestion charges was set up." Eliasson, "The Stockholm Trial," 206.

23. The general technical term is a "congestion charge," some sort of fee to reduce traffic density. This is how it is referred to in the literature. Because of several factors, the specific program in Stockholm was called a *trängselskatt*, which is literally translated as "congestion tax." I will use that term when referring to the specific event in Stockholm, and other terms when discussing the principle more broadly.

24. For details, see Anders Gullberg and Karolina Isaksson, "Fabulous Success or Insidious Fiasco," in *Congestion Taxes in City Traffic: Lessons Learnt from the Stockholm Trial*, eds. Anders Gullberg and Karolina Isaksson (Lund, Sweden: Nordic Academc Press, 2009), 11–204.

25. Jonas Eliasson, e-mail to author, September 27, 2010.

26. Martin Adahl, director of Fores, a center-right research institute, is quoted as saying, "There used to be a maxim in Swedish politics that you never won elections by offering to lower taxes." In Stephen Castle, "Political Earthquake Shakes Up Sweden," *New York Times*, September 20, 2010, http://www.nytimes.com/2010/09/21/world/europe/21iht-sweden.html, accessed May 14, 2011.

27. Jonas Eliasson and Lina Jonsson, "The Unexpected 'Yes!': Explanatory Factors Behind the Positive Attitudes to Congestion Charges in Stockholm," Paper presented at the 2009 European Transport Conference, Leiden, Netherlands, November 19, 2009.

28. Karolina Isaksson and Anders Gullberg, "Introduction," in *Congestion Taxes in City Traffic: Lessons Learnt from the Stockholm Trial*, eds. Anders Gullberg and Karolina Isaksson (Lund, Sweden: Nordic Academic Press, 2009), 7–10.

29. Actual costs of the trial in Stockholm escalated to more than 3,500,000,000 SEK (about $500 million U.S. dollars), far more than anyone expected. This is about twice the entire capital spending budget for the city of Madison, WI in 2010.

30. The Swedes don't mess around with fines. If you park illegally outside my apartment in Stockholm, it costs $100. If you do the same outside my apartment in Madison, it costs $20.

31. Lena Winslott-Hiselieus et al., "The Development of Public Attitudes towards the Stockholm Congestion Trial," *Transportation Research Part A: Policy and Practice* 43/3 (2009): 269–82. See Figure 8, 279.

32. Whether the opinion shift caused the media framing or the media framing caused the shift, we will never know because newspaper readers and nonreaders were not followed over time in any attitude surveys.

33. Eliasson, "The Stockholm Trial," 220.

34. Ibid, 221.

35. *Aftonbladet*, headlines ranged from "Congestion charging: Even more chaos for road pricing" on December 22, 2005 (just before the trial) to "Stockholmers love congestion charging: People have realized the advantages . . . the dirge has

turned into hymns of praise" on January 14, 2006 (11 days after the trial began). Cited in Eliasson, "The Stockholm Trial," 221.

36. See Greger Henricksson, "What Did the Trial Mean for Stockholmers?" in *Congestion Taxes in City Traffic: Lessons Learnt from the Stockholm Trial*, eds. Anders Gullberg and Karolina Isaksson (Lund, Sweden: Nordic Academic Press: 2009), 235–94.

37. Winslott-Hiselieus et al., "The Stockhold Congestion Trial," Figure 8, 279.

38. Winslott-Hiselieus et al., "The Stockhold Congestion Trial," Figure 3, 276.

39. Eliasson, "The Stockholm Trial," 205, 221.

40. As we have often seen, when public opinion becomes more positive, questions get reframed, making it impossible to make reasonable comparisons over time. However, the change in question wording itself is evidence for the continued positive shift in attitudes. The 2009 question read, "Do you think the charges should be increased, decreased, or kept the same?" (no suggestion of doing away with them). Fifty-six percent of the public wanted to keep congestion charges at the current level, and 18 percent wanted the fees increased. One could infer that almost 75 percent favored the tax.

41. Transport for London. Central London congestion charging impacts monitoring. Second Annual Report, London UK, April 2004, available at http://www.tfl.gov.uk/assets/downloads/Impacts-monitoring-report-2.pdf, accessed October 18, 2010; James Odeck and Svein Bråthen, "Toll Financing in Norway: The Success, the Failures and Perspectives for the Future" *Transport Policy* 9/3 (2002): 253–60; See also Geertje Schuitema, Linda Steg, and Sonja Forward, "Explaining Differences in Acceptability Before and Acceptance after the Implementation of a Congestion Charge in Stockholm," *Transportation Research Part A: Policy and Practice* 44/2 (2010): 99–109. I asked Eliasson why his team seemed so surprised at the increase in positive attitudes in Stockholm (one of his papers was titled "The Unexpected 'Yes'") given that previous studies showed positive attitude change. He candidly replied, "We didn't believe them." See Jonas Eliasson and Lina Jonsson, "The Unexpected 'Yes.'"

42. Ibid, Table 2.

43. I first learned of this from Matthew Barzun, the then American Ambassador to Sweden, in his blog. See http://blogomsweden.blogspot.com/2010/04/blog-om-badges-buttons-and-boy-named.html, accessed May 14, 2011.

CHAPTER 9

1. Psychological reactance is a negative attitude that can follow impositions that impinge on freedom and autonomy. This reaction is common when individuals feel obliged to adopt a particular opinion or engage in a specific behavior. Jack W. Brehm, *A Theory of Psychological Reactance* (New York: Academic Press, 1966).

2. C.J. Winand, *Future Deer Management (Part I): Are we on the Right Track?* Bowsite. com, http://bowsite.com/bowsite/features/armchair_biologist/qdm/, accessed May 24, 2011.

3. Ibid.

4. Fiscal years 1997–2007. In 2003, sales began to decline with a big drop from 20,407 to 16,452 plates between 2007 and 2008. These drops might be caused by increased options for special plates, general problems in the economy, or the successful restoration of wolves. However, in 2008 more wolf plates were sold than Green Bay Packer plates. In 2009 the Packers were only slightly ahead of the wolves.

5. John C. Cushman Jr., "G.O.P. Backing Off from Tough Stand over Environment," *New York Times*, January 26, 1996.

6. Ibid.

CHAPTER 10

1. Researchers in an early study of litter cans discontinued a trial in Pocahontas State Park in Virginia because visitors didn't litter enough when there were no cans: "The experiment was to continue for eight weekends. It was discontinued after four weeks, however, since only 94 pieces of litter were found in 48 observations. The picnickers were simply too conscientious for a successful experiment." William C. Finnie, "Field Experiments in Litter Control," *Environment and Behavior* 5/2 (1973): 123–44.

2. Stephen Schmelzer, Wisconsin Department of Natural Resources, interview with the author, December 20, 2010.

3. Robert B. Cialdini, Raymond R. Reno, and Cari A. Kallgren, "A Focus Theory to Normative Conduct: Recycling the Concept of Norms to Reducing Littering in Public Places," *Journal of Personality and Social Psychology* 58/6 (1990): 1015–26.

4. Jack W. Brehm, *A Theory of Psychological Reactance* (New York: Academic Press, 1966); Jack W. Brehm, *Responses to Loss of Freedom: A Theory of Psychological Reactance* (Morristown, NJ: General Learning Press, 1972).

5. Stephen Schmelzer, e-mail to the author, January 4, 2011.

6. Cialdini and his colleagues call this norm salience. Cialdini, Reno, and Kallgren, "A Focus Theory to Normative Conduct," 1015–26.

7. Of course, these signs could make people feel less responsible, but we have no clear evidence of this. Even if it happens, it looks like the awareness of consequences to humans information overcame the possible responsibility denial information.

8. Harold G. Grasmick, Robert J. Bursik Jr., and Karyl A. Kinsey, "Shame and Embarrassment as Deterrents to Noncompliance with the Law: The Case of an Antilittering Campaign," *Environment and Behavior* 23/2 (1991): 233–51.

9. P. Wesley Schultz et al., "The Constructive, Destructive and Reconstructive Power of Social Norms," *Psychological Science* 18 (2007): 429–34.

10. Ian Ayres, Sophie Raseman, and Alice Shih, "Evidence from Two Large Field Experiments that Peer Comparison Feedback Can Reduce Residential Energy Usage," *National Bureau of Economic Research Working Paper 15386*, 2009.

11. Ibid.

12. Dora L. Costa and Matthew E. Kahn, "Energy Conservation 'Nudges' and Environmentalist Ideology: Evidence from a Randomized Residential Electricity Field Experiment," *National Bureau of Economic Research Working Paper 15939*, 2010.

13. David H. Herberich, John A. List, and Michael K. Price. "How Many Economists Does It Take to Change a Light Bulb? A Natural Field Experiment on Technology Adoption." National Bureau of Economic Research. Working Paper, 2012.

14. Aldo Leopold, *A Sand County Almanac* (New York: Oxford University Press, 1949), 207.

15. Maria Börjesson, Jonas Eliasson, and Muriel Hugosson, "The Stockholm Congestion Charges—Four years on. Effects, Acceptability and Lessons Learnt," Paper presented at the 12th WCTR, Lisbon, Portugal, July 11–15, 2010. See Table 1, 4.

16. Jonas Eliasson and Lina Jonsson, "The Unexpected "Yes!": Explanatory Factors Behind the Positive Attitudes to Congestion Charges in Stockholm," Paper presented at the 2009 European Transport Conference, Leiden, Netherlands, November 19, 2009. See Table 3.

17. Linda Steg has described in detail how the norm activation model (NAM) applies to pricing. See Linda Steg and Geertje Schuitema, "Behavioural Responses to Transport Pricing: A Theoretical Analysis," in *Threats from Car Traffic to the Quality of Urban Life: Problems, Causes, and Solutions*, eds. Tommy Garling and Linda Steg (Oxford, England: Elsevier, 2007), 347–66; Erik Verhoef, Michael Bliemer, and Linda Steg, eds., *Pricing in Road Transport: A Multidisciplinary Perspective* (Cheltenham, UK: Edward Elgar, 2008).

CHAPTER 11

1. Aldo Leopold, *Round River: From the Journals of Aldo Leopold* (New York: Oxford University Press, 1952), 3.

2. James T. Addis, interview with the author, December 22, 2011.

3. Richard C. Lathrop et al., "Stocking Piscivores to Improve Fishing and Water Clarity: A Synthesis of the Lake Mendota Biomanipulation Project," *Freshwater Biology* (2002): 2410–24.

4. I first heard this "pizza story" from Steve Carpenter when working on the Northern Temperate Lakes Long Term Ecological Research Project. He still chuckles 20 years later while telling it. "I've told the pizza story in many public presentations, but never wrote it down. There was also the guy who

landed a plane on the ice, rolled a keg of beer over to his buddies who were ice-fishing, got back in the plane and took off. It is a pity I did not get these into print, but editors of limnological journals can be rather humorless." Stephen Carpenter, e-mail to the author, December 29, 2011. Carpenter (like Leopold) has been president of the Ecological Society of America and in 2011 was awarded the Stockholm Water Prize from the hand of the King of Sweden. I was honored (along with 750 other guests) to have dinner with Steve and the King and Queen.

5. It is notable that, of the 33 authors of the 500-page book published on the experiment, not one is a social scientist.

6. As you read the scientific reports you can see the lament, surprise, and thinly veiled disappointment. "At the ecosystem scale for lakes, this role of humans is insufficiently appreciated and poorly anticipated. This predator learns rapidly. It communicates quickly. A modest number of those most experienced and skilled can quickly undo a carefully planned food web manipulation." James F. Kitchell and Stephen R. Carpenter, "Summary: Accomplishments and New Directions of Food Web Management in Lake Mendota," in *Food Web Management: A Case Study of Lake Mendota*, ed. James F. Kitchell (New York: Springer-Verlag, 1992), 539–44, 542.

7. Steve Carpenter, e-mail to the author, January 13, 2012. See Richard C. Lathrop and Stephen R. Carpenter, "Phosphorus Loading and Lake Response Analyses for the Yahara Lakes," Center for Limnology, University of Wisconsin-Madison. This is an unpublished report prepared for the Yahara CLEAN project, December 2011. So, the lack of knowledge of anglers only risked the experiment, but we still know more and can do more about the lake than we know about the farmers, the ultimate source of the problem and the potential solution.

8. In part because of this experience, the limnologists at Madison began to reach out to social scientists and bring them in as partners in the Long Term Ecological Research program and several other NSF funded research and integrated graduate training programs. However, progress has been slow, not because of a lack of enthusiasm by the environmental scientists but because of the lack of sustained involvement by the social scientists, including me. For an extended discussion of the difficulties of bringing social and natural scientists together, see Thomas A. Heberlein, "Improving Interdisciplinary Research: Integrating the Social and the Natural Science," *Society and Natural Resources* 1 (1988): 5–16.

9. Steve Carpenter, e-mail to the author, July 5, 2011.

10. Water Resources Management Program Workshop. *Delavan Lake: A Recovery and Management Study*. Madison, WI: University of Wisconsin-Madison Institute for Environmental Studies, 1986.

11. Bo Shelby and J. M. Nielsen. Use Levels and Crowding in the Grand Canyon. Colorado River Research Technical Report No. 2, Grand Canyon National Park, 1976.

12. Bo Shelby, "Contrasting Recreational Experiences: Motors and Oars in the Grand Canyon." *Journal of Soil and Water Conservation* 35 (1980): 129–31.

13. Ibid., 130.

14. Marv Jensen, Inner Canyon Unit Manager, GRCA 1976–81, "Motor/Oar Combination Trip with Director Bill Whalen, et al. Grand Canyon—1979." Memo to the author, November 7, 2011.

15. Ibid.

16. Bill Freudenburg, e-mail to the author, November 28, 2008.

Bibliography

Abelson, Robert P., and Milton J. Rosenberg. "Symbolic Psycho-Logic: A Model of Attitudinal Cognition." *Behavioral Science* 3/1 (1958): 1–13.

Ajzen, Icek. "The Directive Influence of Attitudes on Behavior." In *The Psychology of Action: Linking Cognition and Motivation to Behavior*, edited by Peter M. Gollwitzer and John A. Bargh, 385–403. New York: Guilford, 1996.

Ajzen, Icek, and Martin Fishbein. "Attitude-Behavior Relations: A Theoretical Analysis and Review of Empirical Research." *Psychological Bulletin* 84/5 (1977): 888–918.

Ajzen, Icek, and Martin Fishbein. *Understanding Attitudes and Predicting Social Behavior*. Englewood Cliffs, NJ: Prentice-Hall, 1980.

Ajzen, Icek, and Martin Fishbein. "The Influence of Attitudes on Behavior." In *The Handbook on Attitudes*, edited by Delores Albarracín, Blair T. Johnson, and Mark P. Zanna, 173–222. Mahwah, NJ: Erlbaum, 2005.

Alwin, Duane F., Ronald L. Cohen, and Theodore M. Newcomb. *Political Attitudes Over the Lifespan: The Bennington Women after Fifty Years*. Madison WI, The University of Wisconsin Press, 1991.

Arlinghaus, Robert. "Voluntary Catch-and-Release Can Generate Conflict Within the Recreational Angling Community: A Qualitative Case Study of Specialised Carp (*Cyprinus carpio* L.) Angling in Germany." *Fisheries Management and Ecology* 14 (2007): 161–171.

Ayres, Ian, Sophie Raseman, and Alice Shih "Evidence from Two Large Field Experiments that Peer Comparison Feedback Can Reduce Residential Energy Usage." *National Bureau of Economic Research Working Paper* 15386, 2009.

Banaji, Mahzarin, and Larisa Heiphetz. "Attitudes." In *Handbook of Social Psychology* 5th ed., edited by Susan Fiske, Daniel Gilbert, and Gardner Lindzey, 353–427. Hoboken, NJ: Wiley, 2011.

Banyard, Philip, and Andrew Grayson. *Introducing Psychological Research: Sixty Studies That Shape Psychology*. New York: New York University Press, 1996.

Bath, Alistair J. "The Public and Wolf Reintroduction in Yellowstone National Park." *Society & Natural Resources* 2/1 (1989): 297–306.

Baumgartner, Robert Mathew. "Attitude Change and Behavior Change: A Field Experiment Investigating Responses to an Alternative Electric Rate." PhD Dissertation, Departments of Sociology and Rural Sociology, University of Wisconsin-Madison, 1987.

Bem, Daryl J. *Beliefs, Attitudes, and Human Affairs.* Belmont, CA: Brooks/Cole, 1970.

Berg, Helen M., and P. K. Bodenroeder. *Hood River Community Conservation Project Evaluation Plan, Report on the Pre-Test Survey.* Corvallis, OR: Oregon State University, DOE/BP-11287-14, 1983.

Berg, Helen M., and P. K. Bodenroeder. *Report on the Pre-test and Follow-After Survey.* Corvallis, OR: Oregon State University, Survey Research Center, 1986.

Bernstein, Carl. *A Woman in Charge: The Life of Hillary Rodham Clinton.* New York: Alfred A. Knopf, 2007.

Bishop, Richard C., and Thomas A. Heberlein. "Measuring Values of Extra Market Goods: Are Indirect Measures Biased?." *American Journal of Agricultural Economics* 61 (1979): 926–30.

Bishop, Richard C., Thomas A. Heberlein, and Mary Jo Kealy. "Contingent Valuation of Environmental Assets Comparisons with a Simulated Market." *Natural Resources Journal* 23/3 (1983): 619–33.

Black, J. Stanley. "The Relationship of Personal Norm, Perceived Social Norms and Beliefs in Lead-Free Gasoline Purchasing Behavior." Master's Thesis, Department of Sociology, University of Wisconsin-Madison, 1974.

Black, J. Stanley. "Attitudinal, Normative and Economic Factors in Early Response to an Energy Use Field Experiment." PhD Dissertation, Department of Sociology and Rural Sociology, University of Wisconsin-Madison, 1978.

Black, J. Stanley, Paul C. Stern, and Julie T. Elworth. "Personal and Contextual Influences on Household Energy Adaptations." *Journal of Applied Psychology* 70/1 (1985): 3–21.

Boglioli, Marc. *A Matter of Life and Death: Hunting in Contemporary Vermont.* Amherst, MA: University of Massachusetts Press, 2009.

Börjesson, Maria, Jonas Eliasson, and Muriel Hugosson, "The Stockholm Congestion Charges—Four years on. Effects, Acceptability and Lessons Learnt." Paper presented at the 12th WCTR, Lisbon, Portugal, July 11–15, 2010.

Bradley, Nina L., A. Carl Leopold, John Ross, and Wellington Huffaker. "Phenological Changes Reflect Climate Change in Wisconsin." *Proceedings of the National Academy of Sciences of the United States* 96 (1999): 9701–4.

Braithwaite, Victoria. *Do Fish Feel Pain?* New York: Oxford University Press, 2010.

Brehm, Jack W. *A Theory of Psychological Reactance.* New York: Academic Press, 1966.

Brehm, Jack W. *Responses to Loss of Freedom: A Theory of Psychological Reactance.* Morristown, NJ: General Learning Press, 1972.

Bright, Alan D., and Michael J. Manfredo. "A Conceptual Model of Attitudes Toward Natural Resource Issues: A Case Study of Wolf Reintroduction." *Human Dimensions of Wildlife* 1/1 (1996): 1–21.

Burn, Shawn M. "Social Psychology and the Stimulation of Recycling Behaviors: The Block Leader Approach." *Journal of Applied Social Psychology* 21/8 (1991): 611–29.

Callicott, J. Baird, Ed. *Companion to A Sand County Almanac.* Madison, WI: University of Wisconsin Press, 1987.

Campbell, Donald T. "Social Attitudes and Other Acquired Behavioral Dispositions." In *Psychology: A Study of a Science,* edited by S. Koch, 94–172. New York: McGraw-Hill, 1963.

Carson, Rachel. *Silent Spring.* New York: Houghton-Mifflin, 2002.

Castle, Stephen. "Political Earthquake Shakes Up Sweden," *New York Times,* September 20, 2010. http://www.nytimes.com/2010/09/21/world/europe/21iht-sweden.html, accessed May 14, 2011.

Christensen Associates (with R. Baumgartner, D. W. Caves, L. R. Christensen, and R. Sweeney). *Analysis of the Wisconsin Electric Residential Rate Experiment, Volume 1: Summary of Findings from the Wisconsin Residential Rate Experiment.* Prepared for Wisconsin Electric, March 1987.

Christofferson, Bill. *The Man from Clear Lake: Earth Day Founder Senator Gaylord Nelson.* Madison, WI: University of Wisconsin Press, 2004.

Cialdini, Robert B. "Crafting Normative Messages to Protect the Environment." *Current Directions in Psychological Science* 12/4 (2003): 105–9.

Cialdini, Robert B., Raymond R. Reno, and Cari A. Kallgren. "A Focus Theory to Normative Conduct: Recycling the Concept of Norms to Reducing Littering in Public Places." *Journal of Personality and Social Psychology* 58/6 (1990): 1015–26.

Cohen, Bernard Cecil. *The Press and Foreign Policy.* Princeton, NJ: Princeton University Press, 1963.

Compton, Joshua A. and Michael Pfau. "Inoculation Theory of Resistance to Influence at Maturity: Recent Progress in Theory Development and Application and Suggestions for Future Research." *Communication Yearbook* 29 (2005): 97–145.

Cook, Howard L., and Gilbert F. White. "Making Wise Use of Flood Plains." United States Papers for United Nations Conference in Science and Technology, Volume 2. Washington, D.C.: U.S. Government Printing Office, 1963.

Cooper, Joel M. *Cognitive Dissonance: 50 Years of a Classic Theory.* London: Sage Publications, 2007.

Costa, Dora L., and Matthew E. Kahn. "Energy Conservation 'Nudges' and Environmentalist Ideology: Evidence from a Randomized Residential Electricity Field Experiment." *National Bureau of Economic Research Working Paper 15939,* 2010.

Craver, Richard. "Adult Smoking Is at a Record Low," *Winston-Salem Journal,* November 15, 2008. http://www2.journalnow.com/business/2008/nov/15/adult-smoking-is-at-record-low-ar-135139/, accessed May 21, 2011.

Cushman, John C. Jr. "G.O.P. Backing Off from Tough Stand over Environment." *New York Times*, January 26, 1996.

DeLamater, John D, Ed. *Handbook of Social Psychology*. New York: Kluwer-Plenum, 2004.

de Kort, Yvonne A. W., L. Teddy McCalley, and Cees J. H. Midden. "Persuasive Trash Cans: Activation of Littering Norms by Design." *Environment and Behavior* 40/6 (2008): 870–91.

Deutscher, Irwin. "Words and Deeds: Social Science and Social Policy." *Social Problems* 13/3 (1966): 235–54.

Dietz, Thomas, Amy Fitzgerald, and Rachael Shwom. "Environmental Values." *Annual Review of Environment and Resources* 30 (2005): 335–72.

Do Valle, Patrícia Oom, Rebelo Efigénio, Elizabeth Reis, and Joãn Menezes. "Combining Behavioral Theories to Predict Recycling Involvement." *Environment and Behavior* 37/3 (2005): 364–96.

Downs, Anthony. "Up and Down with Ecology: The 'Issue-Attention Cycle'." *Public Interest* 28 (1972): 38–30.

Duda, Mark Damian, Steven J. Bissell, and Kira C. Young. *Wildlife and the American Mind: Public Opinion On and Attitudes Toward Fish and Wildlife Management*. Harrisonburg, VA: Responsive Management, 1998.

Dunlap, Riley E. "Trends in Public Opinion Toward Environmental Issues, 1965–1990." *Society and Natural Resources* 4 (1991): 285–312.

Dunlap, Riley E. "Public Opinion and Environmental Policy." In *Environmental Politics and Policy: Theories and Evidence*, edited by James P. Lester, 63–114. Durham, NC: Duke University Press, 1995.

Dunlap, Riley E. "An Enduring Concern: Light Stays Green for Environmental Protection." *Public Perspective* (September/October 2002): 10–14.

Dunlap, Riley E. "The New Environmental Paradigm Scale: From Marginality to Worldwide Use." *The Journal of Environmental Education* 40/1 (2008): 3–18.

Dunlap, Riley E., and Don A. Dillman. "Decline in Public Support for Environmental Protection: Evidence from a 1970–1974 Panel Study." *Rural Sociology* 41 (1976): 382–90.

Dunlap, Riley E., and Kent D. Van Liere. "Land Ethic or Golden Rule: Comment on 'Land Ethic Realized' by Thomas A. Heberlein." *Journal of Social Issues* 33/3 (1977): 200–207.

Dunlap, Riley E., and Kent D. Van Liere. "The New Environmental Paradigm': A Proposed Measuring Instrument and Preliminary Results." *Journal of Environmental Education* 9/4 (1978): 10–19.

Dunwoody, Sharon. "The Challenge of Trying to Make a Difference Using Media Messages." In *Creating a Climate for Change*, edited by Susanne C. Moser and Lisa Dilling, 89–104. New York: Cambridge University Press, 2007.

Eliasson, Jonas. "Expected and Unexpected in the Stockholm Trial." In *Congestion Taxes in City Traffic: Lessons Learnt from the Stockholm Trial*, edited by Anders

Gullberg and Karolina Isaksson, 205–34. Lund, Sweden: Nordic Academic Press, 2009.

Eliasson, Jonas, and Lina Jonsson. "The Unexpected "Yes!": Explanatory Factors Behind the Positive Attitudes to Congestion Charges in Stockholm." Paper presented at the 2009 European Transport Conference, Leiden, Netherlands, November 19, 2009.

Enck, Jody W., and Tommy L. Brown. "New Yorkers' Attitudes Toward Restoring Wolves to the Adirondack Park." *Wildlife Society Bulletin* 30/3 (2002): 16–28.

Ericsson, Göran, and Thomas A. Heberlein. "Attitudes of Hunters, Locals and the General Public in Sweden Now That the Wolves Are Back." *Biological Conservation* 111/2 (2003): 149–59.

Erskine, Hazel. "The Polls: Pollution and Its Costs." *Public Opinion Quarterly* 36/1 (1972): 120–35.

Farman, J. C., B. G. Gardiner, and J. D. Shanklin. "Large Losses of Total Ozone in Antarctica Reveal Seasonal Clox/Nox Interaction." *Nature* 315/6016 (1985): 207–10.

Fazio, Russel H. "On the Power and Functionality of Attitudes: The Role of Attitude Accessibility." In *Attitude Structure and Function*, edited by A. R. Pratkanis, S. J. Breckler, and S. G. Greenwald, 153–79. Hillsdale, NJ: Earlbaum, 1988.

Festinger, Leon A. *A Theory of Cognitive Dissonance*. Evanston, IL: Row Peterson, 1957.

Festinger, Leon A. "Behavioral Support for Opinion Change." *Public Opinion Quarterly* 28/3 (1964): 404–17.

Finnie, William C. "Field Experiments in Litter Control." *Environment and Behavior* 5/2 (1973): 123–44.

Firmin, Michal. "Commentary: The Seminal Contribution of Richard LaPiere's Attitudes vs Actions (1934) Research Study." *International Journal of Epidemiology* 39/1(2010): 18–20.

Fishbein, Martin, and Icek Ajzen. "Attitudes and Opinions." *Annual Review of Psychology* 23 (1972): 487–544.

Fishbein, Martin, and Icek Ajzen. "Attitudes toward Objects as Predictors of Single and Multiple Behavioral Criteria." *Psychological Review* 8 (1974): 59–74.

Fishbein, Martin, and Icek Ajzen. *Belief, Attitude, Intention and Behavior: An Introduction to Theory and Research*. Boston: Addison-Wesley, 1975.

Fishbein, Martin, and Icek Ajzen. "Predicting and Understanding Consumer Behavior: Attitude-Behavior Correspondence." In *Understanding Attitudes and Predicting Social Behavior*, Icek Ajzen and Martin Fishbein, 148–72. Englewood Cliffs, NJ: Prentice-Hall, 1980.

Flader, Susan L. *Thinking Like A Mountain: Aldo Leopold and the Evolution of an Ecological Attitude Toward Deer, Wolves and Forests*. Columbia, MO: University of Missouri Press, 1974.

Flynn-Brown, Cynthia. *Process Evaluation: Final Report, Hood River Conservation Project*. DOE/BP-11287-6, 1986.

Flynn, James, Paul Slovic, and C. K Mertz. "The Nevada Initiative: A Risk Communication Fiasco." *Risk Analysis* 13/5 (1993): 497–502.

Freudenburg, William R., Robert B. Gramling, Shirley Laska, and Kai Erikson. *Catastrophe in the Making: The Engineering of Katrina and the Disasters of Tomorrow*. Washington, D.C.: Island Press, 2009.

Gardner, Gerald T., and Paul C. Stern. *Environmental Problems and Human Behavior*, 2nd ed. Boston: Pearson Custom Publishing, 2002.

Gardner, Martha N., and Alan N. Brandt. "'The Doctor's Choice Is America's Choice': The Physician in US Cigarette Advertisements, 1930–1953." *American Journal of Public Health* 96/2 (2006): 222–32.

Garfinkel, Lawrence. "Trends in Cigarette Smoking in the United States." *Preventive Medicine* 26 (1997): 447–50.

Gedics, Al. http://www.wsn.org/crandon/SOCIMAGN2.html. Accessed May 13, 2011.

Geller, E. Scott, W. Brasted, and M. Mann. "Waste Receptacle Designs as Interventions for Litter Control." *Journal of Environmental Systems* 9 (1980): 145–60.

Geller, E. Scott, Jill F. Witmer, and Andra L. Orebaugh. "Instructions as a Determinant of Paper-Disposal Behaviors." *Environment and Behavior* 8/3 (1976): 417–39.

Geller, E. Scott, Jill F. Witmer, and Margaret A. Tuso. "Environmental Interventions for Litter Control." *Journal of Applied Psychology* 62/3 (1977): 344–51.

Gladwell, Malcom. *The Tipping Point: How Little Things Can Make a Big Difference*. New York: Little Brown and Company, 2000.

Glasman, Laura R., and Delores Albarracín. "Attitudes That Predict Future Behavior: A Meta-Analysis of the Attitude-Behavior Relation." *Psychological Bulletin* 132 (2006): 778–822.

Goldstein, David B. *Extreme Efficiency: How Far Can We Go If We Really Need To?* Proceedings from the ACEEE Summer Study on Energy Efficiency in Buildings. Washington, D.C.: American Council for an Energy-Efficient Economy, 2008.

Goldstein, Nora, and Celeste Madtes. "12th Annual Biocycle National Survey: The State of Garbage in America, Part II." *Biocycle* 41 (2000): 40–48.

Grasmick, Harold G., Robert J. Bursik Jr., and Karyl A. Kinsey. "Shame and Embarrassment as Deterrents to Noncompliance with the Law: The Case of an Antilitter Campaign." *Environment and Behavior* 23/2 (1991): 233–51.

Gross, Steven Jay, and C. Michael Niman. "Attitude-Behavior Consistency: A Review." *The Public Opinion Quarterly* 39/3 (1975): 358–68.

Guagnano, Gregory A., Paul C. Stern, and Thomas Dietz. "Influences on Attitude-Behavior Relationships: A Natural Experiment with Curbside Recycling." *Environment and Behavior* 27/5 (1995): 699–718.

Gullberg, Anders, and Karolina Isaksson. "Fabulous Success or Insidious Fiasco." In *Congestion Taxes in City Traffic: Lessons Learnt from the Stockholm Trial*, edited by Anders Gullberg and Karolina Isaksson, 11–204. Lund, Sweden: Nordic Academic Press, 2009.

Hampton, Bruce. *The Great American Wolf*. New York: Henry Holt, 1997.

Harmon-Jones, E. and J. Mills, Eds. *Cognitive Dissonance: Progress on a Pivotal Theory in Social Psychology*. Washington, D.C.: American Psychological Association, 1999.

Heberlein, Thomas A. "Moral Norms, Threatened Sanctions, and Littering Behavior." PhD Dissertation, Department of Sociology and Rural Sociology, University of Wisconsin-Madison. *Dissertation Abstracts International* 32 (1971): 5906.

Heberlein, Thomas A. "The Land Ethic Realized: Some Social Psychological Explanations of Changing Environmental Attitudes." *Journal of Social Issues* 28/4 (1972): 79–87.

Heberlein, Thomas A. "The Three Fixes: Technological, Cognitive and Structural." In *Water and Community Development: Social and Economic Perspectives*, edited by Donald Field, James C. Barren, and Burl F. Long, 279–96. Ann Arbor, MI: Ann Arbor Science Publishers, 1974.

Heberlein, Thomas A. "Conservation Information: The Energy Crisis and Electricity Consumption in an Apartment Complex." *Energy Systems and Policy* 1 (1975): 105–17.

Heberlein, Thomas A. "Social Norms and Environmental Quality." Paper presented at the American Association for Advancement of Science Annual meetings, New York, 1975.

Heberlein, Thomas A. "Environmental Attitudes." *Zeitschrift fur Umweltpolitik (Journal of Environmental Policy)* 2 (1981): 241–70.

Heberlein, Thomas A. "Time-of-Day Electricity Pricing." In *Consumers and Energy Conservation*, edited by John D. Claxton, C. Dennis Anderson, J. R. Brent Ritchie, and Gordon H. D. McDougall, 194–204. New York: Praeger, 1981.

Heberlein, Thomas A. "Improving Interdisciplinary Research: Integrating the Social and the Natural Science." *Society and Natural Resources* 1 (1988): 5–16.

Heberlein, Thomas A. "Forward." In *Legendary Deer Camps*, by Rob Wegner, 6–7. Iola, WI: Krause Publications, 2001.

Heberlein, Thomas A. "Fire in the Sistine Chapel: How Wisconsin Residents Responded to Chronic Wasting Disease." *Human Dimensions of Wildlife* 9/3 (2004): 165–79.

Heberlein, Thomas A. "Wildlife Caretaking vs. Wildlife Management: A Short Lesson in Swedish." *The Wildlife Society Bulletin* 33/1 (2005): 378–80.

Heberlein, Thomas A., and J. Stanley Black. "Attitudinal Specificity and the Prediction of Behavior in a Field Setting." *Journal of Personality and Social Psychology*, 33/4 (1976): 474–79.

Heberlein, Thomas A., and J. Stanley Black. "Cognitive Consistency and Environmental Action." *Environment and Behavior* 13/6 (1981): 717–34.

Heberlein, Thomas A., and Bruce Laybourne. "The Wisconsin Deer Hunter: Social Characteristics, Attitudes, and Preferences for Proposed Hunting Season Changes." Working Paper No.10. Madison, WI: University of Wisconsin Center for Resources Policy Studies and Programs, 1978.

Heberlein, Thomas A., and Shalom H. Schwartz. "Deactivating the Antilittering Norm: A Field Test of Schwartz's Norm Activation Theory." Paper Presented at the 9th Biennial Conference on Environmental Psychology, Eindhoven, The Netherlands September 26–28, 2011.

Heberlein, Thomas A., and Richard C. Stedman. "Socially Amplified Risk: Attitude and Behavior Change in Response to CWD in Wisconsin Deer." *Human Dimensions of Wildlife* 14/5 (2009): 326–40.

Heberlein, Thomas A., and W. Keith Warriner. "The Influence of Price and Attitude on Shifting Residential Electricity Consumption from On to Off Peak Periods." *Journal of Economic Psychology* 4 (1983): 107–30.

Heberlein, Thomas A., and Matthew A. Wilson. "What Do Attitudes toward Wolves Have to Do with Behavior? Not Much. But That's OK." Paper presented at the International Symposium on Society and Resource Management, Madison, Wisconsin, 2011.

Heberlein, Thomas A., Bonnie Ortiz, and Daniel Linz. "Satisfaction, Commitment and Knowledge of Customers on a Mandatory Participation Time of Day Electricity Pricing Experiment." *Journal of Consumer Research* 9/1 (1982): 106–14.

Heberlein, Thomas A., Matthew A. Wilson, Richard C. Bishop, and Nora Cate Schaeffer. "Rethinking the Scope Test as a Criterion for Validity in Contingent Valuation." *Journal of Environmental Economics and Management* 50/1 (2005): 1–22.

Henricksson, Greger. "What Did the Trial Mean for Stockholmers." In *Congestion Taxes in City Traffic: Lessons Learnt from the Stockholm Trial*, edited by Anders Gullberg and Karolina Isaksson, 235–94. Lund, Sweden: Nordic Academic Press, 2009.

Herberich, David H., John A. List, and Michael K. Price. "How Many Economists Does It Take to Change a Light Bulb? A Natural Field Experiment on Technology Adoption." National Bureau of Economic Research. Working Paper, 2012

Heywood, John L. "The Cognitive and Emotional Components of Behavioral Norms in Outdoor Recreation." *Leisure Sciences* 24 (2002): 271–81.

Hirst, Eric. *Cooperation and Community Conservation: The Hood River Conservation Project.* ORNL/CON-235, DOE/BP-11287-18, 1987.

Hock, Roger R. *Forty Studies That Changed Psychology: Explorations into the History of Psychological Research*, 2nd ed. Englewood Cliffs, NJ: Prentice Hall, 1995.

Hopper, Joseph R., and Joyce McCarl Nielsen. "Recycling as Altruistic Behavior: Normative and Behavioral Strategies to Expand Participation in a Community Recycling Program." *Environment and Behavior* 23/2 (1991): 195–220.

Isaksson, Karolina, and Anders Gullberg. "Introduction." In *Congestion Taxes in City Traffic: Lessons Learnt from the Stockholm Trial*, edited by Anders Gullberg and Karolina Isaksson, 7–10. Lund, Sweden: Nordic Academic Press, 2009.

Jenkins, Robin R., Salvador A. Martinez, Karen Palmer, and Michael J. Podolsky. "The Determinants of Household Recycling: A Material-Specific Analysis of Recycling Program Features and Unit Pricing." *Journal of Environmental Economics and Management* 45/2 (2003): 295–318.

Jones, Edward E., and Victor A. Harris. "The Attribution of Attitudes." *Journal of Experimental Social Psychology* 3 (1967): 1–24.

Jost, John T., and Mahzarin R. Banaji. "William James McGuire (1925–2007)." *American Psychologist* 63/4 (2008): 270–71.

Kanagy, Conrad, Craig Humphrey, and Glenn Firebaugh. "Surging Environmentalism: Changing Public Opinion or Changing Publics?" *Social Science Quarterly* 75/4 (1994): 804–19.

Keating, Kenneth M., Ruth L. Love, Terry V. Oliver, H. Gil Peach, and Cynthia B. Flynn. "Hood River Project: Take a Walk on the Applied Side." *The Rural Sociologist* 5/2 (1985): 112–18.

Keiser, Kees, Siegwart Lindenberg, and Linda Steg. "The Spreading of Disorder." *Science* 322 (2008):1681–84.

Kellert, Stephen. "The Public and the Timber Wolf in Minnesota." *Transactions of the 51st North American Wildlife and Natural Resources Conference* (1986): 152–61.

Kellert, Stephen. *Public Attitudes and Beliefs about the Wolf and Its Restoration in Michigan.* Madison, Wisconsin: HBRS, 1990.

Kellert, Stephen. "Public Views on Wolf Restoration in Michigan." *Transactions of the 56th North American Wildlife and Natural Resources Conference* (1991): 152–61.

Kellert, Stephen. *The Value of Life: Biological Diversity and Society.* Washington, D.C.: Island Press, 1997.

Kitchell, James F., and Stephen R. Carpenter. "Summary: Accomplishments and New Directions of Food Web Management in Lake Mendota." In *Food Web Management: A case study of Lake Mendota*, edited by James F. Kitchell, 539–44. New York: Springer-Verlag, 1992.

Knight, Richard L., and Suzanne Riedel. *Aldo Leopold and the Ecological Conscience.* New York: Oxford University Press, 2002.

Krosnick, Jon A., and Robert P. Abelson. "The Case for Measuring Attitude Strength in Surveys." In *Questions about Questions: Inquiries into the Cognitive Bases of Surveys*, edited by J. Tanur, 177–203. New York: Russell Sage, 1992.

Kühl, Aline, Natasha Balinova, Elena Bykova, Yuri N. Arylov, Alexander Esipov, Anna A. Lushchekina, and E. J. Milner-Gulland. "The Role of Saiga Poaching in Rural Communities: Linkages between Attitudes, Socio-Economic Circumstances and Behaviours." *Biological Conservation* 142/7 (2009): 1442–49.

Kulpa, Jack. "Secret Lakes of the North Woods." *Outdoor Life* 79/5 (1984): 108–9.

LaPiere, Richard T. "Attitudes vs Actions." *Social Forces* 13/2 (1934): 230–37.

Lathrop, Richard C., Brett M. Johnson, T. B. Johnson, M. T. Vogelsang, Stephen R. Carpenter, T. R. Hrabik, James F. Kitchell, John J. Maguson, Lars G. Rudstam, and R. Scot Stewart. "Stocking Piscivores to Improve Fishing and Water Clarity: A Synthesis of the Lake Mendota Biomanipulation Project." *Freshwater Biology* 47 (2002): 2410–24.

Leopold, Aldo. "The Ecological Conscience," *Bulletin of the Garden Club of America* (1947): 45–53. Reprinted in Susan Flader and J. Baird Callicot, Eds. *The River of the Mother of God and Other Essays by Aldo Leopold*, 338–48. Madison, WI: University of Wisconsin Press, 1991.

Leopold, Aldo. *A Sand County Almanac*. New York: Oxford University Press, 1949.

Leopold, Aldo. *Round River: From the Journals of Aldo Leopold*. New York: Oxford University Press, 1952.

Lewis, Thomas A. "Cloaked in a Wise Disguise." *National Wildlife* October/November (1992): 4–9.

Linz, Daniel, and Thomas A. Heberlein. "The Development of a Personal Obligation to Shift Electricity Use: Initial Determinants and Maintenance Over Time." *Energy* 9/3 (1984): 254–63.

Ljung, Per E., Shawn J. Riley, Thomas A. Heberlein, and Göran Ericsson. "Eat Prey and Love: Game Meat Consumption and Attitudes toward Hunting." *Wildlife Society Bulletin* (2012).

Lutzenhiser, Loren. "Marketing Household Energy Conservation: The Message and Reality." In *New Tools for Environmental Protection: Education, Information and Voluntary Measures*, edited by Thomas Dietz and Paul C. Stern, 49–65. Washington D.C.: National Academy Press, 2002.

Lutzenhiser, Susan, J. S. Peters, Mithra Moezzi, and James Woods. "Beyond the Price Effect in Time-of-Use Programs: Results from a Municipal Utility Pilot 2007–2008." Ernest Orlando Lawrence Berkeley National Laboratory (LBNL-2750E). Paper presented at the International Energy Program Evaluation Conference, Portland, OR, August 12–14, 2009.

Magnuson, John J., Dale M. Robertson, Barbara J. Benson, Randolph H. Wynne, David M. Livingstone, Tadashi Arai, Raymod A. Assel, Roger G. Barry, Virginia Card, Esko Kuusisto, Nick G. Granin, Terry D. Prowse, Kenton M. Stewart, and Valery S. Vuglinski. "Historical Trends in Lake and River Ice Cover in the Northern Hemisphere." *Science* 289/5485 (2000): 1743–46.

Mayers, Jeff. "Moratorium on Mines Gains Momentum." *Wisconsin State Journal*, 1C, January 18, 1998.

McCombs, Maxwell E., and Donald L. Shaw. "The Agenda-Setting Function of Mass Media." *Public Opinion Quarterly* 36/2 (1972): 176–87.

McGuinness, James, Allan P. Jones, and Steven G. Cole. "Attitudinal Correlates of Recycling Behavior." *Journal of Applied Psychology* 62/4 (1977): 376–84.

McGuire, William J. "Inducing Resistance to Persuasion: Some Contemporary Approaches." In *Advances in Experimental Social Psychology*, edited by Leonard Berkowitz, 191–229. New York: Academic Press, 1964.

McGuire, William J. "Attitudes and Attitude Change." In *The Handbook of Social Psychology*, 3rd ed., edited by Gardner Lindzey and Elliot Aronson, 238–39. New York: Random House, 1985.

McGuire, William J. "The Myth of Massive Media Impact: Savagings and Salvagings." *Public Communication and Behavior* 1 (1986): 173–257.

Mech, David L. *The Wolf: The Ecology and Behavior of an Endangered Species.* Minneapolis, MN: University of Minnesota Press, 1981.

Meine, Curt. *Aldo Leopold: His Life and Work.* Madison, WI: University of Wisconsin Press, 1988.

Melosi, Martin V. *Garbage in the Cities: Refuse, Reform, and the Environment, 1880–1980.* Pittsburgh, PA: University of Pittsburgh Press, 1981.

Milgram, Stanley. "Behavioral Study of Obedience." *Journal of Abnormal Social Psychology* 67 (1963): 371–78.

Milgram, Stanley. "Some Conditions of Obedience and Disobedience to Authority." *Human Relations* 18 (1965): 57–76.

Mitchell, Robert C. "Public Opinion and Environmental Issues." In *Council on Environmental Quality: The Eleventh Annual Report of the Council on Environmental Quality,* 401–25. Washington D.C.: Government Printing Office, 1980.

Murray, James R., Michael J. Minor, Norman M. Bradburn, Robert F. Cotterman, Martin Frankel, and Alan E. Pisarski. "Evolution of Public Response to the Energy Crisis." *Science* 184/4134 (1974): 257–63.

Naughton-Treves, Lisa, Rebecca Grossberg, and Adrian Treves. "Paying for Tolerance: Rural Citizens' Attitudes Toward Wolf Depredation and Compensation." *Conservation Biology* 17/6 (2003): 1500–11.

Nelson, David E., Gary Giovino, Seth L. Emont, Robert Brackbill, Lorraine L. Cameron, John Peddicord, and Paul D. Mowery. "Trends in Cigarette Smoking Among US Physicians and Nurses." *Journal of the American Medical Association* 271/16 (1994): 1273–75.

Newcomb, Theodore Mead. *Personality and Social Change.* New York: Dryden, 1943.

Newcomb, Theodore Mead, K. E. Koening, R. Flacks, and D. P. Warwick. *Persistence and Change: Bennington College and Its Students after 25 Years.* New York: John Wiley & Sons, 1967.

Newman, Steven P., and Michael H. Hoff. "Evaluation of a 16-inch Minimum Length Limit for Small Mouth Bass in Pallette Lake WI." *North American Journal of Fisheries Management* 20/1 (2000): 90–99.

Nielsen, Joyce McCarl, and Barbara L. Ellington. "Social Processes and Resource Conservation." In *Environmental Psychology,* edited by N. R. Feimer and E. Scott Geller, 288–312. New York: Praeger, 1983.

O'Brien, Michael. *Exxon and the Crandon Mine Controversy: The People vs. Giant Companies A True Story of People Winning.* Middleton, WI: Badger Books, 2008.

Odeck, James, and Svein Bråthen. "Toll Financing in Norway: The Success, the Failures and Perspectives for the Future." *Transport Policy* 9/3 (2002): 253–60.

Paukert, Craig, Michael McInerny, and Randall Schultz. "Historical Trends in Creel Limits, Length-Based Limits, and Season Restrictions for Black Basses in the United States and Canada." *Fisheries Management* 32/2 (2007): 62–72.

Pellow, David N., Allan Schnaiberg, and Adam S. Weinberg. "Putting the Ecological Modernisation Thesis to the Test: The Promises and Performances of Urban

Recycling." In *Ecological Modernisation Around the World: Perspectives & Critical Debates*, edited by Arthur P. J. Mol and David A. Sonnenfeld, 109–37. Portland, OR: Frank Cass, 2000.

Petty, Richard E., and Jon A. Krosnick. *Attitude Strength: Antecedents and Consequences.* Mahwah, NJ: Erlbaum, 1995.

Piper, George. "Only Crandon Wins in Gamble with River." *The Mauston Star-Times*, March 15, 1997.

Policansky, David. "Catch-and-Release Recreational Fishing: A Historical Perspective." In *Recreational Fisheries: Ecological, Economic and Social Evaluation*, edited by Tony J. Pitcher and Chuck E. Hollingworth, 74–93. Oxford, England: Blackwell Science, 2002.

Roder, Wolf. "Attitudes and Knowledge in the Topeka Flood Planner." In *Papers on Flood Problems*, edited by Gilbert F. White, 62–83. Chicago: Department of Geography Research Paper No. 70, 1961.

Rohlfing, A. H. "Hunter Conduct and Public Attitudes." *Transactions of the 43rd North American Wildlife and Natural Resources Conference* (1978): 404–11.

Rokeach, Milton. *The Nature of Human Values.* New York: Wiley, 1973.

Ross, Lee. "The Intuitive Psychologist and His Shortcomings: Distortions in the Attribution Process." In *Advances in Experimental Social Psychology*, edited by L. Berkowitz, 173–220. New York: Academic Press, 1977.

Schuitema, Geertje, Linda Steg, and Sonja Forward. "Explaining Differences in Acceptability Before and Acceptance After the Implementation of a Congestion Charge in Stockholm." *Transportation Research Part A: Policy and Practice* 44/2 (2010): 99–109.

Schultz, P. Wesley. "Knowledge, Information and Household Recycling Examining the Knowledge-Deficit Model of Behavior Change." In *New Tools for Environmental Protection: Education, Information, and Voluntary Measures*, edited by Thomas Dietz and Paul C. Stern, 67–82. Washington, D.C.: National Academy Press, 2002.

Schultz, P. Wesley, Jessica M. Nolan, Robert Cialdini, Noah J. Goldstein, and Vladas Griskevicius. "The Constructive, Destructive and Reconstructive Power of Social Norms." *Psychological Science* 18 (2007): 429–34.

Schuman, Howard, and Michael P. Johnson. "Attitudes and Behavior." *Annual Review of Sociology* 2 (1976): 161–207.

Schwartz, Shalom H. "Words, Deeds and the Perception of Consequences and Responsibility in Action Situations." *Journal of Personality and Social Psychology* 10/3 (1968): 232–42.

Schwartz, Shalom H. "Normative Influences on Altruism." *Advances in Experimental Social Psychology* 10 (1977): 221–79.

Schwartz, Shalom H. "Universals in the Content and Structure of Values: Theory and Empirical Tests in 20 Countries." In *Advances in Experimental Social Psychology*, edited by M. Zanna, 1–65. New York: Academic Press, 1992.

Schwartz, Shalom H. "Are There Universal Aspects in the Structure and Contents of Human Values?." *Journal of Social Issues* 50/4 (1994): 19–45.

Schwartz, Shalom H., and J. A. Howard. "A Normative Decision Making Model of Altruism." In *Altruism and Helping Behavior: Social, Personality, and Developmental Perspectives*, edited by J. P. Rushton and R. M. Sorrentine, 189–211. Hillsdale, NJ: Erlbaum, 1981.

Schwartz, Shalom H., and J. A. Howard. "Helping and Cooperation: A Self-Based Motivational Model." In *Cooperation and Helping Behavior: Theories and Research*, edited by V. J. Derlega and J. Grzelak, 328–56. New York: Academic Press, 1982.

Seaver, W. Burleigh, and Arthur H. Patterson. "Decreasing Fuel-Oil Consumption Through Feedback and Social Commendation." *Journal of Applied Behavior Analysis* 9/2 (1976): 147–52.

Seely, Ron. "Local Governments Say No Thanks to Mine Plan." *Wisconsin State Journal*, November 3, 1996.

Seely, Ron. "Scientists Are Alarmed by Chronic Wasting Disease." *Wisconsin State Journal*, A7, March 21, 2002.

Seligman, Clive, and J. M Darley. "Feedback as a Means of Decreasing Residential Energy Consumption." *Journal of Applied Psychology* 62/4 (1977): 363–68.

Seligman, Clive, L. Becker, and J. Darley. "Encouraging Residential Energy Conservation Through Feedback." In *Advances in Environmental Psychology Volume 3: Energy: Psychological Perspectives*, edited by A. Baum and J. Singer, 1–25. Hillsdale, NJ: Erlbaum, 1981.

Sharpe, Virginia A., Bryan G. Norton, and Strachan Donnelley. *Wolves and Human Communities: Biology, Politics, and Ethics*. Washington, D.C.: Island Press, 2001.

Shelby, Bo, "Contrasting Recreational Experiences: Motors and Oars in the Grand Canyon." *Journal of Soil and Water Conservation* 35 (1980): 129–31.

Shelby, Bo, and Joyce McCarl Nielsen. Use Levels and Crowding in the Grand Canyon. Colorado River Research Technical Report No. 2, Grand Canyon National Park, 1976.

Shelley, Victoria, Adrian Treves, and Lisa Naughton. "Attitudes to Wolves and Wolf Policy Among Ojibwe Tribal Members and Nontribal Residents of Wisconsin's Wolf Range." *Human Dimensions of Wildlife* 16/6 (2011): 397–413.

Siegel, Michael. "Involuntary Smoking in the Restaurant Workplace: A Review of Employee Exposure and Health Effects." *Journal of the American Medical Association* 270 (1993): 490–93.

Slovic, Paul, Baruch Fischhoff, and Sarah Lichtenstein. "Facts and Fears: Understanding Perceived Risk." In *The Perception of Risk*, edited by Paul Slovic, 137–53. London: Earthscan, 2000.

Steg, Linda, and Geertje Schuitema. "Behavioural Responses to Transport Pricing: A Theoretical Analysis." In *Threats from Car Traffic to the Quality of Urban Life:*

Problems, Causes, and Solutions, edited by Tommy Garling and Linda Steg, 347–66. Oxford: Elsevier, 2007.

Stern, Paul C. "Toward a Coherent Theory of Environmentally Significant Behavior." *Journal of Social Issues* 56/3 (2000): 407–24.

Stern, Paul C., and Stuart Oskamp. "Managing Scarce Environmental Resources." In *Handbook of Environmental Psychology*, edited by D. Stokols and I. Altman, 1043–88. New York: Wiley, 1987.

Stern, Paul C., Thomas Dietz, Troy Abel, Gregory A. Guagnano, and Linda Kalof. "A Value-Belief-Norm Theory of Support for Social Movements: The Case of Environmentalism." *Human Ecology Review* 6/2 (1999): 81–97.

Syrek, Daniel B. *Summary of Litter Research Findings Report S-1.1*. Institute for Applied Research, Sacramento, CA.

Tang, Hao, D. W. Cowling, C. M. Stevens, and J. C. Lloyd. "Changes of Knowledge, Attitudes, Beliefs, and Preference of Bar Owner and Staff in Response to a Smoke-Free Bar Law." *Tobacco Control* 13 (2004): 87–89.

Task Force on Federal Flood Control Policy. *A Unified National Program for Managing Flood Losses*. Report No. 67–663. Washington, D.C.: U.S. Government Printing Office, 1966.

Tellis, Gerard. "Advertising Exposure, Loyalty and Brand Purchase: Two Stage Model of Choice." *Journal of Marketing Research* 25/2 (1988): 134–44.

U.S. Environmental Protection Agency. *Municipal Solid Waste Factbook*. Washington, D.C.: U.S. Environmental Protection Agency, 1998.

Van Liere, Kent D., and Riley E. Dunlap. "Moral Norms and Environmental Behavior: An Application of Schwartz's Norm-Activation Model to Yard Burning." *Journal of Applied Social Psychology* 8/2 (1978): 174–88.

Verhoef, Erik, Michael Bliemer, and Linda Steg, Eds. *Pricing in Road Transport: A Multidisciplinary Perspective*. Cheltenham, England: Edward Elgar, 2008.

Water Resources Management Program Workshop. *Delavan Lake: A Recovery and Management Study*. Madison, WI: University of Wisconsin Madison Institute for Environmental Studies, 1986.

Weigel, Russell H., and Lee S. Newman. "Increasing the Attitude-Behavior Correspondence by Broadening the Scope of the Behavior Measure." *Journal of Personality and Social Psychology* 33/6 (1976): 793–802.

White, Gilbert F. "Optimal Flood Damage Management: Retrospect and Prospect." In *Water Research*, edited by Allen V. Kneese and Stephen C. Smith, 251–69. Baltimore: The Johns Hopkins Press, 1966.

White, Gilbert F., Wesley C. Calef, James W. Hudson, Harold M. Mayer, John R. Shaeffer, and Donald J. Volk. *Changes in Urban Occupance of Flood Plains in the United States*. Chicago: University of Chicago Department of Geography Research Papers No. 57, 1958.

Whittaker, Doug, Jerry J. Vaske, and Michael J. Manfredo. "Specificity and the Cognitive Hierarchy: Value Orientations and the Acceptability of Urban Wildlife Management Actions." *Society & Natural Resources* 19 (2006): 515–30.

Williams, Christopher K., Göran Ericsson, and Thomas A. Heberlein. "A Quantitative Summary of Attitudes toward Wolves and their Reintroduction (1972–2000)." *Wildlife Society Bulletin* 30/2 (2002): 575–84.

Wilma, David. "U.S.S. *Lexington* Provides Electricity to Tacoma Beginning about December 17, 1929." HistoryLink.org. The Free Online Encyclopedia of Washington State History. Last modified January 24, 2003, http://www.historylink.org/index.cfm?DisplayPage=output.cfm&File_Id=5113, accessed May 24, 2011.

Wilson, Matthew A. "The Wolf in Yellowstone: Science, Symbol, or Politics? Deconstructing the Conflict Between Environmentalism and Wise Use." *Society & Natural Resources* 10/5 (1997): 453–68.

Wilson, Matthew A. *Appendix H: Public Attitudes towards Wolves in Wisconsin. Wisconsin Department of Natural Resources*, http://dnr.wi.gov/org/land/er/publications/wolfplan/appendix/appendix_h.htm, accessed May 18, 2011.

Wilson, Matthew A., and Thomas A. Heberlein. "The Wolf, the Tourist, and the Recreational Context: New Opportunity or Uncommon Circumstance?." *Human Dimensions of Wildlife* 1/4 (1996): 38–53.

Winand, C. J. *Future Deer Management (Part I): Are we on the Right Track?* Bowsite.com, http://bowsite.com/bowsite/features/armchair_biologist/qdm/, accessed May 24, 2011.

Winkler, Richell, and Rozalynn Klaas. "Declining Deer Hunters: Wisconsin's Gun Deer Hunter Numbers Are Continuing to Decline." Applied Population Laboratory, Department of Community and Environmental Sociology, University of Wisconsin-Madison. February, 2011. http://www.apl.wisc.edu/publications/APL_hunters2011_web.pdf, accessed May 13, 2011.

Winslott-Hiselieus, Lena, Karin Brundell-Freij, Åsa Vagland, and Camilla Byström. "The Development of Public Attitudes towards the Stockholm Congestion Trial." *Transportation Research Part A: Policy and Practice* 43/3 (2009): 269–82.

Wood, Graeme. "Re-Engineering the Earth." *The Atlantic* July/August 2009, http://www.theatlantic.com/magazine/archive/2009/07/re-engineering-the-earth/7552/, accessed May 24, 2011.

Zimbardo, Phillip. "The Pathology of Imprisonment." *Society* 9 (1972): 4–8.

Zuccotti, John Andrew. "A Native Returns: The Endangered Species Act and Wolf Reintroduction to the Northern Rocky Mountains." *Columbia Journal of Environmental Law* 20 (1995): 329–60.

Index